The Internet Strategic Plan

A Step-by-Step Guide to Connecting Your Company

The Internet Strategic Plan

A Step-by-Step Guide to Connecting Your Company

Martin A. Schulman and Rick Smith

WILEY COMPUTER PUBLISHING

John Wiley & Sons, Inc.

New York ▲ Chichester ▲ Weinheim ▲ Brisbane ▲ Singapore ▲ Toronto

Publisher: Katherine Schowalter
Editor: Philip Sutherland
Assistant Editor: Pam Sobotka
Managing Editor: Frank Grazioli
Text Composition: Impressions Book & Journal Services, Inc.
Book Design: Jane Tenenbaum Design

Library of Congress Cataloging-in-Publication Data:

Schulman, Martin A., 1963–
    The Internet strategic plan : a step-by-step guide to connecting
your company / Martin Schulman and Rick Smith.
        p.   cm.
    Includes index.
    ISBN 0-471-14275-1 (pbk. : alk. paper)
    1. Business enterprises—Computer networks—Planning.   2. Web
sites—Design and construction—Planning.   3. Web servers—Planning.
I. Smith, Rick, 1953–.   II. Title.
HD30.37.S337   1997
658′.054678—dc21   96-48418
                                                                         CIP

Printed in the United States of America
10 9 8 7 6 5 4 3 2 1

Acknowledgments

There are many people in my life who made this book possible. Gene Hastings and Dave O'Leary taught me more about networking at the Pittsburgh Supercomputing Center than a library full of textbooks. My manager, Tom Herbst, and my coworkers at Cisco Systems continue my technical education and provide enough flexibility to write without quitting my day job.

My friends at the Internet Society opened the door for me at John Wiley & Sons by offering my name as a technical reviewer. In particular, former Executive Director Tony Rutkowski and Mary Burger gave me challenging tasks and always kept working fun.

Finally, special thanks to my mother, father, and wife. Mom and Dad encouraged me to learn about electronics with my first computer, numerous tools (I'll reassemble the TV next week), and countless trips to Radio Shack. Jennifer always believes in me, and gave me enough time during our first year of marriage to complete this book.

Marty Schulman

This book could not have been completed without the assistance of many people. Assistance from others is especially crucial in writing about the Internet and the Web, because both are changing so much and so fast. No one person or company has all the answers. Anyone claiming otherwise is simply exaggerating to the *nth* degree.

Of course, my wife, Lynda, and sons Ross and Ryan were very helpful in more ways than they know. In my family, I must admit, Lynda is the Internet wiz. Thanks, too, to my parents Evelyn and Willie Smith, who always encouraged me in my passions to read and to write.

On a professional level, I in particular want to thank best-selling author and dear friend Paul Gilster, whose book *The Internet Navigator* (published by John Wiley & Sons) helped educate me about the Internet.

Particular credit goes to a group of people who were so crucial to the founding of Internpath, an Internet Service Provider in Raleigh, NC. I had the pleasure of working with Mike Ramsey, Charley Bratton, Chuck Crews, Alan Clegg, John Tomasetti, Jason Botts, Paul Lowell, Kevin Yost, Joe Harris, Mike Albrecht, Keith Makuck, Curt Hess, Leah Chauncey, Tom Hines, Becky Metcalf, Jenny Jenkins, Joe Ragland, and Jim Goodmon, who founded the company. We built an ISP and Web company from scratch. Those teammates taught me more than they will ever know.

When I began selecting people to participate as case studies for the book, first on the list was Joel Maloff. He is not only known worldwide as an Internet consultant, but also my friend.

The book contains ten other case studies, and I am grateful that each chose to participate. They included: Frank Taylor and Andy Schwab of TriNet Services; Betty Fried, Chip Kelley, and Curt Yeo of SAS Institute; Tom Bartolomeo and Laurie Belock of First Union; Charles Knuff and Mark Sidell of Forté; David Lea of PC Travel; Cliff Allen of Allen Marketing Group; Kevin Yost of TechSolv; Doug Graham of Macro World; Walter Daniels of Daniels & Daniels; and Buck Bohac, Katy Ansardi, and Deborah Kania of Indelible Blue.

Finally, but most importantly, I want to dedicate this book to God. From Him come all blessings.

Rick Smith

The authors jointly thank John Wiley & Sons for giving us this foray into the world of publishing. Phil Sutherland was our first advocate, partnering us on this endeavor and providing unwavering support before moving on to bigger and better things. Pam Sobotka seamlessly picked up where he left off, providing insightful comments and coordinating our final steps to production. Our sincerest appreciation to them and everyone else there who saw this project to completion.

Foreword

Welcome to the brave new world of Cyberspace. For business executives anywhere in the world, it has become increasingly clear that Internet and online services will be critical to conducting business in the future.

This can be terrifying. None of us (over the age of 30) were educated in computer networking such as we have today. Our experiences and skills, learned over years in business, may suddenly be open to question. Direct mail may not work well on the Internet. Traditional advertising may not work well on the Internet. As senior executives, we may *not* know more than junior executives just starting to climb the ladder. We need to get smart about this new world—and fast!

In Douglas Adams's famous five- or six-book trilogy, *The Hitchhiker's Guide to the Galaxy,* we learn that the most important message when faced with adversity is, Don't panic. For readers of *The Internet Strategic Plan,* that message is entirely apt.

Using anecdotes from actual business cases, the authors of *The Internet Strategic Plan* systematically explore Motivation, Dependencies, Goals, People, Location, Resources, Duration, and Issues regarding the challenges faced by real people looking to incorporate the Internet into their businesses. These include case studies from a variety of firms, from First Union Bank to Forté Software, and from a well-known law firm to a systems integrator.

The Internet Strategic Plan asks the questions that you will need to ask yourself as your company begins to take advantage of what the Internet has to offer. In addition to questions and insight, there are real tools that can be put to immediate use. These include an organizational chart with time line (PERT chart) and sample documents in the Appendixes.

In the 16 chapters in this book, the authors have attempted to remove the buzzwords, jargon, and hyperbole of the Internet, and replaced it with solid thinking, planning, and application to important business processes.

As a consultant to major corporations throughout the world, I continue to find many senior executives—CEOs, Chairmen of the Board, divisional Presidents—still uncertain about the longevity or applicability of the Internet.

The Internet has already changed us more than we realize. Five years ago, the Internet was known mostly to university research folks, government labs, and assorted technogeeks worldwide. Now, you cannot open a newspaper without finding some reference to the Internet. You cannot watch television without seeing a URL (Website address) flashed as part of the message. The Internet is everywhere.

The Internet is also very new as far as technology goes. Oh, the Internet has been around since the late 1960s, but the Web has been around only since 1992 and the real push didn't start until 1994. In essence, everything we take for granted concerning the Internet has happened mostly in the past three years. Understanding where all of this is going as it relates to *your* business will be critical to your continued successes.

The service industry executives that could not see how the Internet could reduce his customer service costs has now seen a dramatic change due to the Internet. Customers can access a Frequently Asked Questions document on the Web, and save the time previously spent with a live operator. What is more important is that the customer gets faster and more consistently accurate information. The result has been a significant improvement in customer satisfaction, while at the same time, growth of the number of attendants required has slowed.

Today's executive needs to be prepared to make informed decisions. *The Internet Strategic Plan* will help you do that. In my industry, we speak of time as moving in Internet Years. These are somewhat akin to dog years, although the time span seems to be getting shorter and shorter. As executives, mistakes can be costly. Prepare yourself well before diving in. The days of gut-feel decisions, unsupported by solid consideration, are past. You simply do not have the time to recover from bad decisions anymore. Should you become inclined to make a move based on gut feel alone, take my advice—either take some antacid or get something to eat, and then read this book!

See you on the Net!

Joel Maloff
joel@maloff.com
March 1997

Joel Maloff, founder of The Maloff Company in Dexter, MI, is one of the world's best-known Internet and World Wide Web consultants. His clients include The National Football League, Nationwide Insurance, CompuServe, The Toro Company, and The Discovery Channel. He also has numerous clients in Europe, South America, and Asia.

Contents

Acknowledgments, *v*
Foreword, *vii*
Introduction, *1*
How to Use This Book, *7*

1   **Decide to Connect** 23

Motivation, *23*
Dependencies, *24*
Goal, *25*
People, *25*
Location, *26*
Resources, *26*
Duration, *26*
Security, *26*
Issues, *27*
   Defining the Benefits, *27*
   Exploding the Myths, *34*
   Changing Your Mind, *37*
References, *37*

2   **Educate Employees** 39

Motivation, *39*
Dependencies, *41*
Goal, *41*
People, *42*
Location, *42*
Resources, *43*
Duration, *43*
Security, *44*
Issues, *49*
   Vendor Training, *49*
   Technical Training Curriculum, *49*
   Getting the Most for Your Money, *50*
   Consultants and Cross-Training, *51*
References, *51*

3   **Identify Resources** *53*

Motivation, *53*
Dependencies, *54*
Goal, *55*
People, *55*
    Project Leader, 56
    Rest of Team, 57
    Using Consultants, 58
    Outside Partners, 59
    Dream Team, 59
Location, *59*
Resources, *60*
Duration, *60*
Security, *61*
    Nondisclosure, 61
    Intellectual Property, 61
    Noncompete, 62
Issues, *70*
    Internal Survey, 70
    Budget, 71
    Team Assignments, 72
References, *73*

4   **Define Policy** *75*

Motivation, *76*
    Example: Recording Telephones, 77
    Example: Open Advertising, 77
    Dependencies, 78
Goal, *78*
People, *79*
Location, *80*
Resources, *80*
Duration, *80*
Security, *81*
    Publicly Available Policy Document, 81
    Internal Employee Usage Policy, 81
    Internal Security Procedures, 82
Issues, *86*
    Consistency with Existing Policies, 86
    Limits on Use, 87
    What Cannot Be Limited, 94
    Record Keeping, 95
    Penalties, 96
References, *97*

5   Determine Requirements 99

Motivation, *100*
Dependencies, *100*
Goal, *101*
People, *101*
Location, *102*
Resources, *102*
Duration, *102*
   Company Size, 103
   Geographic Scope, 103
   Technology, 103
   Project Team Availability, 103
Security, *104*
Issues, *104*
   Collecting the Information, 104
   Requirements Format, 106
   Security, 111
   Miscellaneous, 113
References, *119*

6   Architect the System 121

Motivation, *121*
Dependencies, *122*
Goal, *123*
People, *124*
Location, *124*
Resources, *125*
   Technical Writer, 125
   Document Production Tools, 126
   RFPs/RFIs, 126
   Other Sources, 127
Duration, *127*
Security, *127*
Issues, *133*
   General Goals of the Design Document, 133
   How to Organize the Design Document, 135
   Design Methodology, 137
   Outsourcing, 138
References, *140*

7   Estimate Costs 141

How to Use This Chapter, *142*
Goal, *143*

People, *143*
Issue One: Internet Price Overview, *143*
Issue Two: Internet Requirements, *145*
Issue Three: Internet Service Price Factors, *145*
Issue Four: Hardware Shopping List, *147*
    Other Options, 150
    Buy? Rent? Lease?, 150
Issue Five: Telephone Charges, *150*
Issue Six: Web Services, *151*
Issue Seven: Web Requirements, *152*
Issue Eight: Web Shopping List, *153*
References, *153*

8   Design and Acquire Network 155

Motivation, *155*
Dependencies, *156*
Goal, *157*
People, *157*
Locations, *158*
Resources, *158*
Duration, *159*
Security, *160*
Issues, *160*
    Beware the Prefab or Turnkey Install, 160
    Selecting Hardware, 169
    Configuration Document, 169
    Question to Ask Prospective Internet Service Provider, 169
    IP Address/Domain Name Registration, 171
References, *171*

9   Network Connection Testing and Acceptance . *173*

Motivation, *174*
Dependencies, *175*
Goal, *177*
People, *177*
Location, *178*
Resources, *178*
Duration, *179*
Security, *180*
Issues, *184*
    What Is an Engineering Plan?, 185
    Testing Primer, 185
    Written Test Results, 188
    Outsourcing and Consultants, 188
References, *189*

10 Design and Acquire Clients and Servers 191

Motivation, *191*
Dependencies, *193*
Goal, *193*
People, *193*
Location, *194*
Resources, *194*
Duration, *196*
Security, *197*
Issues, *198*
  Selecting Client and Server Software, 198
  Evaluating Web Hosting Services, 199
  Back-End Interfaces, 200
  Outsourcing, 202
  Prices, 205
  Security, 206
References, *207*

11 Install and Test Clients and Servers 209

Motivation, *210*
Dependencies, *211*
Goal, *213*
People, *214*
Location, *214*
Resources, *215*
Duration, *215*
Security, *216*
Issues, *220*
  Writing the Engineering Plan, 220
  What Makes Up the Test Plan?, 221
  Written Test Results, 223
  Outsourcing and Consultants, 224
References, *224*

12 Generate Content 227

Motivation, *229*
Dependencies, *231*
Goal, *231*
People, *232*
Location, *233*
Resources, *233*
Duration, *235*
Security, *236*

Issues, *240*
  Cutting-Edge Sites, 241
  Developing Your Style Guide, 242
  External Web Design Houses, 244
References, *244*

13 **Turn Over to Operations** *245*

Motivation, *246*
Dependencies, *246*
Goal, *247*
People, *247*
Location, *248*
Resources, *248*
Duration, *249*
Security, *251*
Issues, *254*
  Procedures List, 254
  Scheduled Downtime, 255
  Employee User Manuals, 255
References, *256*

14 **Market Your Presence** *257*

Motivation, *257*
Dependencies, *260*
Goal, *260*
People, *261*
Location, *262*
Resources, *262*
Duration, *262*
Security, *263*
Issues, *263*
  Traditional Marketing Techniques, 263
  Internet-Specific Marketing, 266
References, *272*

15 **Review Performance** *273*

Motivation, *273*
Dependencies, *277*
Goal, *278*
People, *279*
Location, *279*
Resources, *280*
Duration, *280*

Security, *281*
Issues, *281*
   Review the Internet Usage Policy, 281
   Revisit the Requirements Phase for Your Project, 282
   Revisit the Design Document, 282
   Review Network Design, Client Design, Server Design, 283
   Review Content Services, 283
   Review the Testing and Acceptance Phases, 283
   Review Your Marketing Program, 284
   Reviewing Your Training Plans, 284
References, *285*

16   Plan Phase II *287*

Motivation, *287*
Dependencies, *289*
Goal, *293*
People, *293*
Location, *293*
Resources, *294*
Duration, *294*
Security, *294*
Issues, *295*
   Adapting This Book's Project Plan, 295
   Additional Capabilities, 295
   Managing the Additions, 300
References, *300*

Glossary of Internet and Telecommunications Terms, *301*
Appendix A: Training Outlines, *309*
Appendix B: Internet Usage Policy for Employees, *317*
Appendix C: Internet Access High-Level Design, *325*
Appendix D: Network Test Plan, *333*
Index, *343*

Introduction

Unraveling a Ball of Confusion

Are you confused by the Internet?
Do you really know what the World Wide Web is all about?
How can you use an online connection to benefit your business?
How do you even get started?

If you said yes to the first question and no to the second, you are not alone. Unknown answers to questions three and four are why you bought this book. Welcome to what is called the Information Age. Some rightly call it the Age of Confusion. The Internet is coming to represent global communications, yet the mystique, hype, and misinformation surrounding it also have created a *Ball of Confusion,* as the old Temptations hit goes.

You no doubt have heard that the Information Superhighway is here today, and it's called the Internet. That's great, you say. But how do I and my business get on?

Oh, and then there is the Web—the tools that will allow Internet users to do everything online, from ordering pizza to videoconferencing to selling all kinds of goods and services. Okay, sounds even better than the Net, you say as a business person. Tell me how I can use the Web?

To help unravel this ball of confusion is what *The Internet Strategic Plan* is all about. Let us stress immediately, however, that this book is not designed to educate you about the Internet's technology or how to use the Web's myriad applications. Rather, we want to help you solve the Internet/Web confusion through planning, organization, and structure as you prepare your business to go online.

Only by applying basic business principles to the Internet and the Web can you minimize the effort to go online in terms of cost, time, and resources. Winston Churchill once said the Soviet Union was a riddle wrapped inside an enigma. The same can be said of the Internet and the Web because of their complexity, acronyms, technobabble, and hype. The Internet and the Web also are still very new to the business community, having been embraced widely only within the past two years. It really is no surprise, then, that the Internet and Web fail to fit within basic business paradigms. Businesses are confused as they try to unravel opportunities from traps.

But the very growth of the Internet to nearly every country and millions of users beckons business people to implement it. With so many people online and with competitive advantages to be gained from electronic commerce, it's no wonder that there has been a cyber rush. However, too many businesses have not bothered to do their homework when it comes to the Internet and Web strategies. The results include confusion, disillusionment, unreal expectations, and in some cases disconnection.

The fact remains, whether you are a sole proprietor or global corporate mogul, government employee or academician, you've seen the handwriting on the CRT. Cryptic strings like http://www.foo.com flash across major network programming; e-mail addresses now crowd business cards; a significant and growing number of people spend their work and leisure hours online. "Surfing" the Net for business and pleasure has become far more than just a fad, so we stress that it's time to think carefully—strategically—about how to get your organization connected to the Internet.

How can you get the most value from your office's connection? It is not just about finding the fastest server, or choosing the most robust applications, or creating the flashiest graphics. If you already have connection or if you are planning one now, you realize the technical, creative, and educational challenges can be straightforward. Expertise is often already available in house, or can be obtained through local consulting or the myriad

How To books and magazines focusing on the Internet. Finding them is important but not enough.

Successful Internet users (and there are many, some of which will be cited in this book) do not perform the individual tasks better than others; they manage the entire process more effectively. This simple axiom is easy to write, but much harder to overcome for many reasons. Unfortunately, small companies rarely possess individuals who can appreciate the relationship of all the tasks involved, from the technical aspects through the marketing implications. Further, large companies often drive the need for Internet connectivity from the bottom up, denying anyone the motivation to consider every department's requirements. All institutions are hindered by the tight deadlines, rapidly changing technologies, and cultural adaptations that usually accompany an Internet connection.

Most importantly, this book takes the top-down approach to the Internet and makes the access planning accessible to everyone. It does not focus on engineering issues or management theory, and to that end is mired neither in technobabble nor MBA-speak. The authors also have remained vendor neutral. Instead, the book contains practical advice about planning the tasks and organizing people so that you can derive maximum benefit from the Internet. Because part of the process is the creation of a common understanding, this book will be used by a variety of people and organizations, including:

▶ Executives, directors, managers, and employees—at every level of the organizational ladder—who will be involved in or benefit from Internet access
▶ Businesses, educational, and nonprofit institutions—who plan to use the Internet to acquire or provide information, promote, sell, or communicate
▶ Large or small organizations—which need help filling gaps in resources or experience, or coordinating different and dispersed groups
▶ Unconnected and connected organizations—that wish to plan a process before beginning, or those who wish to impose one on an existing installation
▶ Anyone—wanting to better understand the process for fully integrating Internet access into an office environment

As stressed earlier, many who learn about the Internet and the Web find that they embody a somewhat undisciplined, almost anarchic culture. If so, it may seem like a structured approach to connecting is at best inappropri-ate, and at worst doomed to failure. Please recognize that all organizations that connect to the Internet perform the steps outlined in this book; the dif-ference is in how they work together to do them better. By taking a more methodical, coordinated approach, you will greatly improve your benefit and satisfaction while minimizing frustration and disappointment. Just as communication and cooperation on the Internet improve daily, we hope this book enhances your journey to Internet access.

To help bring order out of chaos, or to prevent the latter altogether from your Internet/Web process, the book is broken down into a *How to Use* pro-logue and 16 closely linked chapters. We strongly encourage you not to ig-nore any, since each covers issues that will impact on your project.

Additionally, we have included a PERT chart to help you implement a coordinated plan, because we know how complex and daunting an Internet/ Web project can be.

The chapters are as follows and are presented in summary here to help establish the logic to our concept, step by step:

1. **Decide to Connect:** Obtaining Corporate Buy-In
2. **Educate Employees:** Bringing Employees into the Loop
3. **Identify Resources:** Who Will Do What, and Where to Find Them
4. **Define Policy:** Who Uses It and How?
5. **Determine Requirements:** What Are Your Goals and Needs?
6. **Architect System:** How Do You Determine the Equipment, Software, and Telephony Needs?
7. **Estimate Costs:** How Much Money Will It Cost to Continue?
8. **Design and Acquire Network:** Avoiding Pitfalls and Delays
9. **Install and Test Network:** Did You Get What You Paid For?
10. **Design and Acquire Clients and Servers:** What Are the Options?
11. **Install and Test Clients and Server:** What to Look for, What to Avoid
12. **Generate Content:** A Process for Electronic Publishing
13. **Turn Over to Operations:** Making Sure Your System Delivers Consistently and Reliably
14. **Market Your Presence:** Getting Out the Word about What You Are Doing
15. **Review Performance:** Did the Project Work? If Not, What Failed?
16. **Plan Phase II:** Your Next Steps onto the Internet

We also have included eleven case studies from a variety of companies that are reaping benefits from the Internet. Each of these case studies follows a question-and-answer format, with the executives or consultants offering advice about lessons they learned and mistakes they made. The companies include First Union Corp., one of the nation's largest financial institutions; PC Travel, a pioneer in selling airline tickets via the Internet and Web; Indelible Blue, a major IBM OS-2 software reseller; The Maloff Company, an Internet consulting firm with a global client base; TriNet Services, Inc., one of the nation's leaders in Internet and Web consulting; and Allen Marketing Group, a former advertising/public relations firm that has been transformed into a major Internet/Web firm with a long list of clients across the United States.

It is our hope that adding these companies' experiences to the theme espoused by this book's authors will help you turn a ball of confusion into a legitimate business opportunity.

How to Use This Book

If you want your best chance at avoiding Murphy's Law, please read this section in its entirety. It explains how to effectively and efficiently use this book. There are many texts and articles about connecting to the Internet, but the approach here is distinct. Rather than discuss any single piece in particular, this book outlines a process. The following sections set your expectations and describe how to apply the process to your organization. We encourage you not to separate steps out of the process, because we feel that this integrated strategy is the best to follow.

What Not to Expect

Each of the following types of information requires several books for a thorough treatise; do not look for them to be compressed in the following pages.

▶ **Technology Tutorial:** You're assumed to have a basic working knowledge of Internet terminology. If you know that a *router* is a device used to construct internetworks, where long sequences of data are bundled into *packets* that travel independently of each other, you probably know enough to guide the project. Of course, the more you learn as the project progresses, the better.

▶ **Applications Overview:** We cannot describe how to run the project and how to use the programs of the World Wide Web in a single printed volume, yet the success of your project depends on basic understanding of what you can do when you're connected. If you don't already have access to the Internet, get it. Individual accounts are relatively inexpensive, and the lessons you learn online will help expedite your corporate Internet/World Wide Web process. The best way to learn about Internet applications is to use them. Near the same bookstore or library shelves where this book was found, you should be able to locate several books that describe how to get and use a connection. Basic familiarity with electronic mail, newsgroups, and the Web is assumed.

▶ **Detailed Technical Guide:** Tasks outlined in this plan are best accomplished by experienced individuals whose skill sets cannot all be conveyed in a book of this limited length. You should count on locating good people, training them, buying more books, and learning a lot.

▶ **The Fastest Route:** If you are motivated by time constraints, this book is not for you. The thorough process presented here takes a few months to complete without shortcuts. On the other hand, if you are willing to sacrifice a dozen or so weeks to get the most usable connection possible, keep reading.

▶ **Customized Instructions:** No two organizations go through the steps of connecting to the Internet in exactly the same way. This book gives you enough information to customize the process for your needs; do not expect every step to be tailored for you.

▶ **Recommending Vendors:** As stated in the Introduction, the authors are vendor neutral and therefore won't recommend specific companies for any aspect of your project. However, we will offer opinions about how to choose vendors. These opinions are not made lightly and are based on the authors' Internet experience.

A Few Language Issues

In this book, an *organization* refers to any kind of business, educational interest, nonprofit agency, or government branch. To keep it applicable to all, the language is often very general. If the words do not seem appropriate for an office of your size, expertise, or geographic scope, they are probably not intended for you; just adapt them accordingly. Sometimes for variety, we will substitute *corporation*, *business*, or *enterprise*, so do not be distracted if you work for a nonprofit entity, are a sole proprietor or partner, or have an otherwise distinct legal status.

The word *connection* applies to more than just a telephone line; it also means the set of routers that connect you and the computers and software that communicate, along with the people and procedures necessary to run them effectively. The TCP/IP technology is assumed to be reasonably well understood by either you or members within your organization; the main challenges ahead are organizational in nature.

For your assistance and convenience, a brief glossary of Internet terms appears at the end of the book.

Process Overview

As with many services, a traditional product life-cycle model like that of Figure 1 can be applied to the process of obtaining an Internet connection. In this simplified representation, some preliminary work is implied to reach the approval stage. Afterwards, a more detailed sense of the project's goals and the design that achieves them are documented in the planning step. The system is purchased and/or built, installed, tested, and documented during implementation. Finally, the product becomes operational. In practice, the boundaries are often blurred and feedback is always employed as information revealed in the latter stages forces reconsideration of earlier decisions.

The many technical books on the market are designed to help during the implementation and operations phases. This book is intended primarily for

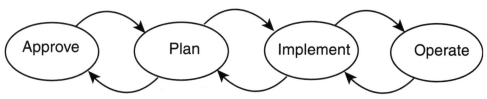

FIGURE 1   Simplified project life cycle.

the planning step, where understanding the relationship tasks have to each other is vital. Since the approval step must be completed first, one chapter has been devoted to that topic.

Who Should Read This Book

In most organizations, and particularly the large ones, different individuals participate in each of the life-cycle model steps. Except for those people with overall project responsibility, this book will not be read completely by everyone. The following sections describe which organizational members have roles in the life cycle, and how each should use this book.

Upper Management

Although the idea and strategy for connecting to the Internet may come from anywhere within the company, upper (or executive) management usually has approval authority. The most important chapters for upper management to read are:

► **Chapter 1:** The reasons for connecting will be visited.
► **Chapter 2:** You will understand how important it is to educate your organization about the Internet.
► **Chapter 4:** You will determine how the connection is to be used.
► **Chapter 5:** You will understand the important requirements process and be able to assemble the appropriate team.

Upper management may also be involved during Chapter 7, where costs are estimated and a decision is made on whether to proceed. Other chapters may be useful as appropriate for your organization.

Project Team

A major premise of this book is that forming a *Project Team* and designating a *Project Leader* to coordinate the Internet/Web project is absolutely essential. Project planning responsibility falls to a small set of individuals.

If you have been assigned to the Project Team, or would like to be, you should read the entire book in detail. Though upper management has already read the prescribed chapters, you may need to help with those efforts. As someone responsible for coordinating everyone's efforts, you must understand the tasks facing each group so that you can help them maintain focus, clear their obstacles, and communicate their progress.

Project Resources

The Project Team will draw on internal resources to help plan and implement the Internet connection. If your specific technical, marketing, sales, production, or other talents have been requested to help develop an aspect of this project (i.e., write a design or procedure, contribute to requirements), these are the chapters that you should read.

▶ **Chapters 1 and 4:** Providing necessary background on this project
▶ The chapter or chapters that describe the specific steps on which you will work
▶ Those chapters immediately before and after the preceding, which will explain the dependencies among pieces of the project

Of course, you will also need to read relevant documentation created during the earlier project steps.

Internet Users

This category can potentially apply to everyone in your organization. To plan a useful connection, it is important to understand what people want to do with their access. Input from across departments is important. In practice, some representatives from as many departments and/or locations will be chosen for the Project Team. They will need to familiarize themselves with the following:

▶ **Chapters 1 and 4:** For important background information
▶ **Chapter 2:** Covering training plans
▶ **Chapter 5:** Describing how the requirements collection phase will proceed

Operations

If the responsibility to maintain any aspect of your organization's Internet access (i.e., operate a computer, supply new information for distribution on the Internet) falls to you, these are the sections of this book you should read:

▶ **Chapters 1 and 4:** Provide necessary background on this project
▶ **Chapter 2:** Discuss education and training
▶ The chapter or chapters that describe the specific steps on which you will work

The Project Plan

The time-honored format for documenting and communicating work efforts within an organization is the *Project Plan.* There are several methods by which it can be represented, each with its own advantage in showing expectations and facilitating tracking. For this book, the PERT chart will be used, in which each box stands for a project function which is usually:

▶ Performed by a specific group of people
▶ Begun and ended at specific points in time
▶ Producing a well-defined result

Each box will display the *task name* (at the top), the *task ID* and corresponding chapter number (bottom left), and the *task duration* (bottom right). Two of the tasks are *milestones,* with no meaningful duration and no explicit result. The remainder are *deliverables,* with nonzero duration and a resulting product. Figure 2 shows how each of these tasks is displayed.

On the PERT chart, these boxes are linked by arrows that indicate the order in which tasks must be performed. Tasks are completed from left to right and top to bottom; all the tasks pointing to a box must be completed before it can begin. Bold lines show critical path items that require more time to complete than other parallel tasks. In practice, the project plan usually provides a baseline from which the actual project evolves. It must remain dynamic to be useful.

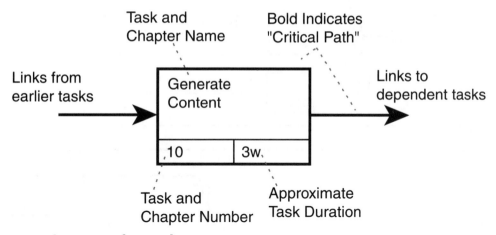

FIGURE 2   PERT chart task representation.

On the following pages, a generic project plan for creating your organization's Internet connection is presented. This baseline must be tailored to reflect your particular needs, and you may decide to eliminate entire branches based on the outcomes described in the first few chapters. Also note that time estimates are approximate and reflect those needed by a mid-sized organization. Additionally, your PERT chart will show additional information, such as cost estimates omitted here for clarity (see Figure 3).

The rest of this book will help you determine which paths are necessary, and how long they may require within your organization. You will likely refer to this chart repeatedly as you read the book.

Following is a more detailed description of each task.

Chapter 1   Decide to Connect

The first step in the generic life-cycle process is a decision. It is often difficult to obtain organizational buy-in to connect to the Internet, due sometimes to a lack of basic information about the Internet at the executive level, often combined with an excess of misinformation. This chapter will help affirm your company's choice to connect by reviewing the reasons it is important, and exploding the myths that keep people away.

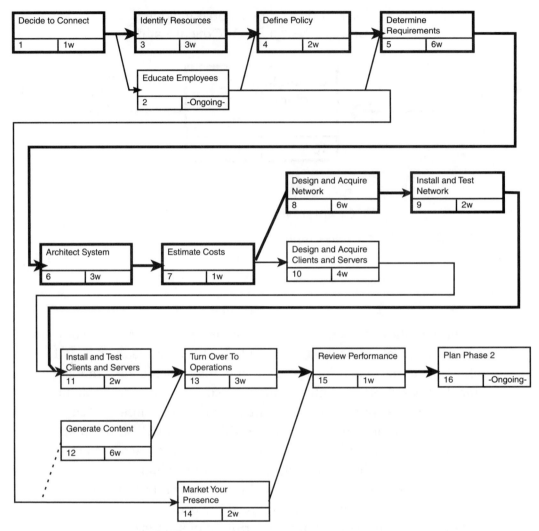

FIGURE 3   The Internet Strategic Plan PERT Chart.

Chapter 2   Educate Employees

When budgets are tight, training programs are often among the first cuts. For effective use of the Internet, skimping on training is pennywise and dollar foolish (or whatever currency you are using). The sooner you begin a calculated training program, the more success you can expect. This chapter will discuss some general guidelines for creating good training plans, and will offer specific recommendations for training employees who have more direct technical responsibilities.

Chapter 3   Identify Resources

Like everything else you do, success depends heavily on the skills and adaptability of the people involved. Most organizations are unfamiliar with the skill areas necessary to launch a successful Internet connection, let alone where to find or how to motivate them. This chapter tells you up front how to assemble a quality team of individuals from within and/or outside your organization. Advice is given on locating hidden internal talent, finding quality consultants, avoiding inappropriate aid, and organizing for success.

Chapter 4   Define Policy

Your company's existing practices—embodiment of your *corporate knowledge*—have been developed from written policies, memos, experiences. On the uncharted roads of the Information Superhighway, no such guidance exists. This chapter discusses boundaries for nonbusiness use, guarding confidential information, and raising awareness of how your electronic voice to the world is used. This preventive approach avoids wasted time and expense implementing undesired features and correcting employee behavior.

Chapter 5   Determine Requirements

The difference between a weekend project and a massive Information Systems (IS) undertaking is in the requirements. This chapter provides a framework for defining what your finished system will do, and serves as an important communications bridge between those who desire and finance the project and those who construct and operate it. No attempt is made to explain every technical service available today; the emphasis is on exposing sufficient general requirements so that a high-level design can be created.

Chapter 6   Architect System

In the familiar context, an architect balances the form and function of a building, but leaves the details to the construction, plumbing, electrical, landscape, and other employees. So too with an Internet connection is it necessary to devise a general plan of how things will work before allowing specialists to construct their components. This chapter covers the architecture or high-level design phase of the project, highlighting key issues and providing a sample plan.

Chapter 7   Estimate Costs

While any project can be terminated at any point due to shifting corporate needs, it is very useful to build in a cost-based decision point. Without experience, it is impossible to accurately predict how much an Internet project will cost to install or run. This step in the project allows you to roughly gauge your initial and ongoing cash expenses so that you can modify the project scope if necessary. It also includes the financial talents within your company on the Internet team.

Chapter 8   Design and Acquire Network

As the old joke goes, The nice thing about standards is, there are so many to choose from. While the Internet embodies perhaps the most successful real-world standardization process to date, things are far from plug and play, with every vendor differentiating their wares with unique and often incompatible features. If as a result of your requirements you decide to connect directly to the Internet, understanding the issues is vital to ensuring a correctly engineered interconnection with the world's largest public packet-switched infrastructure. It is also crucial to minimizing your time to availability, since equipment and circuit leasing are often critical path items in this process.

Chapter 9   Install and Test Network

Whether you have customers or members, they will come to assess you in part by what they see: the cleanliness of your showroom, the courtesy of your sales staff, the responsiveness of your customer assistance. That's why a carefully crafted installation and testing phase are vitally important. This chapter not only builds in that time for your project, but it also provides advice for what to examine to find problems that would otherwise surface down the road.

Chapter 10   Design and Acquire Clients and Servers

Whereas many companies have relatively homogeneous networks, most have very heterogeneous computer environments: PC systems from different vendors and with different peripherals and capacities, Macintosh or UNIX systems, minicomputers and mainframes all coexist. Chapter 10 will help you anticipate problems that arise in typical computer environments when introducing the Internet.

Chapter 11   Install and Test Clients and Servers

As with Chapter 9, the importance of testing cannot be overstated. There is an effect equally noticed among customers and employees who use the Internet: Frustration creates reluctance. If you go online and encounter problems, people who would otherwise come to you, and even your own workers, may not be ready to try again. This chapter will describe some of the testing you should plan to do before opening your service for business.

Chapter 12   Generate Content

Have you ever made a scheduled phone call only to find that neither party had anything to say? Connecting to the Internet to host a Web service without creating a process for content generation is like that—except much more expensive. If you decide to provide information onto the Web, this chapter will highlight the issues—like how to ensure content is reviewed, converted into a suitable format, and loaded regularly—to avoid those silent conversations.

Chapter 13   Turn Over to Operations

Ordinarily, handing off the installed equipment to be operated is a milestone. In practice, however, it is an ongoing process. Procedures to run your system day to day can in part be written in advance, but few organizations allocate the time or resources. This chapter describes how to start the hand-off process, emphasizing the need for ongoing cooperation between designers and operations for continual improvements.

Chapter 14   Market Your Presence

Without a concerted effort to disseminate the word, your organization can remain an unmarked road on the Information Infrastructure. When you have reached this point in the project, you'll be ready to get the word out—to people outside and inside your company. We'll suggest some popular methods for reaching people on the Internet, such as registering with directories and offering cross-advertising to complementary businesses.

Chapter 15   Review Performance

Up to this point, you've received advice for streamlining your company's Internet presence. Now it's time to measure how well we did. This chapter gives some perspective on what to expect based on the authors' experiences with numerous organizations. We'll review where things often go wrong, and highlight some pitfalls you managed to avoid.

Chapter 16   Plan Phase II

As everyone who connected to the Internet discovered, it is not a one-time project, but rather an ongoing process. Sites on the Internet constantly revise their content, upgrade their capabilities, and find innovative new ways to take advantage of their infrastructure. This chapter discusses some of those, including electronic commerce and *Intranetworking*.

Chapter Structure

All but two chapters in this book cover a different step of the project plan using a common outline. The first ten outline headings discuss similar issues from chapter to chapter, but the eleventh varies according to the particular task.

1. **Short Introduction:** An unlabeled set of paragraphs summarizing the chapter's contents
2. **Motivation:** Reasons for doing (or omitting) this step
3. **Dependencies:** Relationship to other chapters
4. **Goal:** What is produced or decided
5. **People:** Description of the skills and roles required
6. **Location:** Where the activities should be performed
7. **Resources:** Set of additional products or services of use for this task
8. **Duration:** How to estimate the time to completion
9. **Security:** When to share information and when to guard it
10. **Issues:** Details about the activities performed and the particular choices faced
11. **References:** Where to go for more information

While most of the sections are consistently brief, the Issues section often becomes lengthy. Please resist the urge to skip this detail, since it contains important information that will save you time and effort.

Use of Case Studies

If you had any reason to think that the Internet is all hype, consider this comment from Charles Knuff, president of Forté, a software company based in California: "The Internet represents a fundamental shift for our company. It has become the major focus of our business efforts. We expect our Internet products to become our primary source of revenue in 1997."

SAS Institute, a global software company based in Cary, NC, is reorienting its products and marketing to incorporate the Web and Internet into its strategy. First Union, one of the largest financial institutions in the United States, is using the Internet to reach new customers, develop new products, and provide better service.

Forté, SAS, and First Union tell their Internet stories in this book. We have always heard that experience is the best teacher, so we chose to include a series of case studies with this book in the hope of giving our readers additional insight into how business people and their companies have dealt with the Internet and World Wide Web.

Eleven companies chose to participate, and they represent a good cross section of business types that can benefit from online services. These firms represent software design and manufacture (SAS, Forté), banking (First Union), finance (MacroWorld Research), online catalogs (Indelible Blue), travel (PC Travel), and legal (Daniels & Daniels). We also selected a world-known Internet consulting firm (The Maloff Company), two Web site and marketing firms (TriNet Services and Allen Marketing Group), plus a systems integrator (TechSolv).

The case studies appear in chapters that apply most to their circumstances. Each follows the same format: an introduction and a series of questions and answers. The Q&A was the same for each but as you will see, many of the answers, although similar, offer different perspectives on problems that are common to the Internet and Web businesses.

As you read these, you will see that the Internet has had a profound impact on SAS, one of the world leaders in database software. First Union is alerting its strategy to capitalize on the opportunities of online banking. MacroWorld and Forté are two companies that have completely reoriented their core business approaches because of the Internet.

Daniels & Daniels, a law firm in Research Triangle Park, NC, not only works with many high-tech firms but also sees the Internet as an opportunity to create new business opportunities. Cofounder Walter Daniels sees the Internet as "a great leveler" in terms of competition, "and we don't want to get leveled."

Intranets are all the rage today, and several of these companies talk about the benefits, or potential benefits, these will deliver.

Readers will find insight about the importance of:

▶ Strategic planning
▶ Internal coordination
▶ Executive buy-in
▶ Identifying revenue and savings opportunities
▶ Marketing research
▶ Gauging impact on customers
▶ Gauging impact on internal departments
▶ Determining customer needs
▶ Determining internal needs
▶ Assessing technical infrastructure

They also discuss how to:

- Identify new products and new markets
- Pick vendors and service providers
- Adapt to changes and new opportunities

Here are samples of comments and tips that you will find in the Case Studies:

First Union: "Before we knew it, we were consumed in the project. We saw the Internet as a way to reach new markets and new customers, and provide better service to our existing customers."

SAS: A strategic plan is important, but "Even more important, however, is executive buy-in at the earliest stages of the process. The last thing you want is to enter into the process of developing an Intranet as a *skunkworks* project."

TechSolv: "Most companies don't have a plan. . . . Without a needs/resource analysis, they are simply buying blind. You shouldn't just throw technology at a problem. Determine the need and then intelligently implement using technology as the vehicle."

Daniels & Daniels: "We have always used technology well and have never regretted any investment we have made in technology. Consequently, incorporation of the Internet into this philosophy has been quite easy."

Indelible Blue: "The Net should be integrated with other plans within a company. Since we are a smaller business, we did not do a formal plan at the beginning. Now we are planning for future implementations."

Allen Marketing Group: "Most of the difficulties we have seen companies face have been related to integrating their Internet marketing activities into their traditional marketing communications activities. In other words, many of the companies with an early Internet presence did not understand the importance of traditional marketing (i.e., print-based advertising and direct mail) in generating traffic to their Web site."

PC Travel: "Nearly every problem was unanticipated, as connecting was like stepping back 15 years in the networking business when everything seemed to be decided on the fly. We overcame the problems with perseverance and with help from [service] providers."

TriNet Services: "One of the worst problems companies have is that because this is a new technology, people underestimate and miscalculate costs and capabilities. There are going to be things that don't work the way they are intended."

The Maloff Company: "The major lessons from my clients were to start thinking first—not after you put the engine in gear. It is important to consider all aspects, including how well the existing infrastructure can handle the new solutions."

First Union: "At First Union, we faced the difficulty of education. Words like *navigators* and *browsers* are foreign to most people who don't dabble in the online world."

Daniels & Daniels: "We are able to charge a premium for our technological capabilities, and our clients still get cost-effective service because of our enhanced responsiveness and delivery capability."

MacroWorld: "It was not apparent in 1993 that the Internet would grow as fast as it did and become so quickly pervasive. However, the decision to scrap the previous upgrade plans and unify all of the services into one sophisticated Web site has, in fact, resulted in greater effeciencies and a flexibility not originally contemplated."

Need for an Internet Account

We would like to leave you with one of the most important points of this Introduction: Get access to the Internet at the start of this plan! It doesn't matter if you get a dial-up account for your home PC (although this is the easiest), make frequent trips to a public terminal at the library, or use that of a friend. The more current, useful resources for getting your organization online are already there! Making sure you have access now will help you check the resources listed in this book, and verify that your plans and policies make sense. You wouldn't design your dream home without going inside a house or two, would you?

CHAPTER 1

Decide to Connect

The most basic and obvious easy step in getting your organization connected to the Internet is sometimes the most frustrating and time-consuming. Gaining approval poses a challenge, often due to a lack of information or an excess of misinformation. There may be no clear understanding of how the Internet helps your organization achieve its goals, or it may seem too expensive, risky, or distracting.

As tens of thousands of organizations are finding out each year, connecting to the Internet is worthwhile. It brings significant business advantages in tangible, sometimes unexpected ways. The cost of a simple connection can be very low (and can be minimized by following this book!) We encourage everyone involved in the process to read this chapter and discuss which reasons apply to your particular circumstances. Cost reduction and growing your customer base are two key issues we discuss.

Motivation

While including a decision milestone as an explicit step may seem redundant, there are several reasons for putting it first:

▶ **Commitment:** Many cautious decision makers do not fund projects without a clear understanding of the benefits, costs, and risks involved. If this is an ongoing step, people involved in the project will become frustrated if repeated efforts to allocate resources are met with reluctance. It is far more efficient to commit to the project, or at least up to the design step after which costs and risks are better understood.

▶ **Create Focus:** The following chapters ask each part of the organization to identify how they will use the Internet. If the reasons for connecting are not commonly understood, it will be very difficult to obtain consensus on how it will be used.

▶ **Identify Resources:** Making a clear statement of intent often prompts experienced individuals to come forward. You may locate internal resources you did not know existed (this is discussed more in Chapter 2).

▶ **Cooperation:** Getting the most from your Internet connection stems from understanding how it helps every part of your organization. Making generally known from the start your decision to connect to the Internet helps ensure cooperation and visibility for the team.

▶ **Signaling Change:** Organizations that choose to attach to the Internet open themselves to new ways of interacting with customers, suppliers, and other external groups. In all institutions—especially those with a long-standing tradition of electronic isolation—it sends a positive message to employees seeking innovation.

Dependencies

As the first step in the project, everything else begins afterward and depends entirely on its successful completion. In practice, this step is often reached because work on a later step was already begun! For example, somebody in marketing may have recognized the need to advertise your services on the Web, or someone in engineering may need to retrieve applications from a popular archive, and what began as a grass-roots effort to connect your company turned into a formal goal. It does not matter how you arrived here—as long as you move forward.

To maximize your benefit from the Internet, it is necessary to consider how it affects your organization as a whole, as indicated earlier. A single existing hardware system, application, or department is rarely enough to efficiently drive the process. Whatever started your interest, from this point on, look at the advantages a connection can bring to your entire enterprise.

Goal

As a milestone, there is no specific output at this stage other than a decision. To communicate that decision, a written or oral report may be delivered, perhaps in the form of a business case or proposal. Whatever form is appropriate for your organization, share it with your employees. Print an article in a corporate newsletter. Send internal e-mail or voice mail. Put a sign on a bulletin board. Since everyone may contribute during the process, sharing the decision from the outset will improve the result.

People

While midlevel managers may possess the authority, deciding to connect to the Internet should be made at the highest level. The chief executive officer, chairman, president, and/or board of directors should all have an interest in seeing it accomplished. The decision should not fall to the leader of a single department, such as the head of Information Systems, or Marketing, or Sales.

While this may be unavoidable in small organizations, the benefits of centralizing the goal for Internet access in large organizations can be dramatic. Large companies whose branches install independent connections could easily save tens of thousands of dollars in service-provider fees, hardware costs, and personnel time with a single, consolidated approach. Many large companies waste tens of thousands of dollars because Internet access is fragmented across divisions. When consolidation eventually occurs, it is extremely costly to reconcile disparate systems and practices.

Again, we stress that the Internet/Web decision be made not on intuition or a hint. It should be based on solid information gathered by responsible, knowledgeable employees, or with the help of outside consultants.

Location

Since the decision should be made by those highest in the organization, this step will probably be performed wherever headquarters are located. The basic reasons for connecting do not depend on geography. In fact, a consequence of the Internet is that a single access point to the network infrastructure can easily and economically facilitate global computer exchanges.

Resources

This step requires time from those able to make the decision and commit funds. If they need to understand how it will help the organization, they can draw on the knowledge of employees from marketing, IS, or those who otherwise gained an appreciation of how the Internet can help.

We'd like to think there's sufficient motivation from the growing public awareness of the Internet along with the information in this chapter to convince you.

Duration

As a milestone, this step should take a minimum of two weeks. The decision should not be rushed, and if outside expertise is needed the time line may have to be extended. The project time line starts when the decision is made to proceed. In most organizations, it takes many weeks or months to reach launch time. If you are trying to drive or participate in the process, it is not cause for discouragement. When the advantages and disadvantages are clearly explained, the correct decision will be made. If you are responsible for making the decision, a following section on Issues may help you get there more quickly.

Security

As the output from this step is a decision, the security considerations are simple: Should we let the world know of our decision to connect? For many businesses, there is a strong desire to hide this decision. Many prefer not to tip the competition to their plans, others simply have a policy against sharing technical plans, and some simply keep quiet as a hedge against changing their minds. All will need to enter Nondisclosure Agreements (NDA) with the companies discussed in the coming chapters.

Be aware that early in this process, you will likely need to register a *domain name* that identifies your address on the Internet. This address must be globally registered in a freely accessible database. While others cannot discern your exact plans, intentions to have some connectivity cannot be hidden forever.

Issues

Many organizations make the decision to connect to the Internet agonizingly difficult. Why is it sometimes so hard? We believe there are two root causes: Either the benefits are not clear, or they are obscured by misinformation. Each is addressed separately in the following sections.

Defining the Benefits

Driving every significant business decision is a set of questions relating choices to your organization's mission. In the context of connecting to the Internet, those questions include:

► How could the Internet and/or Web help your company?
► How could either, or both, hurt?
► What mechanisms do you use to communicate with your customers? With vendors and partners?
► How do you keep tabs on the competition?
► What are the internal constraints, such as budgets and personnel time?
► What other options exist?

Ultimately, you are responsible for ensuring the four Ps of your organization are successful: product, price, place, and promotion. The Internet can help usually in more than one way. As you conduct your cost/benefits analysis, consider the following ways in which it can help.

Improving Communication with Customers

In 1996, the home PC stood up and demanded attention, when domestic purchases actually exceeded those of TVs by a healthy margin. As PCs depart the niche realm of early adopter toys bound for mass-market acceptance, their ability to create compelling , interactive graphics and sound enable richer user interfaces than TV, magazines, and other conventional media. Their tireless availability also lets your customers order and seek information or support 24 hours a day, 7 days a week, with nary a busy signal or musical hold. Numerous companies provide dynamic product tutorials, a way to customize product sizing, and online ordering for one-stop convenience; and e-mail is becoming a standard and socially acceptable form of communication.

Expanding Customer Base

The nearest things to global yellow pages are the *Internet WWW Directories*, which provide near instantaneous search capabilities on trillions of characters of information. To create a Web site is to have an entry, enabling customers thousands of miles away to find you. E-mail also breaks down geographic barriers—providing a store-and-forward, intrinsically documented form of communication that is not billed based on distance, and is highly suited to busy people on opposite sides of the globe, a user population recently estimated at over 40 million and growing.

Reducing Cost

The direct cost advantages of Internet connectivity are directly related to the technology. Unlike traditional telephony, the capacity of Internet circuits are efficiently shared among multiple computers *at the same time*. Thus, your computer can send electronic mail, mine can browse the web, and another can conduct a real-time videoconference on the same circuit simultaneously. When my mail session is finished, the capacity is made available for a faster Web download. This graceful sharing leads to overall cost reductions over other technical approaches. The current pricing models of the Internet also help—billing is not based on distance (as with long distance), and sometimes not even on utilization. The largest cost component of any wide-area network, the transmission capacity, cannot be shared with any greater efficiency than offered by the Internet. As a technical advantage, these costs can be quantified.

There are also numerous indirect cost savings associated with Internet access. The Internet's newsgroups offer huge repositories of human knowledge willing to answer questions, often in a few minutes. The WWW sites contain trillions of characters of information readily available without leaving one's office. Software archives on the Internet also provide free and shareware applications. It not only saves time, but connecting to the Internet culture also has a tangible benefit that is difficult to measure in dollars.

Enabling New Business Models

The Internet does more than just improve the way things are done; it also enables new things. Many of these are high-tech businesses, such as Internet-based data archiving, software sales and support, online multiuser interactive gaming, and remote monitoring and diagnostics. But the Internet has also enabled new partnerships in low-tech businesses, too, such as the online ticket sales, marketing, and related services.

FIRST UNION CORPORATION

First Union Corp. (Figure 1.1), one of the nation's largest financial institutions, is building what it believes is the bank of the future. And the future depends upon the company's ability to deliver new products and services to customers who want to bank any time, any place, any way.

While continuing to offer traditional banking products, the company also will focus on delivering electronic commerce and online banking to its customers through its virtual bank *branch* on the Internet.

"Online banking is definitely where things are heading," said Tom Bartolomeo, Vice President of Information Security responsible for rolling out the Internet project for the Charlotte, NC, banking leader. "Everything we see in this area has been validated in recent months with Visa, Microsoft, and others changing their strategy to incorporate TCP/IP into their efforts. This tells you that the Internet channel is a channel to be reckoned with."

But Mr. Bartolomeo cautions that just building a Web site and getting Internet access is not enough to ensure success. "The Internet is constantly changing and evolving, and some of this technology will become obsolete, as with any other venture," he said. "So marketing your products and

(continued)

FIGURE 1.1   The First Union home page.

offering value-added services to your customers become crucial to success on the Net."

First Union is at the forefront of *cyberbanking* (SM), which allows customers to access their accounts through the Internet using a secure Internet browser. Cyberbanking functions will include account inquiry, funds transfer, bill payment, and loan applications.

Mr. Bartolomeo joined First Union's Card Products Division in early 1994, and soon after he and his team in Internet Marketing realized that online banking through the Internet had potential for helping the company to grow. By January of 1995, First Union had a Web site, becoming one of the first Internet bank pioneers.

Mr. Bartolomeo stressed that companies wanting to develop an Internet/Web strategy have to be willing to deal with several challenging issues:

► Create a sound business strategy
► Develop a strategic plan

▶ Learn to adapt and change quickly
▶ Stay abreast of technology

What follows is the Q&A with Mr. Bartolomeo:

Question: What factors and/or research led to your company's decision to develop an Internet/Web strategy? What approach should other companies take?

Answer: In 1994 we started to explore the possibility of using online services and looked at Prodigy, which had a credit-card application. We decided we could do the same thing and when we got an account with a local Internet service provider, we began discovering the power of the Internet. Eventually, we realized we could develop a Web site on the Internet for the entire company. Before we knew it, we were consumed in the project. We saw the Internet as a way to reach new markets and new customers, and provide better service to our existing customers.

I recommend that newcomers ask themselves one important question before jumping head-first into a project like this: What do you want your Web site to do for you? For instance, is it a marketing tool to introduce products and services? Will it be transaction-based? Will it offer commerce-enabled transactions? Will it be totally interactive?

Once you've determined what you want, the next step is figuring out how you'll support it internally and deliver it externally. Developing a Web site just because the other guy is doing it will almost certainly guarantee disappointment.

Question: Often in this startup process, there are many difficulties to be overcome, technical and otherwise. What are some of the most common? Did companies anticipate these? What were they able to do to overcome these obstacles? What lessons should companies learn from this experience?

Answer: The major hurdle companies must overcome is the impact the Internet has on how they do business. And to be honest, I don't know if companies are aware of the vast opportunities that lie on the doorstep of the Internet.

At First Union, we faced the difficulty of education. Words like *navigators* and *browsers* are foreign to most people who don't dabble in the online world. So our job has been to teach employees and customers the

(continued)

capabilities of the Internet, to explain its viability as a key business tool, and to keep them abreast of the constant evolution of this fascinating medium.

Security on the Internet is our other major (and most important) hurdle. Our challenge is twofold: changing customer and employee perceptions of security on the Internet and building the systems, policies, and procedures to protect customer and bank information from the inside and outside. Electronic security will continue to evolve as we conduct more and more of our business online. And First Union will have to constantly upgrade its security procedures and systems to ensure a secure transaction environment for its customers.

Question: What is some advice you would give others?

Answer: No matter what the technology is, it always comes back to good, fundamental business decisions and core disciplines, such as marketing, finance, and communications. Before First Union spent millions of dollars on technology we were unfamiliar with, we tested and learned as much as we could about the Internet with the help of a small project team. It is always important to develop a product-business case that will allow you to research the Internet channel.

We started with soft, information-based marketing of First Union products and services on our Web site. Then we added transaction-based and commerce-based applications and an interactive customer comment section. As we continue to refine our remote banking strategy, customers will eventually be able to transact all their banking business online.

The key point is, we couldn't have built this Web site without corporationwide support (Systems Development, Information Services, Customer Service, Marketing). It all overlaps.

Question: How important is it to have a strategic plan?

Answer: It's important to first understand *why* you are developing the Internet channel. (What is your business objective?) This will serve as your foundation. If your goal is to reach new markets, new customers, and offer something of value—whether it's information, products, or services—then your strategic plan is there to guide, to measure, and to determine what works well and what doesn't; and how these elements contribute to your long-term goals.

One of the most valuable benefits we gained from the planning process was the ability to proactively navigate through the peaks and valleys of the research and development efforts. We learned about the Internet's vast potential and also its possible shortfalls.

As technologies rapidly evolve and new initiatives arise, you must always have focus on your major objectives.

Question: What are some of the mistakes that you see other companies making as they delve into the Internet? Why are they making them?

Answer: Companies that set up Web sites just because other companies do so are making a mistake. They are not making the decision based on sound business objectives and principles. If you are outsourcing your Web site, make sure you carefully investigate your alternatives, seek references, and visit with their technical and marketing personnel.

If you're building your site in-house, then remember it's a corporationwide effort. The initiative will cut across and touch all areas within your organization. By involving your whole employee population, you help expand the level of interest and knowledge in the Internet and enhance the quality of your Web site.

Question: What has access to the Internet and use of the Web meant to your business?

Answer: It has given us the ability to offer our customers banking where and when they want. Now our customers are telling us we're meeting their needs by delivering a new way to transact their banking business that's fast, easy, and convenient.

Question: If you were new to the Web/Internet and looking for a book to help you plan/coordinate/execute an Internet strategy, what are some of the points you would want covered?

Answer: I would like to see tips on: building a successful Web site, selecting the right consultants, preparing people for how the Internet can positively impact their businesses, and also becoming a cost-effective way to reach customers.

Question: What are some of the factors companies should be looking for when selecting an ISP, Web site developer, and/or consulting firm?

Answer: Companies should select a group of people with the expertise to understand the technology and the marketing aspects of the project. They need to think strategically and not only understand where the Internet is headed today, but also where it will be in five or ten years.

We talked to several advertising agencies and media companies before selecting a consultant (TriNet Services, Inc., of Raleigh, NC) with the right

(continued)

marketing and technical background. You have to check references and samples of their work.

Question: First Union was among the pioneers in banking on the Internet. How were you able to persuade management that this was a risk worth taking?

Answer: We did our homework and learned as much as we could about this new channel, then we effectively communicated our strategic plan to senior management. We developed a vision and strategic plan to explain how we could use this channel to better serve existing customers and to reach new customers and markets. Once management accepted our plan, we went to the rest of the bank and asked for their support and explained the value of this channel.

Exploding the Myths

Everybody has heard something about the Internet, either from the news media or literature or word of mouth. Sometimes, the information conveyed is inaccurate or incomplete. This section dispels some of the misinformation that has been circulated.

Myth: Connecting to the Internet costs thousands or tens of thousands of dollars.

Fact: While large corporations can spend hundreds of thousands of dollars for hardware and tens of thousands each month in recurring telecommunications charges, the vast majority of groups with dedicated connections buy or repurpose less expensive hardware costing only a few thousand dollars. Recurring charges may be less than $1,000 per month or substantially lower, depending on the access speed and distance to the telephone company's central office.

For the smallest organizations, dial-up and ISDN access can drop recurring charges to $100 per month or less, and equipment under $1,000. There is even the possibility of letting someone else provide the connection and hardware for only a substantially smaller monthly fee.

The ISP business also has become very competitive, especially with many of the regional Bell operating companies now offering Internet access and Web services. You should screen vendors, seek the best prices possible, and negotiate for discounts on equipment and installation.

Myth: The Internet is still only a research project.
Fact: Neither the infrastructure nor the purposes are relegated to research anymore. Originally, the National Science Foundation (NSF) funded the *backbone*—a collection of devices and long-distance circuits that connected key locations across the United States. Now they fund only the InterNIC, a network operations center, and places where Network Service Providers (NSPs) can attach to each other. All current backbones are commercial.

While NSF backbone users followed an *Acceptable Use Policy* that required applications to be research oriented, current NSPs permit any purpose. As such, commercial organizations have caught up to noncommercial ones and are growing at a faster rate. The next chapters will suggest how those organizations are relying on the Internet in ways that make it far more than experimental.

Myth: Nobody runs the Internet; anarchy rules.
Fact: There is no single entity that controls the Internet; it depends on the cooperation of entities that compete with each other. In the strictest sense, so does the telephony network, which requires local exchange carriers, interexchange carriers, and other telephone companies to cooperate.

While the Internet lacks the same coordination model as the telcos, it does have one. There are three network information centers for information in the Americas, Asia-Pacific, and Europe where problems can be resolved. There is also the international IETF (Internet Engineering Task Force) and several regional operations forums where problems are often avoided. As the NSPs begin to emulate the performance requirements of existing telephony services, watch for more quality of service guarantees and specifications.

Myth: If you build a Web site, *they* will come.
Fact: In 1995, this probably was true as Internet surfers trolled the Net looking for any new source of information. Now, with hundreds of thousands of

sites available, these surfers have choices. And they will go only to sites that have information relevant to them or products and services that meet their needs. A coherent Web strategy based on research of your customer needs, or on your need to offer new distribution channels or new products, is absolutely essential. Even the best-designed Web site on the fastest server with the latest high-end graphics and applications will whither and die if no one knows where it is or it has nothing anyone needs.

Myth: The Net is too big and will break under its own weight.
Fact: Recently, the number of networks connected exceeded the number it was designed to handle. A cooperative effort among the NSPs was launched, and it successfully staved off the exponentially growing memory requirements, and even succeeded in shrinking them slightly. Meanwhile, a long-term fix will be provided by the recently approved next generation of the Internet Protocol, version six.

There are numerous other risks as the size of the Internet scales beyond expectations. For each, there are short and long-term technological fixes known or planned. With the amount of investment and continued daily use of the Internet, no single technical hurdle will permanently disable it.

Myth: The Internet is full of hackers breaking into companies for fun.
Fact: The Internet has its share of infamous security breaches, and for each one many others likely go unreported. Some may stem from the large population of idle students, although a growing number are profit-motivated professionals and disgruntled employees.

Risk is inherent in every communication with the outside world, including telephony. PBX fraud costs corporations millions of dollars, yet they are used because the benefits dominate. The risks of Internet access can be drastically reduced in many ways, by using firewalls or even building completely isolated systems. Considered in the light of the benefits, many organizations are still choosing to connect.

Myth: The Internet is home mainly for college students and techies.
Fact: To use the Internet from home years ago required the patient coaxing of temperamental PC software more typical of the techie population.

Now built-in network support and turnkey packages are making access more available to anyone. Recent statistics show a cross section of Americans going online, roughly split between men and women, 38 years old on average, with slightly higher than normal incomes and years of education.

Changing Your Mind

Organizations are under constant change, and the factors that motivate Internet access cannot be shielded from it. Here are some things to keep in mind if you must reevaluate your decision.

▶ **Design Phase Decision Point:** When the design phase is complete, you will have identified enough issues to estimate costs and time frames. If possible, wait at least until that phase is complete, so your decision will be based on accurate information. If the project is canceled, the team's momentum will have been saved, and the project can be more easily resumed in the future.

▶ **Start Over:** A change in the reasons to connect may simply require that you reconsider the first steps in your plan. Think about starting the policy, requirements, or design phases again before canceling the project entirely.

▶ **Point of No Return:** Strictly speaking, the plug can be pulled at any time.

However, there are some steps at which you must make financial commitments. Unused hardware can often be returned, but not software. Contracts with companies with local circuits or Internet access may have cancellation charges, as can consulting or development arrangements. Finally, if you need to hire anyone to support your efforts, try to make the decision to see the project through before they are on board.

References

Where can you go for more information? To retrieve current statistics on the World Wide Web, visit such sites as: http://www.generalmagic.com/, http://www.nw.com/, http://www.mids.org/, and http://www.cyberatlas.

com/. Additionally, the following search engines are extremely useful—using them you can find information on almost any topic. Keep these handy in your Bookmarks or Favorite Places file: http://www.altavista.digital.com/, http://www.lycos.com/, http://www.excite.com/, http://www.hotbot.com, and http://www.yahoo.com/.

CHAPTER 2

Educate Employees

Knowing how to drive a car and repair a car are two entirely different things. And even if your mechanic has a good, general track record for general repairs, today's cars are so specialized you want the mechanic to be trained on your particular make and model. There's no doubt that general aptitude for supporting PC applications and internal networks can apply to supporting the applications on the Internet, but there are still substantial technical and process distinctions or differences that are unique, and you should not just assume that on-the-job training will provide the quality of support you want.

Your company has two choices in regards to technical training and support for your Internet and Web project. You can train people (either new hires, or retraining existing staff), or you can retain consultants and/or vendors to provide continuous support and maintenance. This chapter is geared to companies who want to develop their own TCP/IP and Web expertise, with the obvious benefit that in-house experience will help you screen external help.

Motivation

In 1993, the Internet was a toy for most companies. In 1994 and 1995, much the same could be said about the Web. No longer. As the 16-hour outage of

America Online in the summer of 1996 indicated, electronic, Internet commerce has become mission critical for thousands of companies and millions of individuals around the globe.

Smart executives were immediately questioning if their firms had the on-hand expertise to deal with a problem such as AOL experienced. Sadly, many companies do not, relying on vendors, contractors, or consultants. That lack of self-reliance can be reason for concern.

But solutions are not easy or cheap. The relative newness of the Internet combined with its ever increasing popularity has led to a considerable shortfall on qualified technical personnel who can effectively maintain and manage Internet and Web services. People who are available are expensive, and technical consultants charge $150 per hour or more in many cases. (Of course, a big price does not mean they are worth it!) Chances are, your company lacks the internal expertise to handle the intricacies of a TCP/IP or HTML world, and may not possess enough to screen new hires or outside consultants.

The technical people at your company need to be a part of using the Internet and the Web. They need to have a say in the goals and a sense of involvement; they don't need to have heaps of standards thrown on them, such as how long they can wait before responding to a query, the standards for responsiveness. They need to be a part of establishing the procedures.

The consequences of not adequately training personnel include:

▶ Lower quality of support and maintenance than you expected
▶ Guaranteed frustration when problems occur
▶ Delays in resolving problems
▶ Loss of revenue from missed sales
▶ Customer complaints about outages, delays—or both
▶ Lack of self-reliance

The staff that wants to do a good job wants the tools that are needed in order to be good. This is very much in line with the Demming Philosophy of Continuous Improvement. He sensed that most employees want to do good work and as management you have to provide them with the tools. In that sense, training is one of the best tools you can buy.

Dependencies

Technologies change and employees turn-over, so education needs to be a continuing process in your organization. That makes it difficult to give specific dependencies for this step. In fact, by reading this book before you start, employee education has already begun. Just try to plan ahead to ensure the necessary training has occurred before all future tasks begin. The dependency lines from this task on the chart indicate how some tasks have special training needs.

Goal

Again, this is an ongoing goal. You don't walk away with a specific written product, although there may be slides, booklets, and procedures involved. You come away with people who are prepared to deal with the inevitable operational issues and some plan for ensuring continuity, since people do get new jobs. Turnover is especially high in the Internet and Web business, and there are no signs of this abating.

From the day your Internet system is operational, you can expect that the designated support staff will not be able to fix every possible problem. Murphy's Law struck Internet startup company Interpath in Raleigh, NC, on the day it was to go online on April 1, 1994. Everything was operational, from T1 backbone connection to phone lines when the nearly 50-line phone rotary went dead. Unknown to the company, a change had been ordered regarding the local telephone circuits, and Interpath's technical staff—strongly qualified in all Internet matters—was left wringing its hands while waiting for help from the phone company. But they did know enough to determine what the problem was and to get corrective measures started. Having enough basic knowledge to determine what a failure or challenge is can be crucial to getting your company back online as quickly as possible.

The rapid technical pace of the Internet can make some skills insufficient or even obsolete. No sooner did the PERL programming language become the *de facto* standard for writing server-based applications for the World Wide Web than JAVA stole the show. The sudden popularity swing happened quickly—and another could occur before your project is finished! Count on training to continually update skills for the most relevant protocols and products.

Look ahead to the future steps of this plan, and think in terms of preparing people for each one. What information is necessary in-house to determine requirements? (Hint: Some hands-on experience, at the least!) What about design? Operations? Target training for tasks, and plan ahead so that the information is obtained in advance. Some of the training outlines we provide can help ensure you cover the topics needed.

People

There is no surprise here. The people with the operational roles in this product are going to be involved on the student side of the classroom. In terms of the instructors, unless you are blessed with very skilled employees with a lot of extra time, you should strongly consider looking to external resources for technical training.

The authors shared firsthand tales of top technical people who spent weeks preparing for and delivering detailed, insightful training for employees—at least while their pagers were not being activated. Providing good training is not a problem *per se,* but inefficient allocation of resources is. With a few hours of interviews, those same people could have identified qualified external trainers who could deliver the general information easily, leaving them more time to do organization-specific training and their routine network design jobs. You wouldn't want highly paid CEOs making their own copies, would you?

Also consider the trained person's perspective. Junior people will listen to anyone who has a clue; but they can tell when a person is clueless, so adequate screening of companies chosen to provide instruction or guidance is absolutely critical. You also don't want teachers or instructors who will mislead or misguide your technical staff. That could lead to disastrous consequences when problems occur. We recommend that when training is contracted, the trainers be evaluated beforehand and specified by name. (Avoid bait-and-switch techniques.)

Location

Operations people always function better with an understanding of the entire system. If your company is geographically distributed, consider holding training at or near the headquarters and making a time at the hub or operations center part of the training plan.

The ability to visualize all parts of the system can greatly enhance some people's ability to work with problems. If that's not possible, or if your company isn't geographically distributed, then clearly you will want to have the training at the most central, cost-effective location. Another factor in the choice of training location is the availability of laboratory resources, discussed more in the following sections.

Resources

Everything that was true for training your users applies for training your technical staff, but this must be deeper because the technical staff will be employing special tools of their trade. You will want to make sure they spend time hands-on with as much of the equipment as they will actually be using. This includes the actual network components and the troubleshooting tools to help conquer difficult problems.

This is where use of a training center can have another strong advantage, because there are hands-on, troubleshooting courses that can make a network analyzer available for each pair of students. That's rarely the case in the organization itself, where a much higher equipment-to-student ratio is the norm.

Some equipment vendors will provide routers, CSU/DSUs, and other hardware as part of their own instruction courses. But training on one brand doesn't necessarily apply to another, so bear that in mind as you move through the acquisition process.

For more information about needed resources, please refer to the same section in Chapter 3.

Duration

Operations training is ongoing just as it is for the rest of your staff. Employee turnover, the continual introduction of new capabilities, and refinement of skills necessitate that this task never really stops. However, you should plan on three weeks of training per full-time operations staff member without prior experience before they step up to their jobs. You want them to be proficient and able to deal with a battery of tests (hypothetical or real situations), testing out in the 95-percent range or higher.

Isn't that a lot of time, you ask? Yes.

Won't that be expensive, given that technical training can run several hundred dollars per day, let alone the production time lost from normal duties? Yes.

This also may require shifting of job responsibilities and cross-training. However, this step is essential, and the necessary funds, staff time, and resources must be dedicated if you are to sufficiently train your staff.

But look at it in perspective. If you have somebody whose full-time job is to monitor and/or maintain your Internet access and they have never done this before, then three weeks of full-time training is the rough equivalent of a single college class accounting for time spent doing homework, projects, and exercises. The complexity of the Internet easily rivals that of introductory psychology or calculus. There is just so much for a full-time operations person to know. Even in those classes it is often difficult to attain a 90-percent to 95-percent comprehension level, so if you are bringing in people cold and expect them to do a good job it will take at least three weeks to get them prepared.

In practice, most people have a little prior experience that can be applied. And unless you are a large company, Internet maintenance is not a full-time job, anyway.

Security

General training is just that—no customer-specific or proprietary information is exchanged. There is a tremendous amount of general training necessary—either explicitly planned or obtained by your employees and consultants through other means—motivated by the project plan or obtained prior. So it's easy to omit the notion of security in your early training plans (except as relates to the creation of a secure network design).

If your plans include the creation of proprietary systems, or the handling of confidential information, you will have to include it in the training! So many times, designers have expected operations to protect information that was not explicitly marked sensitive, and without clear directions on how to act. They just thought it was known! Make security a part of your operations and employee training—especially if your business depends on it.

FORTÉ

When an opportunity is seen, successful companies strike, even if the opportunity requires a retooling of the firm from the products it produces to the way the company is run.

Such was the case with Forté (see Figure 2.1), a privately held software company based in San Diego, CA, which saw a need on the Internet for a USENET news reader. Forté developed one and then made it available through the Internet and Web. The result has been a smashing success even though the company had to develop a new line of products, sell them in a new way (over the Internet), and deal with a shift in paradigms from managing sales of occasional $20,000 packages to sales of thousands of smaller packages. But Forté managed the challenges and now is a well-known name in Internet software circles.   (continued)

Figure 2.1   Forté's home page.

"It was clear that if we developed a product that did for USENET what Netscape had done for the WWW, we could rapidly capture market and mind share," said company President Charles Knuff.

In just over a year, Forté has succeeded with two successful news reader and e-mail products, called Free Agent (which is free) and Agent. "Free Agent and Agent became the number-one rated products in their category, and have the largest market share for news and e-mail reader products in the world," Mr. Knuff said. "There are currently hundreds of thousands of users of Free Agent and Agent worldwide."

Success also produced several problems. According to Mr. Knuff, the demand for the products exceeded expectations; the company also had to reorient itself from selling expensive software packages in conventional fashion to selling many inexpensive packages via the Internet. This led to changes within the company, as he explains in the Q&A segment to follow.

Mr. Knuff also pointed out that his company had not done enough market research before rolling out its products. He cautioned other companies against relying too heavily on a set of software features, since the Internet and the Web are evolving so quickly.

Another reason he believes Forté succeeded with its Agent and Free Agent products was the company's decision to beta-test the product before its general release. Two people were assigned to the products and worked with the thousands of people who wanted to test the software.

Forté, which was founded in 1982, had on staff people who had been monitoring the Internet due to its incredible impact on the software industry. And the company was able to leverage some of its existing technology to develop its new Internet products.

"Research and development focused on two areas, 3D animation software and Internet software," Mr. Knuff explained. "The company was successful with its 3DPC product line (a screen saver) winning many awards and capturing reasonable market share. However, after releasing Free Agent and Agent it became obvious that there was a greater opportunity in the Internet market for both consumer and business-related applications."

Before developing its Internet products, Forté focused on telecommunications software products that helped medium and large corporations manage their PBX (private branch exchange) telephone systems. More than 2,500 companies worldwide now utilize Forté's tools.

What follows is the Q&A with Mr. Knuff:

Question: What factors and/or research led to your company's decision to develop an Internet strategy?

Answer: The factors that led to the decision to move into the Internet space were the growth of the WWW and the lack of a powerful news reader for USENET. It was clear that if we developed a product that did for USENET what Netscape had done for the WWW, we could rapidly capture market and mind share. In addition to this, Forté had spent significant amounts of money in the creation of a groupware-based (software that allows people to collaborate) logistical infrastructure to meet the demands of supporting and developing global products for global markets. The collaborative component of our logistical infrastructure was very similar to the collaborative nature of USENET; therefore, we were able to extend our infrastructure model and combine it with the Agent model to create a new set of Intranet applications. Our new Intranet applications provide for communications, collaboration, and business cycle management externally via the Internet and internally via Intranets.

Question: Often in this startup process, there are many difficulties to be overcome, technical and otherwise. What are some of the most common? Were you able to anticipate them? What were you able to do to overcome these obstacles? What lessons did you learn?

Answer: The single most difficult problem we experienced was the amount of demand for the product, and the desire for more features. The fundamental shift from our business model from selling $20,000 telecommunications software packages to giving away software for free and selling it electronically over the Internet represented significant challenges to management.

The groupware-based logistical infrastructure we had in place allowed the company to rapidly move into this new business space. During the field trial process a team of two people was able to manage the over 20,000 beta testers and very efficiently funnel the feature and problem reports to development. Once the products were commercially released our infrastructure accommodated the efficient integration of our sales and marketing groups into the commercialization process.

Question: If you had the process to do over again, what are some of the things that you should/would do differently? What lessons were learned? What is the advice you would give others? (continued)

Answer: We did not perform sufficient market research to identify the real potential demand for our first Internet product, therefore we did not optimally apply our resources to maximize our initial opportunities. The lesson we learned was to never overcommit on the feature evolution of an Internet software product, because there are too many independent variables that will adversely effect your estimates, not the least of which are changing standards and the availability of good development tools.

Question: How important is it to have a strategic plan? If you were to write a strategic plan, what would be some of the highlights?

Answer: An Internet strategic framework was established. However, it acted more as a guideline than a tactical plan due to the evolutionary nature of the Internet.

Question: What are some of the mistakes that you see other companies making as they delve into the Internet? Why are they making them?

Answer: While it is difficult to comment on the nature of mistakes being made by other companies, I suspect that many companies that enter this space underestimate the need for a strong logistical infrastructure to organize, communicate, and manage the information that is created under this new and evolving business model.

Question: What has the Internet/Web meant to your business?

Answer: The Internet represents a fundamental shift for our company; it has become the major focus of our business efforts. We expect our Internet products to become our primary source of revenue in 1997.

Question: If you were new to the Internet/Web and were looking for a book to help you plan, coordinate, and execute an Internet strategy, what are some of the points you would want covered?

Answer: I think the best approach for the book would be the use of case studies that deal with the various issues facing business. However, the spin should be from the Internet perspective of high speed and high customer expectations.

Question: What are some of the factors companies should be looking for when selecting an ISP, Web site developer, and/or consulting firm?

Answer: The quality of customer service is the most important factor when selecting an ISP.

Issues

Fortunately, the issues surrounding this task are familiar if your company is involved in any training activity—as most are. In the following sections, we mention those aspects most specific to the Internet.

Vendor Training

Targeted system training from your vendors is likely available, from the servers to the network components to management tools. You can sometimes negotiate training as part of the discount. Vendors obviously want to make as much money as they reasonably can, but they also know an educated customer spends less time pointing fingers and purchases more equipment. Don't be afraid to ask. Also, be clear that you want technical training, and not another sales pitch. Some vendors see any opportunity with an overhead projector as a chance to make a sale—even if one has just been made.

Technical Training Curriculum

Despite the challenges presented by TCP/IP, routing, and Web server issues, more and more colleges, universities, and community colleges offer Internet-related courses plus hands-on Internet and Web instruction. Most have computer labs with Internet access, and their prices can be much less expensive than those found in the business community.

News groups also can be a good place for Internet systems administrators to exchange ideas, gripes, and concerns.

The engineers that design and build your web will be very specialized. The WWW has highlighted the number of areas in which one can focus. Computer experts alone can spend the good part of a career delving into the details of, for example, a particular computer operating system such as UNIX without necessarily becoming an expert in the particular application programs it runs! To appreciate the depth this involves, visit a site like UNIX Guru Universe, which can be found on the Web at http://www.polaris.net/ugu/, and you'll see what we mean (see Figure 2.2).

FIGURE 2.2   Home page of the UNIX Guru Universe, where systems administrators trade ideas and concerns.

Getting the Most for Your Money

Here are some things to consider when evaluating particular training facilities and courses.

▶ Hands-on instruction at a computer lab or on your premises
▶ Hands-on experience with tools and equipment that are to be used
▶ Training materials and curriculum
▶ Instruction from one or more expert trainers with a strong Internet background
▶ Arrangements for follow-up training and/or questions

Just as we recommend in Chapter 13, be sure to check references and ask for samples of manuals/guides and instructional materials. It also would be a good idea to send a team member to a class to determine how effective the classes are.

Consultants and Cross-Training

A viable option is to find experienced Internet technicians who can maintain and manage your equipment remotely. They often will work on a contract basis, offering a specified number of hours per month to monitor your network and to address problems as they arise.

While outsourcing certainly can be a cost-effective, wise option, there are risks. For example, if you choose this option you neglect the development of internal talent. This means you are at the mercy of a nonemployee who has other clients and may not put your interests first.

A better solution is to retain an expert initially and have him or her cross-train selected members of your company. An operations person is going to have to learn the basics of TCP/IP, plus spend one or two days learning the basics of router operation and maintenance, as well as a day or two learning the server and applications protocols.

You should draw up a contract with the consultant that specifically lists each deliverable item, from network installation and server setup to specific steps to be taken during training of your staff. The contract also should include nondisclosure and noncompete clauses if your company is dealing with a proprietary product and/or service.

In the case of a large company with a substantial Internet infrastructure and a large staff of Information Services people, programming and network tasks can be subdivided. Some people may already have Internet-related experience, so not everyone will have to hit that three-week training target. Instead of one person hitting all aspects of training, you will have one person focusing on network issues, a different one to learn servers, another to learn Internet-working. Although training often becomes more technical and focused in large organizations, be on the lookout for opportunities to cross-train.

References

The most current printed training information about the Internet can be found in periodicals. Numerous choices exist, including many that are sponsored completely by advertising. Among the useful options are: *PC Computing, InformationWeek, PC Magazine, NetGuide, Internet World, HotWired, Communications Week, Network Computing, LAN Times, PC Today, Online Access, Web Week,* and *Red Herring.*

Many of the best sources of information suitable for training are in text books. If the same bookstore where this text was acquired does not offer a large selection, seek a store with a wider offering. Of particular use are the technical bookstores common in major cities, and the college and university stores at which courses are offered.

Other excellent sources of reference materials are local colleges and universities, although only those with labs may provide the most beneficial detailed technical training. Training classes are also often advertised in professional magazines and in major newspapers. Be certain to check references.

Appendix A provides a basic training outline that you may use to educate your own employees. Because no two companies have the same needs, you should modify this training document to suit your company's requirements.

While the previous chapter mentioned the utility of Web searches, do not expect to locate an expert-level, online training site that meets all your needs. Most quality training presentations are worth money, and are not sold. For training, the Web should be used as practice and for supplementary information only, and for evaluating the consulting organizations, magazines, and bookstores that will provide more help. By following mailing lists, novices can eventually become experts—a practice their training instructors should mention.

CHAPTER 3

Identify Resources

One of the key project management tasks is that of obtaining the necessary human and financial resources necessary to bring a plan to completion. This chapter stresses the importance of locating good people—within or outside your organization—before you begin. Subsequent chapters will provide more detail on obtaining task-specific needs.

Motivation

"I don't even know where to get started."

That's what a senior vice president of a $150 million technology company said as she discussed with a consultant what the Internet and the World Wide Web could do for her company. "I know we can benefit from this technology, and I am under pressure to use the Internet and to build a Web site. But where do I even start?"

Senior management of this company, like many others, has made a decision to connect to the Internet and has assigned a senior executive the task of doing so. But the firm has done so without defining a clear mission and without putting together a Project Team, as suggested in Chapter 1.

This executive was left alone and immediately sought support outside the firm even though some valuable resources existed internally. Unfortunately, she was not authorized to employ those. Even after talking to her superiors a proposal that had been designed with the assistance of a consultant, she was told she now had to find funding within her division to implement the project. As you might guess, the project came to a screeching halt.

This is a good example of what happens too many times within companies and corporations that are exploring the Internet. To help avoid this problem, we will spend this chapter discussing the importance of identifying resources (internal and external) and forming a Project Team. The best laid strategic plan is useless without raw materials for implementation.

Even if your company is good at mobilizing resources for other projects, this chapter can help save time and money in building your Internet connection. We'll help you tailor the type of help you need specifically for Internet projects, locate resources you didn't know existed, and provide tips for finding qualified assistance the first time.

Dependencies

It should not take too much convincing to take this step after the decision to connect. Acquiring resources can be time-consuming and expensive, taking people's focus away from other responsibilities and tasks. Deferring this step until the fundamental decision to connect is made avoids wasting resources if it's not appropriate for your organization.

Once you have decided to connect, identifying resources is the next step—a vital step—in your plan. Successful connections depend on the convergence of skills from a wide range of people—computer, networking, purchasing, operations, marketing, writing, graphics, sales, and so on. If you're not convinced of this, read ahead to the "People" and "Resource" sections of later chapters, and assess whether all requisite abilities reside in a single person in your organization. (If they do, put down this book and give them a raise!)

By not drawing in your resources from the beginning, you risk increased cost and greater employee turnover. Consider the small east-coast firm that understaffed its initial Web efforts. Three individuals were chartered to acquire the facilities, configure the computer, and create the instructions for connecting 100 employees to the Internet with a Web site and e-mail. Clearly, the project was not considered important at the time. Four months later, the employees had learned a great deal, but executives could not understand why the now more important access was not ready. They hired an outside firm to redo the initial design for substantially more money than originally allocated. Their site now takes thousands of hits per day, and work almost halts when external e-mail stops. Two of the employees who learned so much now help run it were hired back as consultants.

Goal

The output of this step is the list of people and outside organizations along with the roles each will play in fulfilling your plan. These are the individuals who will read the remaining chapters in detail and lead your organization in the completion of your plan; this book will help ensure those individuals possess the knowledge and experience critical for your success.

You're not likely to adopt a new set of workforce management tools specifically for this project—and it's best you do not try. Use whatever techniques you currently adopt—a personnel matrix, daily progress reports, weekly status meetings, Statement of Work, or a combination—to define what and how much everyone is contributing. Unless the project is part of your formal work goals, it is likely to slip into oblivion.

Many of the steps in this book are ongoing, repeating as needs change or your project grows. This is especially true of this chapter, since the list of resources changes due to natural project evolution, attrition, and (hopefully!) the acquisition of new people with applicable skills.

People

In this chapter, this section discusses who will identify the human resources necessary to complete your Internet project. In subsequent chapters, the people discussed will be those who actually implement it.

There are many ways to organize the various team members for your project. In this section, we take a hierarchical approach—beginning with the roles with the highest responsibility and working downward.

Project Leader

The project leader has the singlemost influential role in determining the success of your plan. It is almost always a full-time employee, usually someone with at least a year or more of corporate experience, and definitely someone with a successful track record. Selecting this project *czar* is the most important decision this book will help you make. Some of the qualities you should seek include the following:

▶ **Organization.** The leader is someone who can coordinate all aspects of the project and isn't reluctant to delegate authority.

▶ **Vision.** This is a person who can envision the strategic and tactical business advantages that the Internet/Web project has for the company.

▶ **Thorough.** Building a successful Internet/Web project is complex, so someone who will expect each person to fulfill each task in a timely and orderly fashion is required.

▶ **Flexible.** Your leader must be able to adjust to new demands and requirements, and seize upon new opportunities, because the Internet and Web technologies are changing so quickly.

▶ **Comfortable with technology.** The leader doesn't necessarily have to be proficient in the use of the Internet and Web but must be eager to learn and to share that knowledge with others.

▶ **Innovator.** The right leader is someone who has a record of accomplishment and showing initiative.

▶ **Team player.** This is a corporate project, not an individual career builder. The leader must be able to reach across departmental lines to recruit the necessary support that will unite the company behind this new venture.

▶ **Decisive.** Crucial decisions will have to be made, and the company's executive management must have confidence that the team leader will make the best ones.

In addition to these qualities, this individual must be empowered to push the Internet/Web plan to completion, with authority to delegate tasks, expedite and define processes, cut through red tape, mobilize the necessary resources, and keep all parties on track. The higher placed this individual, the quicker and better your chances for effectiveness.

Rest of Team

The size of the team is dependent upon the size of the company, the number of departments, and the judgment of the Project Leader. The team could be 2 people or it could be 12, although large groups can prove to be difficult to manage and prone to stagger over microscopic details.

Only after you have picked the leader should the rest of the team be assembled. This group should represent key departments within your organization, most certainly starting with IS. Not too far behind should be Human Resources, since these people know who works for the company and also need to stay abreast of how the project will affect all employees.

Any department, such as IS and telecommunications, that will be directly affected by the project should be asked to participate in some fashion. This will avoid any surprises and help build support across departmental lines.

Team members should reflect the qualities of the team leader. They also should be enthusiastic but realistic about the project. Naysayers can delay, if not doom, the project. On the other hand, a dose of reality will be needed occasionally to keep the team's perspective. Hands-on experience with the Internet technologies, content production, electronic marketing, or any other related elements are strongly recommended.

The Project Leader also needs to compile a list of every corporate department, and then mull over possible Internet and Web applications for each. The knowledgeable person you have picked will be able to see opportunities perhaps where no one else has. Based on this overview, the Project Leader should brief all department heads about the project, and then ask them to recommend staff members for the Project Team. By involving department heads, you are less likely to anger supervisors who stand to lose talented people—and time. If the managers are involved and thus see personally how they can benefit, they are much more likely to be supportive.

For example, a large health care provider in the southeast wanted to pursue an Internet/Web project. The plan received approval at senior executive levels, but department heads ended up scuttling the project by refusing to fund it from existing budgets. This was very costly turf protection.

Note that sometimes, qualified resources already exist—hiding in ongoing projects or unrelated jobs. The Project Leader also should conduct an internal corporate survey to determine just how much Internet and Web knowledge already exists on the payroll. This not only could save the company money, but also creates the opportunity to recruit more champions for the project.

Using Consultants

There are many circumstances in which using consultants makes perfect sense. When the requisite technical or production skills are lacking in-house, when internal resources are already stretched thin, or when staff has difficulty seeing how an Internet or Web application can be useful, it's time to look for outside assistance.

Technical and business consultants can be found through existing vendor relationships (Who would you recommend?), or by asking peers who have gone through a similar Internet/Web exercise. Also, many firms can be located by searching the Web and by looking through various local, regional, and national computer or Internet publications, where these companies are most likely to advertise.

After compiling a list of prospective companies, you can further screen them by submitting a Request for Information. This series of questions should ask for a wide range of information, including:

► Scope of service, from Web site development to maintenance
► Types of Internet connectivity and support that are available
► Experience in providing security and firewalls
► Experience in dealing with electronic commerce
► Resumes of contracted individuals
► Rates
► Samples of work (especially online samples you can visit and evaluate!)
► References

You should also use this screening process with prospective consultants to brief them about your project, and to ask them for ideas and suggestions. For example, ask them if they or any of their clients have had experience in the particular area you are exploring, and if so do they have any information, horror stories, or warnings they can share (without violating confidentiality agreements with other clients).

An important fact to remember, however, when retaining outside expertise: Unless they are contracted (often at great expense) to remain onsite every day, they will work with other clients and therefore may not be ready to respond quickly to your needs. Be sure to engage whatever facet of your organization authorizes contracts early, so outside contracts can be written and enacted quickly.

Outside Partners

In consideration of external resources already employed by your company, you need to consider whether they can assist, and to what extent you need to involve them. Technical consultants, advertising and marketing, order fulfillment, and even banking partners can play valuable roles in your Internet project in addition to their ongoing responsibilities.

If circumstances do not permit their full involvement, keep your partners advised of relevant decisions and progress. Often, they can provide unexpected aid, or can at least make better decisions based on your input.

Dream Team

To summarize this section, here is what your project dream team will consist of:

▶ A manager with strong leadership
▶ Creative yet realistic individuals
▶ Empowered representatives from key corporate departments
▶ People (on staff or external) with technical knowledge of the Internet and Web
▶ A team-oriented group excited about their assignment

Location

The project and organization headquarters will likely be in the same location, feeding the tendency to seek internal and external resources that are nearby. This makes sense—to a point. The project leader should be in a position to obtain visibility and resources, which makes headquarters ideal. Furthermore, choosing external resources that are located near the company simplifies the logistics of ongoing business and technical meetings.

Just remember that valuable experience exists in the field. Spread the resources across the corporation, and go where the employees are. If your organization is geographically dispersed, expect teleconferencing and travel. Advanced access to the Internet (see the following section) may also let team members gain experience with Internet applications, and increase their project efficiency.

Resources

Locating resources can itself be a time-consuming process. Use of internal communication mechanisms, like interoffice mail, notes on the bulletin board by the coffee machine, teleconferences, and other standard means will greatly aid your ability to locate resources inside your company.

The best way to locate resources outside your company while sparking innovative applications is to acquire temporary Internet access. Numerous companies provide software and a telephone number so that any PC and modem can dial up the Internet. This will be invaluable in identifying, communicating with, and evaluating consultants and external sources of Web assistance. The cost of dial-up accounts and modems is extremely low—and the PC is already available.

Duration

A reasonable minimum goal to set for this process is ten working days, assuming a team leader (who should have at least a year with the organization) and other necessary resources are available internally. It's the team leader's goal to recruit internally, conducting informal phone or in-person interviews to assess candidates.

If external resources are required, it may take 20 to 30 working days to finish. Potential companies need to be identified, respond to RFIs, have their work evaluated, and sign contracts. These tasks are time-consuming in most organizations. While internal resources get involved in latter project steps, it is best if everyone is on board from the start. This is a key up-front step which the Project Leader should drive fiercely.

Security

Much like the prior step, your decision on how public your decision should be determines what security is appropriate. If there is no need to hide your intent to connect, security is simplified. However, if outside help is used, the following should be considered.

Nondisclosure

Nondisclosure agreements prevent your external help from discussing your plans with other companies. This is an important agreement—timeliness to appear on the Web is nowadays a competitive advantage. Keep ahead of your competition by not tipping your plans to them.

Intellectual Property

When your site is complete, its design, operational procedures, and content all represent valuable intellectual property—whose value is at least equal to the resources expended in their creation (and hopefully worth much more to your business). As such, other organizations—especially those that played a part in their creation—will be interested in retaining some rights.

Most organizations will obtain all rights pertaining to the content itself. These items usually represent deliverables of little value to those who created the site. The design may be *reworked* by the vendors for use with other clients. This is probably a reasonable practice unless your site includes such unusual design as to be difficult to reproduce. For most readers, this is not the case.

If you are a large organization with sufficient resources, you may be able to negotiate to keep the intellectual property of applications or computer *scripts* that automate aspects of your Web's system. These are often easy to reuse, and will likely find their way to other customers of your external vendors unless you require otherwise. If your vendors will consider it, discuss the cost implications of these options with them up front.

Noncompete

It may be possible to restrict your outside vendors from simultaneously working for competitors, or from recruiting employees from your organization. Some organizations also place restrictions on future employers in pre-employment agreements. If your company has special concerns in any of these areas, engage legal counsel at this time.

Daniels & Daniels

Daniels & Daniels, the first permanent law firm resident in the techno-logical hotbed of Research Triangle Park, NC, saw that the Internet and World Wide Web offered many opportunities—and some risks. But the firm did not rush into deploying its solutions even as it began to represent a host of high-tech companies.

"We did a lot of research before we did anything," said Walter E. Daniels, cofounder of the firm and a graduate of the University of North Carolina law school. Among the factors driving the firm toward the Internet was competition with other firms. He explained that the Net is "a great leveler, and we don't want to get leveled."

Many other factors also entered into the firm's thinking, from quality of life and communications improvements to profit potential. Thus, the firm developed a comprehensive strategy, dealt with a host of difficult issues, planned how to take advantage of still evolving technologies, and launched its Web site in the summer of 1996.

What follows is the Q&A with Mr. Daniels:

Question: What factors and/or research should lead to a company's decision to develop an Internet strategy?

Answer: For Daniels & Daniels, the factors leading to our development of an Internet strategy are manyfold. First, our law firm represents technology companies. Our trademark has been our willingness to use technology to serve our clients. Our clients expect it. Even without the Internet, we have had e-mail capability since 1982. We have used portable computers since 1986. We have electronic access, internally and externally, to electronic research information involving thousands of databases. We have the ability to obtain remote access to our office via the telephone network from anywhere in the world; from almost anywhere in the world, we can view, print, and redirect faxes received in our office, we can access e-mail and can send and receive documents. In sum, we have always used technology well and have never regretted any investment we have made in technology. Consequently, incorporation of the Internet into this philosophy has been quite easy.

In this light, the Internet is not something that is a toy. We view it as fundamental to our business. For example, many of our clients are developers of Internet software or development tools, are Internet service providers, are Web publishers, are online advertisers, or are providers of online content. We have other clients that are not in the technology business at all but who use the Web to tell their story. Our clients include scores of companies that already have Web pages fundamental to their business. We are able to charge a premium for our technological capabilities, and our clients still get cost-effective service because of our enhanced response time and delivery capability.

A second factor is that we wish to maintain our firm as a transaction-oriented firm, and we know that the Internet is on the verge of being a major transaction environment. The principle holdbacks to date have been the relatively slow speed of modems, and the lack of standards for encryption and security, but those are now at hand.

I fully expect that in four to five years time, perhaps sooner, there will be as many sales of products over the Internet as are done today via paper-based, mail-order catalogs, that perhaps one-third of all retail banking will be done over the Internet, that over one-half of all individual hotel and airline reservations will be made via the Internet, and that the Internet will be seamlessly integrated with the public switched Network for voice communications.

Business meetings will be held via video conferences over the Internet, perhaps including many participants that work out of their home with no office at all. Doctors will practice telemedicine over the Internet. This is not pie in the sky. All of this can be done today. Those who don't get ready to play this game will suffer the fate of the pony express when the telegraph was invented. From where we stand today it would only take marginal investments to do any of these things.

A third factor is that the Internet is a great leveler, and we don't want to be leveled. It is often said that to have information is to have power.

(continued)

With the Internet, more and more information is being made widely available, information that was once only available to a privileged few. This means that those who once maintained their competitive position because they had access to restricted information will now find more inroads to that competitive position. We always want to be in a position of having clean, organized access to information so that we can maintain our competitive position.

A fourth factor relates to quality of life. The distributed nature of the Internet will make it easier for our attorneys and clients to communicate with each other electronically regardless of their location. We've already exchanged documents with clients traveling in Hong Kong while we have been looking at the sounds on the Outer Banks of North Carolina.

Question: What is your Internet strategy?

Answer: Our Internet strategy is very simple in concept. We want to:

- Connect our office to the Internet on a dedicated basis, and continuously migrate to higher bandwidth as more cost-effective delivery becomes available
- Prevent unauthorized access to our office from the Internet, and prevent the introduction of viruses
- Use the Internet as an organized resource tool, particularly as it relates to external legal, governmental, and business information
- Use the Internet as a communications tool; for now, text; soon for voice and video commensurate with the use of these means by our clients

We also view the *intranet* as a complement to the Internet so that people within our office can have seamless access to the resources they need. Documents such as office manuals are all slated to be placed on our intranet. We also fully expect that our future groupware applications will be based on the Web-like operating system.

The components of our initial Internet setup are also simple:

- Our Internet access is via Sprint Communications, initially 64Kpbs frame relay, expandable to T1 (1.544 Mbps) frame relay
- Cisco router, capable of handling a T1

- ▶ NT-Based Internet Server running Netscape Enterprise Server for Domain Name Service and World Wide Web Server functions
- ▶ NT-Based Raptor Firewall
- ▶ Intranet server running Netscape Mail Server, Netscape Proxy Server, Netscape Catalog Server, Netscape News Server, and Netscape Enterprise Server
- ▶ Use of a Citrix gateway for restricted remote access via the Internet via Compuserve notes worldwide, and via the public switched telephone Network
- ▶ Use of HAHTSITE and Corel development tools

We also laid the groundwork for the eventual voice and video applications by installing a wiring system based upon category-5 cable capable of handling 100 megabits per second.

Stage 1 is to offer Internet e-mail with full mime capability; Stage 2, World Wide Web service and news service; Stage 3, intranet Web; Stage 4, Internet-based voice and video communications integrated with a computer telephony server; Stage 5, use of an ATM or fast ethernet switch to handle all office communications.

Stage 1 has been implemented. Stage 2 will be implemented soon, but this will be a never-ending process. State 3 will be implemented within three months, but this too will be a never-ending process. The Stage 4 computer telephony server will be installed within one year, and integration with Internet-based voice will be dependent upon product availability, higher bandwidth, and the interest shown by our clients in such communications. The ATM step, or its equivalent, is probably three years away.

Our computer telephony will most likely be implemented in conjunction with Microsoft Exchange, but we are monitoring other universal mailbox solutions offered by providers such as Netscape and Novell; and we are studying how these products will work with such groupware functions as calendaring, scheduling, voice mail, and document exchange.

Our Internet Web page will be designed to provide a number of community service functions, as well as services specifically designed for our client base. We cannot announce the services at this time, but we do expect to generate revenue from our Web page. Our intranet catalog server will be used as a way of organizing information on the Internet in a proprietary

(continued)

way for use by persons from within our office LAN, or who access that LAN via the Citrix remote access gateway. We fully expect our intranet catalog server to be a resource that will help provide our firm a competitive edge.

In sum, we've thought about the Internet opportunity quite a bit and we are committed to move forward to take advantage of this opportunity on a staged basis. We fully expect that the Internet will sag a bit as the infrastructure backbone strains to keep up with the demand, but we anticipate that the major carriers will continue to make the necessary investments to make sure the infrastructure keeps up with the demand. We are not refraining from making investments because of the tales of Internet doom.

Question: Often in this startup process, there are many difficulties to be overcome, technical and otherwise. What are some of the most common? Were you able to anticipate them? What were you able to do to overcome these obstacles? What lessons did you learn?

Answer: Among the biggest problems we faced were:

▶ The decision to be the master of our own fate, that is, obtain our own dedicated access and own servers vs. relying on Web service and mail service from Internet service providers

▶ Coordination between the local telephone company and the Internet service provider

▶ Finding people who understood both the Internet/TCPIP world and Novell Networks

▶ Deciding what TCPIP stacks to use on our Windows workstations, or whether to use Netware Loadable Modules (NLMs) to accomplish the same function

▶ Figuring out a firewall solution that didn't bankrupt the firm or take legions of UNIX gurus to maintain

▶ Integration of direct Internet e-mail with legacy e-mail systems

We did a lot of research before we did anything. Our solutions were as follows:

1. Opt for open systems (and avoid any proprietary solution)
2. Require the Internet service provider to handle end-to-end coordination for both the Internet and local loop link
3. Get our Novell Netware and Internet consultants to work as a team

4. Use an NT-based fireware
5. Upgrade: first to Windows for Workgroups for 486-class machines, then use Microsoft-provided TCP/IP stacks; and second, upgrade to Windows 95 for Pentium-class machines, thereby drawing upon the TCP/IP functionality built into the operating system

Question: If you had the process to do over again, what are some of the things that you should/would do differently? What lessons were learned? What is some advice you would give others?

Answer: At the time we began our planning process, Netscape was still being hatched, Mosaic freeware controlled the browser world, all Internet servers were UNIX boxes, there were only a few Internet service providers available, there were only a few books available at all on the Internet (much less topics like firewalls), and most Novell consultants knew little about UNIX commands or TCP/IP. Were we starting today we would acquire many good books on topics ranging from communicating with NT Servers, to Internet firewalls and Network security, to computer telephony.

My advice would be to purchase about 20 different good books now available in major chain book stores to use as resource guides, to procure a subscription to *Network Computing* magazine, and once this is done, to actually read the materials. Very rarely will one of these books answer all of the questions, but together one can get a pretty good understanding of the important practical and technical considerations.

Timing and coordination are important. It is very important to plan to get everything to come together at the same time. It takes long lead times to get service, and may take equally long lead times to get critical components, like a router. In our situation, the Internet connection and the router had a lag time of six weeks to two months. Installation professionals are also a critical resource and sometimes it is difficult to get together all of the parties necessary at the same time. As a result one may end up paying for the costs of communications lines they are not using.

Question: How important is it to have a strategic plan? If you were to write a strategic plan, what would be some of the highlights?

Answer: I think it is very important to have a strategic plan. Ours exists but is not written in a formal way. We do feel like we know where we are going, and when we make equipment purchases we try to anticipate where

(continued)

we need to be. For example, we are committed to purchasing high-end laptops for each of our legal professionals, but we are also requiring that these machines have multimedia capabilities and jacks so that we will be able to handle the computer telephony, voice, and video capabilities in our plan.

The highlights of our strategic plan were discussed previously.

Question: What are some of the mistakes that you see other companies making as they delve into the Internet? Why are they making them?

Answer: Some companies, I think, are expecting too early a return from their entrance into the Internet. In doing so, they are underestimating the value of becoming familiar with the medium.

Question: What has the Internet/Web meant to your business?

Answer: The e-mail functionality is an absolutely critical part of our business today. The World Wide Web has been important in helping us to find product information related to software and hardware systems. More important, the Internet has been extremely useful in helping us to find some types of legal information that would otherwise be very difficult to obtain.

For example we serve as counsel to the North Carolina Health Care Information and Communications Alliance, Inc. (NCHICA), a nonprofit comprised of major medical centers like Duke and the University of North Carolina, computer companies like IBM, carriers like AT&T and Bell South, and insurers like Blue Cross Blue Shield and Health Shield, all of which are working on ways to share health information electronically to improved patient care and reduce costs. In this capacity we have been developing legislation to address the privacy needs of individuals, with respect to their health information. In doing this research we have been able to use the Internet to monitor legislative activity in many states and in Washington; consequently, we have been able to draw from the best of many ideas and have had the benefit of being able to review comments and criticisms, with respect to other legislative initiatives. The result is that we have been able to be cost effective in obtaining the information, we have enhanced the quality of the legislative work product based upon the broad-based input, and we believe that we are close to developing a legislation that will significantly benefit the State of North Carolina and may be a model for the nation. This would have been an extremely difficult and an extremely expensive task without the Internet.

Question: If you were new to the Internet/Web and were looking for a book to help you plan/coordinate/execute an Internet strategy, what are some of the points you would want covered?

Answer: The most useful books are those that that provide the nuts and bolts related to setup and installation of Networks, that deal with the mechanics of what you do at the workstations to provide Internet connectivity, and that illuminate how the various Internet servers and firewall machines work together.

Question: What are some of the factors companies should be looking for when selecting an ISP, Web site developer, and/or consulting firm?

Answer: An Internet service provider should have the type of service needed by the customer, whether it be a dial-up account, a Serial Line Protocol Account (SLIP), a Compressed Serial Line Protocol Account (CSLIP), ISDN switched access, dedicated Frame Relay (at various speeds), or other dedicated line, such as a T1. The carrier should not overpack lines, should have responsive customer service and technical support, should be willing to coordinate relations with the local telephone company (if dedicated access is required). The more end-to-end or turnkey solutions that can be provided by any vendor, including the carrier, the better. Responsiveness and costs also are important.

Contracts with Internet carriers should have some protections against downtime (or low downtime) due the fault of the carrier, the ability to upgrade service without penalty, and the ability to terminate with reasonable notice for substantial outages or downtime. Where dedicated service is provided, contracts should provide systematic monitoring service. The carrier should be able to know that your line is out before you are able to report it.

With respect to Web site developers, it is important to make sure that your developer has the requisite experience so that you are not paying for on-the-job training. A good checkpoint would be to go and look at other sites that have been done by the developer, and to check with the customer at that site to verify what work on that site was done by the developer. Mere HTML programming doesn't do it anymore, so it is important to see if your developer has licensed access to new-generation, powerful development tools. Your contract with the Web developer should ensure that all work is original or appropriately licensed by the owner of the development tools used, and should ensure that the work that is created is to be owned by the customer, not the developer.

Issues

Some of the best experience resides in companies that provide Internet hardware, software, and/or access services. We think as sole partners, they are the wrong choice. Their focus may be to sell you things you do not necessarily need, for their own short-term gain. Independent companies that have no interest in your selecting particular hardware or access providers seem more likely to act in your own best interests. Consider involving others only after their selection has been justified by the requirements and design steps.

There also are no guarantees that you will be able to find the necessary internal resources to handle this project. But the best champions you can recruit are already on your staff. They can preach the Internet/Web gospel across the company, and by using staff your company can save money as well as time. Your company's confidence and budget may be tested if it is determined that outside resources are needed. To bring outsiders on-board is a challenge to many firms. If you are not prepared to listen to recommendations that may force some paradigm adjustments, or recommendations that run a bit counter to corporate culture, you are in for difficult times. If you determine that outside resources such as consultants are needed, you also need to understand that the cost is not cheap. Top-level consulting firms charge $150 an hour or more.

Internal Survey

The internal survey is crucial to determining what the Project Team will need. Here are some questions that should be included in any survey:

▶ Which employees already have Internet/Web experience? To what extent?
▶ Which employees already have used online services? To what extent?
▶ Which employees already have experience with routers and TCP/IP?
▶ Which employees have C++, HTML, or other programming experience?
▶ Are any departments currently utilizing the Internet or Web? If so, how?
▶ When was the last top-to-bottom survey of corporate computing needs? Is one already due? Did the most recent cover any topics related to the Internet/Web?
▶ What plans and budget already are in place for technology upgrades, new computers, and related hardware?

▶ What budget money is already available for corporate training?

▶ Is there excess computing capacity?

▶ Does the company employ client/server or dumb terminals and a main-frame?

▶ If a mainframe is in use, is budget available to upgrade existing computing system?

▶ What type of local area network already is in place?

▶ Is there a corporate wide area network?

▶ Has any thought been given to developing a corporate intranet as an alternative to a private WAN?

▶ What security procedures are already in place?

▶ Is a TCP/IP stack already available?

▶ How many phone lines and modems already are available at desktops?

▶ How is long-distance service provided to the company? If high-speed T1 circuits are used, are there 56k channels available that could be utilized for data?

▶ Does the long-distance provider offer Internet/Web services? If so, could these be bundled as part of a new, lower-cost telecommunications contract?

▶ What vendors do you already work with that already have Internet/Web experience?

▶ How many fax machines, which could be replaced by Web servers, are being used within the company? What is the long-distance bill associated with each?

▶ Who would be interested in working on this project? If so, why? What skills would you add?

▶ If your department had access to the Internet, how would you use it?

▶ How do your friends' employers use the Internet/Web? Are there any possible applications for your company?

Budget

Once the internal survey has been completed, the Project Team has a much better idea of what costs will be involved and where some cost savings might be identified.

While it is beyond the scope of this book to recommend specific budget items for every project, some general points to consider include:

▶ Travel and/or telecommunications for team members

▶ Dial-up Internet accounts for team members

▶ PC, modem, and phone line availability

▶ Staff personnel availability for team assignments

▶ The scope of need for outside consultants and their costs

▶ Prices for a broad range of Internet and Web services

▶ LAN and/or WAN establishment or improvement costs

▶ Cost to update from a mainframe/dumb terminal environment to a client-server

▶ Cost of training for IS personnel

▶ Cost of additional personnel that might be needed to implement an Internet/Web solution

Once you are further along in the design, Chapter 7 will give you more information on estimating overall project costs as a checkpoint for continuing.

Team Assignments

The Project Leader needs to sketch out the scope of the Internet/Web assignment and then find people to make sure crucial points are addressed.

Each team member needs specific assignments and responsibilities. All team members should have to respect deadlines and be held accountable.

Some areas to which individuals should be tasked include:

▶ Writing and administering the internal survey

▶ Reviewing of survey results and preparing a report with observations and recommendations

▶ Interviewing prospective consultants and/or vendors

▶ Writing, distributing, and reviewing RFIs

▶ Meeting with IS department to determine needs and resources

▶ Performing competitive analysis

▶ Shopping for ideas and possible applications

▶ Taking notes as well as preparing periodic updates and reports

▶ Keeping department heads and corporate management informed of progress

▶ Monitoring the implementation of early steps of the project, such as assigning individual Internet accounts and making sure employees receive necessary software and training

References

Where can you go on the Internet/Web to find more information on the Internet regarding this kind of information?

Check out the following Web sites operated by companies that offer articles and reports about some of the key issues addressed in this chapter:

www.jup.com (Jupiter Communications)
www.pcmag.com (*PC Magazine*)
www.informationweek.com (*Information Week* magazine)
www.webweek.com (*WebWeek*)
www.cobb.com/int (*Inside the Internet*)
www.internav.com/index.html (InterNav)

CHAPTER 4

Define Policy

A recent Internet/World Wide Web survey reported that two well-known men's magazines have among the most popular Web sites. The reasons are obvious. Sexually explicit material is widely available on the Web, and probably will be despite the recent organized efforts to curtail it.

What was surprising about the survey was the origin of many of the Web site *hits,* or visits. High on the list was NASA.

Not too much later, the sales force of a major telephone company was introduced to *Pointcast* (www.pointcast.com) software, the impressive PC screen saver and Web browser that can automatically retrieve from the Net information of interest to individual users. Several immediately downloaded the software onto their desktops, unwittingly violating corporate policy by bringing nonnative software onto the company's network.

An embarrassed manager soon put out the word to the sales folks that this was not permissible.

Corporate executives want to prevent problems before they occur, and this chapter is designed to help you avoid what these anecdotes illustrate. Employers have legitimate concerns about employees surfing on work hours, or downloading obscene or other types of questionable material. Lost productivity is one reason; another is corporate image. There also are security and virus concerns as well.

Another problem is the already mentioned telecommunications bill. While the 1996 effort stalled, future legislation could call for penalties if pornographic material is passed over networks, and a company could find itself in court if its Internet access is abused in this fashion.

While policies may seem boring to some, they simply are essential, because organizations are run by their policies. Long and short, written or oral, rooted in history or continually updated, a set of guiding principles is at the heart of every decision. In the same way, a policy for an Internet connection should examine how it is used in the broadest terms. Who will access it? When may it not be used? What can or cannot be transferred across the connection? These are examples of the questions to address.

Every group that connects to the Internet gains an explicit approval at some point in the process, but few create a written policy to govern its use. Some may expect employees to know why they are connected and to act accordingly. Others may assume existing policies will cover it, or may wish to gain experience with the connection before deciding how to govern its use. The majority of organizations have no policies, or those with such gaps or lack of enforcement as to be meaningless.

These approaches are fraught with problems. Even if the reasons for connecting are well understood, not every user will know how to use it appropriately. Existing policies rarely cover the unique methods of interaction that the Internet allows. Most importantly, without a well-defined policy up front, it may not be possible to agree on reasonable requirements for all parts of the organization.

This chapter guides you in the creation of a corporate Internet policy. Those who made the decision, and everyone who is part of managing the project should read and participate in this step. Those who work to define requirements and design the system should be familiar with its outcome.

Motivation

Perhaps the easiest way to understand the importance of an Internet policy is to imagine the characteristics of Internet-based communication applied to more familiar devices. The following examples are not intended to scare you away, but to emphasize the value in completing this part of the project.

Example: Recording Telephones

Suppose every phone in your office recorded both sides of every conversation. How would you adapt your corporate telephone usage policy? You might modify it in several ways. For example, you might set standards for when it was appropriate to share these recordings with other individuals. The nature of your job might depend on keeping some interactions confidential. You may also wish to strictly limit what employees may offer or agree to over the phone. A well-intended offer of help might later become a corporate liability. Finally, you might even set a corporate standard for how long to keep messages, in case you need evidence for litigation later.

Every electronic message traversing the Internet is stored in computer memory and possibly on a hard disk; migrating those messages to a more permanent medium, such as a floppy disk or magnetic tape, is trivial. Even though there is still some debate over what constitutes a contractual agreement on the Internet, using a store-and-forward mechanism for everyday communications requires some forethought.

Example: Open Advertising

If your organization chooses to advertise over the radio or TV, imagine what it would be like if all your employees could create commercials on the air, live. What impact would that have on your corporate communications policy? Your first tendency would be for outright prohibition; you would probably require all corporate communications to be cleared through a careful process, as they are probably done now. If you could not stop it, you might at least offer guidelines about what could or could not be said.

On the Internet, an electronic message or document created by a single individual can easily be distributed to tens of thousands of readers with a few keystrokes. The more controversial the statement, the more likely it will be redistributed to hundreds of thousands or millions of others. Once it attains some degree of notoriety, the print, TV, and other media will further spread attention. Employees may not be accustomed to or prepared for their statements having such far-reaching implications.

Dependencies

As the last chapter conveyed, the reasons for connecting to the Internet motivate the policy, not the other way around. Still, it is prudent to understand the risk before one commits to a project, and a strong policy statement can convey to a decision maker how dangers will be minimized. Therefore, in some cases, a little thought given to the policy and the drafting of an outline can help gain approval. Given the current concerns in the workplace about security and abuse of Internet/Web access privileges, you might be able to overcome a supervisor's worries with a preemptive strike.

It is not advisable to proceed to the next steps on requirements gathering without a common understanding of the policy. The next step will require people in different departments to decide how the connection is to be used. If people expect different types of use to be allowed, their requirements will be inconsistent, and the resulting design would be inadequate or wasteful. Therefore, you should not proceed with your plan before this is complete.

Goal

The policy statement is a freely distributed, relatively short document. During its development, keep these suggestions in mind:

1. **Keep It Readable:** It is very important that employees with access be familiar with this policy. Since long documents often go unread, try to make it easily digestible, limiting its length to five or ten pages in a clear, friendly style. Use tables wherever it summarizes information well. Ignore unnecessary sections that explain the technology or history.
2. **Make It Available:** Announce its availability using your organization's internal document system. Create overheads that highlight the main features, and offer brief presentations to interested employees. Your company's Human Resources Department also needs to be involved to ensure that other corporate policies are adhered to and any disciplinary steps included in the Internet/Web policy meet established criteria.
3. **Do Not Mention Specific Applications:** A policy that tries to determine exactly which programs may be used will quickly fall out of date. Determine

general types of use, and allow the requirements to dictate which specific applications are selected.

4. **Keep It Flexible:** Define the means by which the policy can be changed. The Internet is changing in size and applications; a policy that must be rewritten with each major shift will quickly be forgotten.

5. **Legal Overview:** Be sure your company's legal department or counsel reviews the document, particularly in light of the telecommunications act. Your counsel will want to make sure your company's legal risk is limited.
   A usage policy document should cover the following key points:

▶ Overview of the company's mission statement that covers its Internet/Web strategy

▶ Who is responsible for what areas of the Internet/Web operation, from operation to content issues

▶ What the responsibilities are for the end users

▶ How policies and procedures can be appealed or revised

▶ In general, what Internet usage is permitted

▶ In general, what Web usage is permitted

▶ How corporate Internet/Web access can be used from the employees' homes (if that capability is to be made available)

▶ In general, how usage will be monitored

▶ What the penalties are for misuse

▶ What the appeals process is for those accused of misuse

The specific details of each step are best left to your company, and in particular your Human Resources Department.

People

The project team responsible for Internet access—the one that manages the process described in this book—should develop the policy. It starts to assemble the members at the earliest part of the process, giving them more time to build an effective group. They will also constitute a wealth of internal experience, and will therefore create the best policy possible. Whoever approved the project should review the policy when complete.

In small organizations, the team may have only two or three people; one is not enough to ensure diverse viewpoints are considered. In larger organizations, five or six may suffice, while ten is probably the limit for productive group sizing. Everyone is expected to work only part time on this project, but ensure the total person-hours available will suffice to meet the project time line.

Location

The policy can be developed at any location. Since the team may represent a cross section of the corporation, whatever location is most logistically reasonable should suffice. Note that this team will continue to manage the project throughout its duration, and the meeting environment should be convenient and conducive to productivity for the group to be successful.

Resources

Since this most likely will be a short, text document, little in the way of unusual resources will be required. If a consultant is chosen, money must be allocated. Some additional administrative or word-processing support may be required if people creating the document have very limited time.

Duration

With the suggestions in this book, a focused, experienced team of two or three people working for a small organization could probably define a comprehensive policy in approximately one full week of their time. Therefore, allow at least two weeks for the inevitable interruption or schedule hitch.

A large organization should probably allow at least four weeks to coordinate the team, produce the document, conduct one or two revision cycles, and obtain the necessary levels of approval. In practice, it may take closer to six.

Given how anxious many are to connect to the Internet, can your group wait? If not, and this step is squeezed, try to do two things. First, derive whatever draft working policy you can from the contents of this chapter. While it may not be accepted, at least your assumptions will be written. Second, be sure to share the entire project plan, showing the dependencies and deliverables. Try to obtain buy-in to the overall process; it takes a little longer but it does save time and effort down the road.

Establishing regular group meetings at this stage is desirable, since continued coordination of activities minimizes the total project time. Thirty minutes or an hour once per week or every other week will probably be sufficient to maintain internal communications.

Security

To be certain, security is one of the biggest reasons to write your policy. But how widely distributed should that policy be? It may seem like an obvious question—but it isn't that simple. For example, a security policy that explained in great detail what measures were used to safeguard corporate information might present a *challenge* if acquired by a competitor. Yet that same plan might hold decisions on customer information that you want to make available to everyone!

We think you should consider three levels of security just for your policy! This is not as much work as it sounds, since one will contain most of the information found in the other two. Think of them as:

Publicly Available Policy Document

This version is the smallest, containing only those words that you feel comfortable sharing with the outside world (or perhaps a new hire candidate) about how the Internet is used within your company. This should make it clear to potential investors and the public how you treat your connection and seek to use the Internet.

Internal Employee Usage Policy

This is the document shared with your employees on what they may and may not do in detail on the Internet. This document is for internal use only, and may contain information that—if learned by other companies—could make it slightly easier for them to infiltrate your network, or that could save them effort and time in connecting their companies.

Internal Security Procedures

This final security document may be used only by your internal security department (if you are large enough to have one). It's not a very farfetched concept—every company depends a little bit on secrets kept by a few to keep their companies secure. For example, the copier codes, or the location of the keys to the storage area, may be restricted. *Security through obscurity* may help protect your corporate network by keeping details of its security detection and prevention mechanisms in the dark.

THE MALOFF COMPANY

Joel Maloff is not one of those people who believe in the Internet and World Wide Web as a Field of Dreams. "If you build it, it's not a sure thing anyone will come," he likes to say. And he speaks with considerable experience (see Figure 4.1).

His advice to companies contemplating a Net or Web strategy is simple: Treat this as you would any business issue or venture.

Maloff also recommends that companies should designate an *Internet Czar* internally, who is empowered to see the Internet and/or Web project through to completion. "In too many cases," he said, "companies let projects get bogged down because responsibilities cross departmental lines, which creates confusion and dissension."

Maloff, founder of The Maloff Company in Dexter, MI, is one of the world's best-known Internet and World Wide Web consultants. His clients include The National Football League, Nationwide Insurance, CompuServe, The Toro Company, and The Discovery Channel. He also has numerous clients in Europe, South America, and Asia. Before forming his own business, Maloff was a senior executive with ANS, which at one time was the largest Internet service provider in the world. He also has considerable experience in running major networks and in telecommunications.

Here is the Q&A with Mr. Maloff:

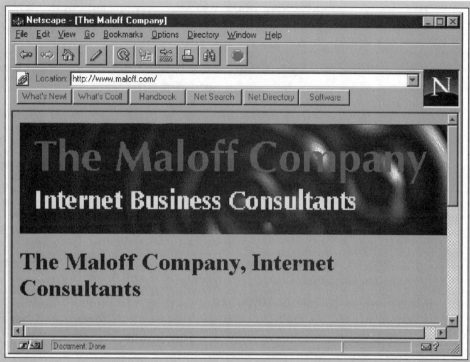

FIGURE 4.1   The Maloff Company home page.

Question: What factors and/or research should lead to a company's decision to develop an Internet strategy?
Answer: Business issues. Companies should not consider using any tool if it is not clearly beneficial to them from the start. Why buy a Porsche when you need a pickup truck? Businesses must start out with a quantifiable business issue (i.e., reducing inventory costs, reducing customer turnover rates, increasing sales from the western region). "We gotta be on the Net or the Web" is not a business problem.

Understanding the specific requirements, its current cost and impact on personnel, and the investment required to implement an electronic commerce solution is critical from the beginning. Not knowing why something is being done or having properly set expectations almost ensures failure.
Question: Often in this startup process, there are many difficulties to be overcome, technical and otherwise. What are some of the most common?

(continued)

Did companies anticipate them? What were they able to do to overcome these obstacles? What lessons should companies learn from those?

Answer: The major lessons from my clients were to start thinking first—not after you put the engine in gear. It is important to consider all aspects, including how well the existing infrastructure can handle the new solutions.

- ▶ Is there a common e-mail system throughout the enterprise?
- ▶ Are there multiple administrators from separate lines of business?
- ▶ How well do they coordinate?
- ▶ If you publish an e-mail address for customer inquiries, who answers the questions and in how timely a manner?

There are many issues such as these that must be considered before implementation.

Question: If these companies had the process to do over again, what are some of the things that they should/would do differently? What lessons were learned? What is some advice you would give others?

Answer: Much of that has been described previously; however, the one major mistake many companies have made is believing that electronic commerce, Internet, and Web are part-time jobs and can be done by a technical person with *spare time.* This is hardly true.

Electronic commerce will be a critical part of how businesses engage in commerce in the future. It is more than a full-time job for people who understand not only technology, but also business implications. It is a senior management role and hardly technical only. I have repeatedly recommended to many Fortune 100 companies that they create such a position, and most are doing so. When calculating investment, return rates, and likelihood of success, this is one of the key factors. Many companies fail to include personnel expenses in their budgets, and are doomed to many unpleasant surprises.

Question: How important is it to have a strategic plan? Do they normally cover all of the necessary points? If you were to write a strategic plan for others, what would be the highlights?

Answer: It isn't important; it's essential. If you do not know where you are going, any road will take you there! Most companies are now beginning to recognize this and, rather than letting technology drive them, they are beginning to plan for technology's role. Many financial institutions are good examples of this, especially the insurance industry. They recognize that their businesses could be substantially changed through the displacement of agents, replaced by online *insurance malls.* All businesses will need to step up to the issue of planning sooner or later, formally or informally. You cannot succeed without some level of clear strategic planning.

Question: What are some of the mistakes that you see other companies making as they delve into the Internet? Why are they making them?

Answer: Lack of planning and thinking of the Internet and the Web as self-fulfilling plans are two of the biggest mistakes being made. Others include failing to develop proper plans, procedures, and training materials; and subsequently distributing them to everyone that needs to know.

Question: What has the Internet access meant to your business? Can you share any numbers in terms of sales and additional revenues? Return on investment? Did you establish a separate budget for the Internet plan?

Answer: I could not conduct the business that I do today without the Net. I publicize myself, sell my research reports, conduct my consulting, and make contacts for new business via the Net. I even do interviews electronically.

Question: If you were new to the Internet/Web and looking for a book to help you plan/coordinate/execute an Internet strategy, what are some of the points you would want covered?

Answer: Well, I would probably want a how-to, but that tends to be specific to each organization. You should cover common sense issues here, but keep in mind that technology is changing very rapidly. The Web has been around only three years, RealAudio is only a year old, and Internet Phone is barely a year old. New security measures come out every day, and Java will change everything. Few companies can afford to go it alone and hope that their staff keeps up on everything. This is why it is important to use competitive outsourced services, such as consultants or Web hosting organizations, who are up to date and can answer questions relevant to each individual company or division.

Question: What are some of the factors companies should be looking for when selecting an ISP, Web site developer, and consulting firm?

(continued)

Answer: Clear experience, an ability to listen and understand what the company is trying to achieve, and comparable, demonstrable references are all criteria to be used for any of these categories. From there, it changes. ISPs must be able to provide 24-hour-per-day, seven-day-per-week customer support. They must offer a variety of access services that suit the potential needs of the customer—from SLIP/PPP to ISDN and leased line services. Someone needs to be competent to address security issues—from plans to policies to implementation tools.

Issues

While access to the Internet does throw some twists on existing practices, most organizations have individuals who can distill appropriate usage guidelines from an understanding of the business. The most time-consuming part is determining a suitable approach to the problem. A large, distributed, low-tech company would likely implement a completely different set of restrictions than a small, high-tech firm.

The following sections provide suggestions for how you can and cannot proceed in developing a policy for your group. Read through all the sections and select only those that are appropriate. You should also consider whether there are other issues particular to your own circumstances.

Consistency with Existing Policies

Start the effort by assembling all the relevant existing policies. Gather those that apply to computer systems, communications systems (i.e., telephones, FAX, internal e-mail), and corporate security. Everyone on the team should become familiar with their provisions.

If your company lacks written policies, take time to summarize the informal office regulations of which you are aware. Write down your understanding about how information is classified, who speaks for the company, and what rules apply to computer account passwords. Determine to what extent if any personal use of telephones and PCs is allowed, whether any restrictions on time of use exist, and if some employees have more communications privileges than others. Remember: The more difficult you think it is to capture these rules for devices that are used every day, the more important it is that they be clearly written out for Internet access.

Limits on Use

The easiest policy to write allows everything and prohibits nothing. In general, this will provide maximum benefit from the connection, but may not balance risks correctly. For example, a software company may allow its development department to connect to the Internet so that they can maintain contact with other programmers, thus saving time. However, if an intruder uses the connection to steal or modify code being developed, it could cost the business dearly.

Your policy should define the limits on access that are consistent with your organization's goals. The following sections discuss some ways in which access may be constrained. Some of these constraints can be mandatory, implemented by technology, while others are discretionary and require user compliance. Your particular policy may provide a matrix with one of these categories on the vertical axis, and several columns for each of the others, detailing what may or may not be done.

By Applications Type

The previous chapter showed how the Internet provides a common mechanism by which organizations and consumers may interact through computers. It is convenient to continue to use this high-level model to divide Internet applications into four basic types, as discussed in the following sections.

Human-to-Human Communications.   The first type, *human-to-human* communications, is illustrated in Figure 4.2. Applications such as electronic messaging, chat, multiuser games, and audio/videoconferencing enable humans to respond to each other using the computer as an interface.

This type of application is among the most useful and popular. Electronic messaging alone is already a popular internal application, and a significant contributor of traffic on the Internet. It makes it easy to reach busy people with a single attempt, and softens the effect of being in different

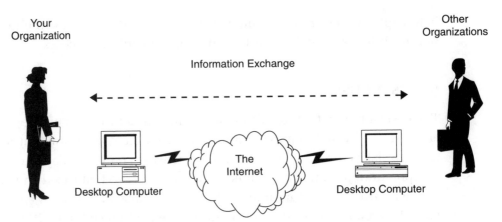

FIGURE 4.2   Human-to-human communications on the Internet.

time zones. E-mail can also be less expensive than telephone calls or faxes, as electronic chats and videoconferencing can be cheaper than traveling.

Human-to-human applications have their downsides also. When employees subscribe to numerous mailing lists, or casual business correspondence use increases, it can become a significant time sink. With no mechanism to guarantee delivery or failure notification, electronic messaging may be inappropriate for soliciting certain kinds of timely responses. Neither e-mail nor electronic chat conveys vocal inflections that carry warmth and humor, and both require greater attention to semantics and spelling. While audio and video over the Internet eliminate many of these drawbacks, they impose more severe bandwidth requirements.

Unless your organization is extremely sensitive to drawbacks associated with e-mail, strongly consider allowing human-to-human interactions in your policy. The requirements will determine whether simple e-mail or more advanced interactive applications should be used.

Information Dissemination.   Figure 4.3 shows the second type of communication your organization can enable over the Internet: *Information Dissemination*. In this mode, you place information on a computer server that makes it available for retrieval by people. The most popular set of computer programs for performing this activity belong to the Web. Current Web sites are very sophisticated, supporting data retrieval, posting, searching, referrals, and even transactions. In fact, there is some crossover to human-to-

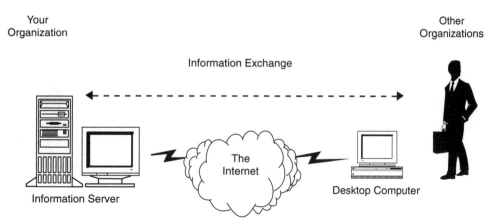

FIGURE **4.3**   Information dissemination on the Internet.

human applications, in that electronic messages may be sent as a consequence of Web use even though the primary interaction is from human to machine. Furthermore, the ultimate source of information is usually from a person—but the use of a computer server eliminates his or her direct involvement in its transmission.

This is an extremely popular area of participation, which has recently attracted many organizations. In addition to supporting numerous activities, Web applications allow engaging user interfaces with formatted text, graphics, audio, video, and *hyperlinks* that allow simple point-and-click option selection. It is a powerful way to market your organization, distribute software products, support customers, or otherwise share information that can be printed, filmed, or broadcast.

Not every organization's charter allows for active promotion or information distribution. Others, such as local lawn-care service, may simply find a more targeted distribution, such as local mailings, more effective.

Success can also be a drawback, with very popular Web sites using large amounts of network bandwidth and server capacity, requiring even more money to maintain quality service.

To make this key decision, do not let a vague sense of cost or security concern you. Decide whether providing a presence on the Internet is relevant to some aspect of your business; whether these other factors are worrisome will be determined in the design.

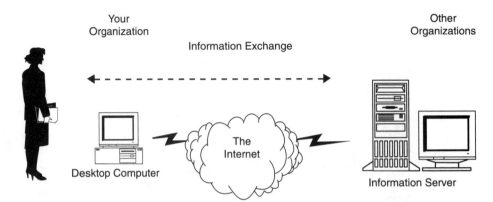

FIGURE 4.4   Information collection on the Internet.

Information Collection.   When the roles of servers and clients are reversed, Information Collection, as shown in Figure 4.4, results. It is very important to understand the distinction between these: in the former, users on the Internet were able to retrieve information about you, while in the latter, your employees can obtain information about other organizations.

Most organizations can benefit in some way from this capability. If your organization disseminates information on the Internet, it may be instructive to see the formats and capabilities that others use. It is also helpful to gather information about companies that can help you (i.e., suppliers, consultants), or those against which you compete (competitive analysis.) Access to libraries, directories, and online shopping services may also save time and money.

Using the Internet in this manner is not without drawbacks. Like electronic messaging, it is easy to spend large amounts of time browsing. There is also a limit to what is available electronically without charge, and to what you can believe.

If you disseminate information on the Internet, you should use it to collect information as well. It will help you understand what others see. Otherwise, you will have to decide whether your people can reasonably take advantage of what is available; with few exceptions, most can.

Machine-to-Machine Communications.   The final method of communication over the Internet is shown in Figure 4.5. *Machine-to-machine* access

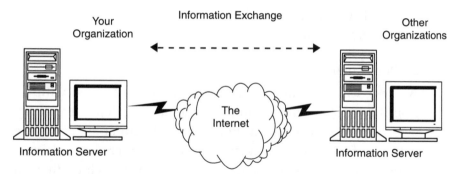

FIGURE 4.5   Machine-to-machine communications on the Internet.

allows geographically distributed computers in the same or different organizations to share data over the Internet. Though the machines were configured by people, the data exchanges take place according to the programs
executing inside the computers, and not under the immediate control of
users. In this case, the Internet acts like a private virtual network of dedicated access lines or switched services, such as Frame Relay or SMDS.

A considerable cost reduction is the prime advantage to this method of
use. Using dedicated links, private networks have recurring charges that
depend on the number of circuits, their length, and speed. The costs can be
minimal for a few close offices, but they increase rapidly as the number of
sites or their distances grow large. Network services, such as Frame Relay
and SMDS, may be slightly more or less expensive, depending on the number of sites, the particular configuration, and operational costs.

There are two major downsides to this type of use. First, the current
technology and operational issues make it more difficult to guarantee availability and throughput on the Internet than through virtual private networks. Second, traffic traversing some parts of the Internet may be easily
monitored or modified, risking possible unauthorized access to systems
and information. Certain types of security breaches can be avoided by using devices that encrypt data before transmission.

If there is a high cost associated with network unavailability or security
breaches, or if encryption does not completely address your security concerns, this type of application is clearly inappropriate. If these are not issues, it is worth allowing the potential cost advantages of building a virtual
private network over the Internet. In the near future, as security standards

and quality of service mechanisms gain acceptance, expect a rapid growth in this fourth type of interaction.

By Department

Another way in which Internet access can be limited within an organization is by group. For example, an engineering department may need to access particular discussion groups or software archives on the Internet to better perform their jobs, while for customer service such access would be a distraction. There are several mechanisms by which this can be accomplished.

The possible result of such a division is to create separate classes of information, *haves* and *have-nots*, within the company. Haves inevitably tell about and share their capabilities with some of the others, while the have-nots keep asking for occasional help or the same kind of applications. The result may be less conducive to productivity than granting everyone the same level of access.

By Individual

Unless employees dial up from home, or terminals and PCs have special software installed, no login is required when gathering information from the Internet. (Electronic messaging does require individual mailboxes that can be controlled somewhat.) Therefore, granting access by individual can be more difficult to enforce than by department, and equally problematic.

By Local Machine

There is a straightforward (but not impenetrable) technical mechanism by which access can be limited on a per-machine basis. Only certain PCs in some offices or groups would have access, partially converting a network security problem into a physical security problem. This could be used as part of the solution to granting access by department or individual.

A limited set of computers configured to disseminate information is certainly prudent, and a limited set of computers configured to retrieve information has its advantages—among them, a reduced number of applications to purchase and maintain, and a sense of certainty in knowing where and when these applications were being used.

In some organizations, an open area or library might be home for the Internet access terminal.

The main consideration before taking such action is whether the reduction in spending is worth a possible reduction in efficiency. Consider how many dedicated machines could reasonably serve the office versus how many individual machines would require the application. Factor in the possibility that some people will be less efficient working from a terminal that is not their own. While some small organizations may consider this approach, most with fairly robust systems administration support will find it more convenient to include this application on people's desktops.

By Time

While in most cases, employees will self-limit their time on the Internet, it may be appropriate to define reasonable hours of use or total hours spent. These limits may be implemented voluntarily or automatically. While in most cases, this type of limit seems as unwise as limited access to telephones or libraries, there may be some instances where it is appropriate.

For example, some retail business may wish to connect primarily to disseminate information on the Internet, with information collection abilities as a convenience. Prior to the holidays or busiest times of the month, it may be appropriate for users to voluntarily restrain or to have access disabled.

By Content

Trustworthy mechanisms by which content can be filtered are being developed, and a policy will likely have to address the nature of the information transferred over the Internet. Following are some general categories of information that may be appropriate for your policy; you should consider whether other categories of importance exist for your organization.

► **Business Information:** If there is a list of topics that are inappropriate for discussion over the telephone, the Internet policy should remind users of the same procedures and guidelines. Information that is usually not to be discussed, such as impending acquisitions, marketing plans, and phone lists, would be easily circulated electronically.
► **Software:** The Internet provides a very large software archive, with free *source code* (a high-level language), compiled software (ready to execute on specified computers), *shareware* (which trusts the user to pay the author a reasonable fee), and commercially supported products (which require separate purchasing agreements).

Part of the computer systems policy should determine whether users or systems administrators may download applications onto their computers. The policy may constrain this activity, limiting the number of applications, or requiring some internal request. It may also dictate the terms under which shareware may be acquired.

If developing software is part of your business, you will have to address these policies from the other side. Determine under what terms downloaded software can be incorporated into products. Determine the disclaimers you must attach to software you provide.

▶ **Netiquette:** All e-mail users should be familiarized with the organization's standards for *Netiquette*, a set of informal rules for behavior on unmoderated news and mailing lists. These types of guidelines exist in numerous books, reminding users that anonymity is not license to insult.

▶ **Intellectual Property:** Many people on the Internet have spent considerable time creating useful information on a variety of topics. With current Internet tools, cutting and pasting that information into internal documents becomes trivial. Because that information may be of questionable origin or contain copyright notices, a policy should dictate how that information should be cited. Similarly, if your organization plans to create useful text or unique graphics, a policy for attaching an appropriate restriction should be defined.

▶ **Illegal Material:** Presumably some organizational policy already precludes the transfer of text, audio, images, or video that are pornographic, libelous, or otherwise illegal. It may be wise to reference these statements in your Internet policy.

What Cannot Be Limited

While some reasonable mechanisms exist by which to constrain access, it is important to understand that some types of use cannot or should not be limited. When an improved security infrastructure is put in place, some of these constraints may disappear.

Incoming E-Mail

Since the original electronic messages on the Internet are easily forged, and being able to receive incoming messages from new users is desirable, limiting the receipt of incoming e-mail by sender is not advised. While a particular message handler may have a maximum message size or maximum amount of e-mail per user, this generally should not be made artificially low, either. A message containing a large document or computer file may not pass the first criterion, while a flurry of unwanted messages may fill up the latter.

Retrieved File Size

While it is possible to request users to avoid large file transfers during working hours, it is difficult to enforce. A voluntary request to limit known large files during daytime hours would be appropriate for organizations with low-speed connections, but may not be heeded.

Redistribution of Information

Unlike a printed book that must be copied page by page, information encoded for electronic transfer across a network is easily re-sent numerous times. In general, you may request that correspondence, communications, or information disseminated onto the Internet undergo limited retransmission, but it is difficult to prevent. Before sending information, consider the risks if it becomes available to the entire world.

Internally you may exercise somewhat greater control over what information is recirculated. It is appropriate to set guidelines for what may and may not be shared when received over the Internet, but remember that as with printed paper, it is hard to prevent.

By External Machine or Organization

While every machine on the Internet is assigned a unique identifier, there are ways to pretend to be another computer. Therefore, it is difficult to implement a policy that restricts external access to particular machines or companies. If the outside community is to be restricted, it should probably be required to support a strong authentication method, in which a password is never transmitted in the clear.

Record Keeping

As discussed earlier, the information transfer via electronic messaging is always stored in some form as it traverses the Internet. Electronic messaging applications and many others also provide the means by which to record actions, such as the transmission of a message or request of a file. Several of these forms of record keeping are discussed in the following.

Archives

Ensure the computer systems policy on maintaining reasonable hard-disk usage extends to cover archiving of e-mail and other collected information. There may be a different set of standards for maintaining e-mail that cannot be recreated, and other downloaded data that can be reacquired.

Access Logs

Many systems that support the ability to disseminate or collect information allow every transfer (and an indication of its success or failure) to be recorded. How much of this information may be recorded and how long it will be kept should be a matter of policy.

On the one hand, maintaining utilization statistics allows capacity planning and allows those who disseminate information to determine how effective it is. On the other hand, keeping logs requires additional disk resources, and implies the need for processing the raw data into a useful form. Also, if logs are kept on information collection, there may be issues of privacy. Users should be aware of what is being tracked.

Billing

The preceding usage records may be used to bill internal departments, in the same way some telephone and fax systems charge to department or project codes based on utilization. However, raw logs usually require considerable scrutiny to translate into an accurate bill. This practice, while reasonable in some circumstances, should be carefully implemented and tested before used.

Penalties

To be effective, a policy must specify the consequences of noncompliance. This can both deter willful violations and avoid lengthy debates concerning appropriate punishment. When invoked, the action taken will probably depend on many factors, including the severity of the violation, the impact it had on the organization, the penalties specified by related policies, and whether it is a repeated offense.

For some organizations, misuse may result in loss of Internet access privileges, a restriction that can be challenging to enforce in large organizations with technically skilled individuals. Be certain to decide whether removing users is desired, and to discuss how it can be achieved in the design phase.

References

External resources are somewhat difficult to provide for this section, since your decisions must represent your individual organization's culture and goals. There is a useful reference for proper Internet behavior at ftp://ds. internic.net/rfc/rfc1855.txt, which discusses network etiquette, or *Netiquette,* as it has become known. Your Internet service provider may also provide a usage policy of its own. Be sure to retrieve the *Site Security Handbook* at ftp://ds.internic.net/rfc/rfc1244.txt. Finally, the Internet Usage Policy for Employees in Appendix B provides a sample policy document written for a small non–high-tech company. This example document illustrates appropriate language and the degree of detail needed in a clearly defined policy statement.

CHAPTER 5

Determine
Requirements

Now that everyone in your organization knows an Internet connection is arriving and guidelines for its use are established, it is time to decide precisely what you will do with it. The traditional name for this description of necessary capabilities and characteristics is *requirements*, but that name connotes everything it contains is mandatory. In reality, since most documents include levels of importance, such as *Need to have*, *Like to have*, and *Nice to have*, the document is really *desirements*.

In many organizations, grass-roots efforts drive the need to connect to the Internet. Due to the source of motivation the solution often does little more than serve those who requested it. The intention of this step is to assist you in getting the most out of your Internet connection. The key is collecting requirements from as many people as possible. A secondary advantage of this step is the creation of a common set of expectations across all departments, eliminating disappointment and unwanted surprises.

This chapter will guide you through the process of collecting requirements. This information should be shared more than other chapters, since everyone who takes advantage of the Internet can have input even if they do not contribute to the implementation. Be sure to have the policy in hand when working, to focus this step on uses that are permitted. In this chapter everything will be discussed as if it had been allowed in the policy; you should modify your requirements accordingly.

Motivation

The technical network and systems designers on whose skills this project must rely in part have many passions in life. One of them is drawing block diagrams of computers and routers connected by LANs and leased circuits; another is to collect several such pictures from different people, and argue about which is best. The only problem with this valuable and sometimes entertaining ritual is that it does not necessarily make your connection to the Internet happen more quickly or better.

At the same time, your marketing, sales, and other employees have their passions—which are often as far away as possible from thinking about networks and computers. We guarantee this project can expand to need all the resources you can make available: a black hole for people, money, time. When it's done, it may still fail to meet the needs or expectations of departments that were not involved in its definition.

The requirements document can help avoid this by helping you design a solution that meets corporate needs and desires, not just the needs or wishes of a certain group or groups. It avoids disputes among designers—who often set out to solve slightly different problems. It also permits the solution to be evaluated against solid criteria, and to communicate to everyone in the organization how the connection may be used. This step will help avoid confusion and expedite your Internet process. Better that designers should argue over the last soda in the vending machine, anyway.

Dependencies

Policies make requirements definition tractable by offering constraints. Methods of use that are not aligned with the corporate goals are eliminated early, avoiding time spent discussing their details, and possibly designing them. Thus, do not begin writing requirements until their compliance with policy can be ensured. Although the policy definition is relatively short, if it can be written and approved in short pieces, some requirements work can begin early.

The design step is being primed while your team is collecting requirements, since technical expertise is required to ensure the requirements are reasonable. It may also be appropriate to begin discussions with vendors, service providers, or internal resources that could provide a more economical or efficient design. However, no design should be finalized until this stage is complete.

Goal

The requirements document should be a moderate collection of tables and text that describes how the connection will be used. To be meaningful, the entries should have a first level of sanity checking already performed. Specific computer applications and any special circumstances will need to be identified. This document may need to be revised as the company evolves, but should be frozen at the completion of this phase. You should consult and involve the designers early to ensure it will meet their needs, since they are the end users.

In practice, this step is ongoing, since your connection to the Internet will evolve along with all automation steps in your company. At some point, the document needs to be finalized so that a design can begin—but it's okay to treat the document as *living*, allowing changes down the road, as long as people know they may not be incorporated in the initial implementation.

People

The requirements document will be written by the same Project Team that developed your Internet plan and usage policy. When selecting participants from the technical departments, ensure the person or people who are likely to be chosen for the design function are included. Their early input will help keep requirements reasonable.

Location

While the policy was done at the convenience of the team, this step is at the convenience of the end users. Count on collecting the bulk of the information from people distributed throughout the organization. This implies at least phone interviews, internal e-mail, and possibly written question-naires.

Since many people may not yet understand how the Internet can help them, some education is required to complete this step. This could include executive overviews and briefings. An idea would be to videotape a brief-ing for showing at remote locations or at an employee's convenience. And since those discussions are usually most efficient in person, collecting re-quirements often requires travel. If possible, work this step in with other duties that take the Project Team to everywhere the organization extends.

Resources

Some resources for travel may be needed, as suggested previously. Also, given that requirements are probably longer than the policy, administrative or word-processing support is even more desirable during this phase.

Consultants can possibly play a more substantial role in this phase. If technical resources are not available within the company, or if departments would like guidance in defining their applications, an external consulting group may be useful. One that possesses both familiarity with your organi-zation and experience using the Internet successfully will offer the best value.

Duration

There are many factors to consider when estimating the duration for this task. Rarely can a small company perform the task reasonably in under a week, while a large, technologically advanced company might require sev-eral months for a thorough job (assuming they could wait that long!). Here are some guidelines for estimating the time it will take you. When you're done with the real estimate, you may have to compress it to meet your overall project goals—just beware of how that may cost more money down the road.

Company Size

The only way to represent the needs of your company is to talk to a statistically significant percentage of it. The exact percentage depends on how similar individual jobs are. Clearly, a company with 100 people doing exactly the same thing can be interviewed more quickly than one with 20 people whose daily tasks are markedly different. Consider how many employees you have, and whether their job descriptions overlap or are unique, and start with a baseline of one to three weeks accordingly. It is difficult to plan with any greater precision, so be generous with your estimate and strive to finish early.

Geographic Scope

A company that is spread across several buildings or cities requires extra time to coordinate reaching people, either by car, plane, or even phone. Those spread across countries have to worry about time zones, language, and office culture differences. Allow another week or two, depending on how easy it will be to reach all parties involved.

Technology

Just as a professional craftsman's power tools are far more complex than the weekend handyman's, your Internet project sophistication is highly dependent on how much technology your company uses. If you're a technologically oriented company with a high degree of existing information infrastructure, add another two weeks to the total. If you're small and not technology focused, your initial entry into cyberspace will not require additional time.

Project Team Availability

While we'd like to think this is the most important project at your company, we know better. You have other things to do, and maybe even some major deadlines approaching—like the end of your quarter or fiscal year. The Project Team may only be working on this 25 to 50 percent of their time (hopefully more!), which further prevents them from creating the finished product. Add another 50 to 100 percent of your current running total based on the fraction of team time available.

Security

At this step, there can be ideas and plans that are very valuable to your company. The Project Team should continually decide if the point is reached that the document should be restricted to employees and contractors who signed nondisclosure agreements. For example, if you decide you want to be the first organization to sell mail-order soda via the Internet, that information getting out early could give the other companies a chance to compete. Be aware that the information in this document may represent some value to your company, and should be protected accordingly.

Issues

Defining requirements for Internet access is an imposing task. You're expected to take a technology that continues to evolve and specific programs that are constantly improved, and use them with a service provider that often cannot precisely state what data throughput or availability you will receive, in a market where prices are generally being driven downward and the number of users on the Internet grows exponentially, and apply all that to help your business plan. It's now time to wish you luck.

Of course, you can do a little better than that by considering some of the hard learned lessons of numerous Internet pioneers, as summarized in the following issues.

Collecting the Information

While requirements collection is challenging in general, it is particularly troublesome for Internet access for the reasons presented in the following sections.

Lack of Applications Understanding

Depending on the nature of your organization, few or many employees will understand how a connection to the Internet can help them do their jobs. Part of the requirements collection process (and part of the reason it takes so long) is the need to explain what it can do. You should plan to spend some time explaining its uses for every department interviewed. It may also be worthwhile to schedule some of the training discussed in Chapter 2 before these interviews begin.

If you have not already obtained access to the Internet—through a dial-up account or a friend's access—this is your next best chance. People who have used applications make much better decisions about what they need than those who hear them described.

Another useful technique is to approach people with recommendations instead of options. Very often, people in various departments will be excited about the prospect of using the Internet, and any potential application on the entire palette will be eagerly sought. Instead, the Project Team may wish to start with some recommended Need to haves, Like to haves, and Nice to haves for each department.

Internet Requirements Creep

If left to the technologists, your connection to the Internet might be called upon for everything from WWW surfing to remote toaster control. What is often needed is a discussion between nontechnical people, who understand the business requirements, and technologists, who understand the cost and complexity implications. This prevents requirements from inching along toward the *entertaining*, and also avoids another design iteration to reduce costs. At the same time, a little headroom is desired—since many companies that attach to the Internet upgrade the speed of their connections, and sometimes their network hardware and servers, within a few months. If your policy permits it, don't underestimate the interest Web surfing will generate.

Organization and Presentation: The biggest challenge to requirements acquisition is simply agreeing on and conveying exactly what the document should include. Everyone will have different experiences with requirements collection in the past, and a different opinion about what should be included and how to present it. Consolidating different topics and formats into a single, integrated requirements is time-consuming and may not yield a thorough result.

Requirements Format

There are numerous ways to represent your requirements: from the obvious plain text document to the excessive video documentary. Something in the middle is probably ideal.

In general, people do not like to read long documents. (This book being an exception, of course.) Wherever possible, a needs matrix makes the document easier to develop and use. In fact, the problem is more than just two-dimensional. You may have to fill in each element in the matrix with more than just a check mark. Following are some of the aspects to consider.

Location

One of the first considerations in structuring your requirements document is how you will treat multiple location. If you have several offices in the same country with similar requirements, each could be represented in the same requirements document. Otherwise, if your multiple locations have slightly different needs, it helps to write a document for one (the most complex perhaps) and then use it as a starting point for the others. If your offices differ in some significant way—like in different countries, or the type of work performed is completely different—it makes even more sense to break it up into separate documents. A subgroup could work on each independently, but they should share a common template and format.

Department

Breaking out requirements by department helps segment the task so that it can be worked in parallel. It also makes it easy to create a staged implementation that aims to help those departments in most critical need first. You may choose to use functional groups within departments, or break down need by location.

Applications

You will need to specify what programs you plan to run that make use of the Internet. This can be difficult to do, since new programs emerge often, and the functions that general-purpose programs such as Internet browsers do continue to increase. For example, many browser vendors recently began to incorporate *real-time audio* capabilities that used to be separate computer programs. Depending on when you start your requirements plan, you may find that the exact programs used can be changed later.

Following are some examples of applications requirements you'll want to consider. The Project Team should engage in a more complete survey to identify other uses of interest. One way to do this is to visit the home page of the company that provides your dial-up access, or write your browser. Often they will have links to other related software packages you can download and evaluate.

Electronic Mail.   One of the most ubiquitous applications, we find that every department will find e-mail useful. Marketing can reach potential customers and conduct small- or large-scale research. Sales can accept unsolicited inquiries and contact target markets (although *junk e-mail* must be generated with care). Together with customer service and possibly engineering, participation on mailing lists that are particular to the industry or a product can provide invaluable perspectives from existing and potential customers.

With so many companies providing electronic mail for their employees, everyone will want to add their addresses to their business cards. Depending on who your company contacts, it can reduce long-distance tolls and the frustration of telephone-tag. Everyone with an industry contact, supplier, or peer can reach someone via e-mail.

Web Access.   The Web, which transforms the Internet into a graphical point-and-click environment, will most likely be heavily requested by your staff. Because of improvements in browser software, a number of search and other functions (such as gopher, FTP, and newsgroups) can take place with a GUI. Other tools also enable the Web to support video and audio.

However, since your users can pull down graphics and use all these various functions, bandwidth utilization also will increase. Your design plan should prevent you from having 200 people accessing the Web simultaneously over one 56/64K leased-line connection. Such demand would reduce throughput to a crawl. Bandwidth needs can be controlled by what functionality you allow employees to have. If audio and video aren't essential, then neither should be supported.

Newsgroups. Newsgroups are similar to mailing lists in that the entire readership can see messages from and post messages to each other, but the protocols used make finding a discussion on a particular topic and distributing them to remote sites more efficient. There are tens of thousands of topics covered in the free newsgroups circulated on the Internet, and many more available for monthly subscription fees.

The breadth of topics covered makes newsgroups of use to many organizations, and the best way to identify which ones in particular is to subscribe to several (using a dial-up Internet Service Provider) and locate discussions of relevance. Marketing can find candid discussions about products and companies for their research. Engineering can locate helpful forums for the products and services they use. Sales can conduct limited outbound campaigns, subject to the rules of Netiquette. Human resources can post positions and check out the competitors. Executive management can find, for a modest fee, a daily feed of relevant industry headlines and highlights.

Many distinctly nonbusiness-related newsgroups do exist on the Internet, and to some their distraction outweighs any benefit. If discussed as a group during the requirements process, spurious groups can be filtered out and only useful topics retained. The group writing the requirements is in the best position to decide how to proceed.

Newsgroups typically are updated overnight, and the size of the feed is now so large that a 56/64K Internet connection simply can't support it. You may want to see if your ISP will screen newsgroups to your site, thus reducing the flow. Internal controls of newsgroups can be controlled by your IS department. Some limitations will need to be put in place unless your company designs a robust system.

Chat. Communicating interactively via split-screen terminal windows has been around for a long time, but recently the capabilities have been expanded through the Internet Relay Chat application, or *chat* for short. By contacting one of numerous computers configured as a *chat relay*, hundreds of users spread around the world can locate and join ongoing discussions by topic. Like newsgroups, the right groups offer frank exchanges about products, services, and companies from a diverse population. There are also several niche discussion groups, like those where computer programmers (and sometimes *hackers*) live that can provide perspective and expertise to engineering staff.

Though lacking the warmth of a human voice, there are many innovative applications for chat. By running your own relay, you can organize your own network forums, providing subject matter expertise, focused discussion groups, or speedy customer support. Consider whether your customers would join you online for an *ask the experts* hour, during which their interactive questions would be answered immediately. If your product is hi-tech in nature, accessing customer service through an online window may also be attractive. This Internet capability is still being developed, and creative ideas are welcome.

Audio and Video Conferencing.   For years, live audio or video information has been transmitted on the Internet, combining the low-cost and interactive capabilities of chat with the inflections and facial cues of in-person conversation. The types of conferencing break down into three general categories. The first is point-to-point audio or video casting, which is possible over the Internet using moderate bandwidth links and relatively inexpensive hardware with two client PCs. While the number of users with the proper setup is relatively small now, it will grow. Sales, marketing, and customer support can take on added dimensions using these capabilities.

The second type of conferencing involves from perhaps two to a dozen users interacting together through a server or *reflector*. Since only the capabilities supported by a user's platform will be enabled, it is possible to connect home PCs with limited or no video to office workstations with color video support. Multiuser conferencing can easily support project coordination with vendors, consultants, and customers distributed across the country. It can also facilitate better coordination among the operations groups of different companies, or executive conference calls (of a nonsensitive, noncritical nature).

Multicasting is the third method of audio/video conferencing; it uses the virtual Multicast Backbone (MBONE) to send a small number of videoconference quality streams to a large number of recipients. For years, many topics of particular interest to those who design and operate the Internet have been broadcast, including key IETF sessions and relevant research lectures. More recently, topics of general interest, such as NASA events, telecommunications seminars, and even some live entertainment, are shown. Thus, the ability to receive MBONE broadcasts will be of interest to the engineering and training departments, while your public relations group may one day find the need to broadcast on it.

Another activity to keep in mind is electronic white board. Interactively modifying the contents of an electronic drawing (and other *groupware* applications) is being used on the Internet. While it can have applications for coordinating designs and documents with suppliers, vendors, and customers, its availability through the Internet is somewhat limited at present. Again, creative uses are waiting,

Online Commerce.   If your company plans to sell products over the Internet, your plan will have to address concerns about security, encryption, and transaction processing. This will add substantially to the cost of your plan, from design to hardware, consulting to continuing maintenance. A detailed discussion of this topic is best left to you, your IS department, and a consultant.

Special Sites

If you are on the Internet and so is another organization, you'll be able to communicate, right? Wrong. Communication on the Internet depends on the *Peering Agreements* made between companies that provide Internet Services. While many companies do have arrangements, there is no guarantee that you will be able to reach a particular organization from your service provider. (Actually, similar situations exist in telephony, where, for example, a cellular phone provider may not allow you to roam in all areas!)

If your employees are counting on reaching certain sites in particular—vendors, customers, partners, and so on—this is the time to find out. Include these in the plan, so the service provider with whom you do business can be queried in advance.

Time of Day

Somebody needs to decide how much capacity your link to the Internet will allow. There are some general rules of thumb for doing this, but occasionally a power user can blow these out of the water. For example, if 99 percent of your company uses only e-mail and the link is sized for them, their messages may be slowed down markedly by a single individual using a real-time audio application or exchanging large amounts of data with another site. Additionally, if you create a Web site that becomes popular, it can generate enough queries to saturate most servers and links easily. This often happens when one person posts a recommended URL to a newsgroup or mailing list, and many readers check it out simultaneously.

One way to reduce peak load on a link is to average it out. Thus, it's worth noting the time of day when special transfers need to be done. Also, if sites are in different time zones, this should also be noted. If you have some control over when transfers are done (like when a newsfeed is received or an unattended backup is performed), indicate that, too.

In practice, nobody can predict their network traffic in advance. Internet traffic on backbones often shows two peaks—one in the morning, and one midafternoon. The exact amounts vary according to the day of the week and special events; the only generally agreed upon trend is that the average amount of traffic is continuing to rise.

Data Formats

Though the Web represents some of the most interoperable technology currently deployed, there are still more than two ways to do almost everything. Encoding images, compressing files, attaching files to e-mail, transferring files to browsers, and even representing simple text can all be done in a variety of ways.

If someone in your organization depends on information presented in a particular format, now is the time to notice. For example, suppose marketing wants to use the Internet to retrieve current forecast information from a contractor. That contractor may mail it out as a uu-encoded attachment file, but your e-mail reader may understand only the more popular MIME format. Similar situations can arise with the transfer of audio, graphic, and video formats. Make sure you research the format needed for any special information transfers you will need.

Security

With which would you feel safe: a large, illuminated, door-sized opening on the front of your house, or a small, unlit, hole hidden behind a shrub around the back? Most would prefer the former, yet network connections resemble the hole: tiny, difficult to watch, and capable of allowing as much loss as the door. This is in part why the Internet—which provides connectivity to an increasing number of the world's computers—and this topic often go hand in hand.

For very complex requirements, the security considerations can constitute their own substantial document. Clearly, this book cannot address all the security-related issues involved—you will have to rely on internal or external people with expertise in this subject. The following sections are intended to stimulate the discussions you can expect to have.

Estimating Risk

When somebody offers you a network with absolutely zero probability of intrusion, our best advice is to find somebody else. The scientists who study computer security do not express reliance in absolute terms, but rather as a probability of failure—something consultants should know and convey. Writing requirements that say "no change of intrusion over the course of a year" are about as meaningful as buying a car with zero probability of mechanical problems after one year. The best you can do is a car that's less likely to have problems—but it still might.

Given that, one way to deal with the reality is to express security requirements in terms of the expected duration between successful attacks. For example, a system can be engineered to allow successful breaches once a day, or once a year, or once a millenium. Expressing your needs in these terms will keep your document grounded in reality.

Another means of dealing with this problem is to deal not with the chances of break-in, but the potential for damage. This allows the design engineers to perform a cost benefits trade-off. For example, your requirements might note that "As a worst-case scenario, if an attacker was able to modify our Web site to contain alternate pricing that looked valid, we could lose up to $1,000 in business." This quantifies the loss, and lets engineers know that a $10,000,000 solution is overkill, but that a $250 fix is more than reasonable. The scenario, by the way, is not at all unlikely—happening to numerous sites, including some representing government agencies.

Intentional vs. Unintentional Attacks

To many, security implies only those actions of intentional origin. In the most general sense, security also protects against unintentional attacks: flooding from a major storm, a power outage, a defective software application can all do as much harm as a hacker. As you write your requirements, don't limit your considerations to intentional acts.

Another way to express this need is in terms of availability. A class of attacks called *Denial of Service Attacks* make your system unavailable to others. If you have critical applications or the potential to lose revenue, document it in this section.

Prevention vs. Detection and Correction

In the end, your site will be vulnerable—it's only a question of degree. After you've used the basic security measures, there comes a point where preventive measures are not sufficient, or are just too costly. That's the time to consider detection and correction.

Part of security is not just keeping things from going wrong—it's about finding them when they go wrong and fixing them quickly. As you derive your requirements, list everything that could be a source of problems for you. Those that cannot be stopped beforehand can be anticipated, and a disaster recovery plan can be developed to deal with them.

Miscellaneous

As your requirements document is assembled, there are a few more things to consider that do not fit neatly into the preceding categories. They are offered in stream-of-consciousness format in the following.

Domain Name

If your marketing department is counting on using a particular domain name for its e-mail or WWW site, now is the time to mention it. In fact, this should be reserved ASAP, since domain names are currently being reserved in droves. There is the potential that new top-level domains (TLDs) will be introduced that will ease the naming crunch somewhat.

Accounting and/or Billing

For some organizations, keeping track of internal resource usage is important. It can be used to charge back budgets, or track growth. If this is necessary for your company, it should be included in this document. Some usage tracking is beneficial if only to show the project's results. Reporting can be done based on department, application, time of day, or even per user. All of these have implications on the design, so now is the time to discuss them.

Cost

Any budgetary constraints expressed in advance can save time later. If there is a hard limit, or perhaps some guidelines in place, these need to be communicated with the team from the start. Consider how much time one could save in the high-end luxury car lots by knowing the car had to cost under $20,000. (Make that the *new* car lots.)

Evolution

If there are any future plans for your Internet connection known in advance, share them. The design step is not an exact methodology, but rather a creative examination of options that can be steered more quickly to a better solution by all available information. Anything that can be anticipated and shared—major changes in the corporation, strategies, IS department, personnel—could all impact the best choice down the road.

TRINET SERVICES, INC.

Some of the nation's largest companies have turned for help in developing and deploying their Internet strategies to TriNet Services, Inc. of Raleigh, NC (see Figure 5.1). Among them are First Union, NorTel (formerly Northern Telecom), Nationwide Insurance, Pfizer, Bayer, The American Banker, and Centura Bank.

Frank Taylor, the company's founder and president, believes one of the reasons for his company's success is its business approach to the Internet and the World Wide Web. "Companies should do their home work and not rush into this just because one of their competitors has," he said. "They should treat their Internet decision just like they would any Internet decision."

TriNet helped First Union, based in Charlotte, NC, and Centura Bank, based in Rocky Mount, NC, develop their electronic banking efforts. The firm also assisted telecommunications giant NorTel in deploying an aggressive Internet plan for both internal and external applications.

"The first reason to design an Internet strategy is if it will generate a return on investment," Mr. Taylor said. Other reasons could be to cut costs or to improve internal communications through an intranet.

As for how the Internet project should be deployed, Taylor said forming and empowering a Project Team is essential for it to be a success. He

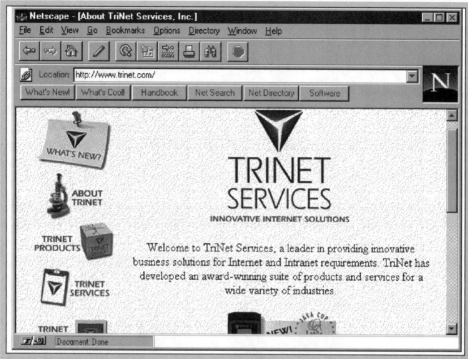

FIGURE 5.1   TriNet Services, Inc. home page.

also cautioned that any Internet and Web project must be dynamic, given the tremendous changes taking place with the technology.

Here is the Q&A with Mr. Taylor:

Question: What factors and/or research should lead to a company's decision to develop an Internet strategy?

Answer: Take a business approach. If you have something that is going to generate an ROI, then that is the first reason to generate a strategy. One factor is whether the company intends to use the Internet utilizing internal or external resources. Some companies have enough resources to do this internally, but they still should consider working with an outside company that has direct expertise with what they are trying to do. They can save considerable time and money by doing this.

As an alternative, they should look at what companies similar to them have done, or perhaps seek out noncompetitors and ask for their input.

(continued)

They also should use the Internet itself to communicate with others in industry, or to gather information from the Web about what it is they want to do.

They also may not be doing things for their customers; it may be an Intranet for internal use. They simply must pay attention to the audience: who their users are, and if there are any customers for what they are attempting to do over the Internet as a business strategy.

They also may use these technologies to solve some sort of internal business process to supplant or replace, for example, a proprietary network for EDI with a value-added Internet strategy.

Question: Often in this startup process, there are many difficulties to be overcome, technical and otherwise. What are some of the most common? Did companies anticipate them? What were they able to do to overcome these obstacles? What lessons should companies learn from those?

Answer: The most common difficulty is lack of familiarity with the technologies. Unless they have resources internally, they have to go outside for expertise, and those resources are in high demand and short supply. The hardest problem most companies have is finding a good resource that has a track record, because this industry is so new. There are few companies that do have a track record.

One of the worst problems companies have is that, because this is a new technology, people underestimate and miscalculate costs and capabilities. There are going to be things that don't work the way they are intended. For example the Internet itself is not 100-percent reliable, so people don't anticipate variables that they can't control about the medium. They get into it and go, "What? I can't count on 100 percent up time like I can with my phone?" Or, "I can't have these big, beautiful graphics on my page?"

A big problem with Web sites is that companies want full control of what people can and can't do. Lo and behold, they can't due to technology or bandwidth constraints or the technical capabilities of their customers. A lot of people have trouble adjusting to that.

For example, companies want to put their traditional marketing staff for materials on the Web. In fact, they may not work or be appropriate. Marketing people are used to dealing with traditional media and often have a difficult time adjusting to the limitations and advantages of the Web. It's totally alien to them. How can they overcome this? I can't stress enough that they listen to the experience of others, whether by hiring consultants or listening to others who have done this before.

Companies also should develop a team of individuals that is flexible, willing to listen to the advice of experts, are enthused by the technology, and most ideally already understand the Internet culture.

Question: If these companies had the process to do over again, what are some things that they should/would do differently? What lessons were learned? What is some advice you would give others?

Answer: The biggest one that I have found that people should do differently is that I wouldn't involve the marketing people as the decision makers. They should be involved in the process, but not as the decision makers. If you are doing a marketing project, they should not be in charge because of the problem I mentioned earlier: overcoming traditional preconceptions. You also don't want to have the wrong people making decisions, people who aren't enthused or aren't willing to listen to the experts.

A lot of companies are not doing their homework as well. A lot are rushing into the Web or the Internet just because their competitor did. They should do this for the right reasons, by finding ways to help their business, whether directly or indirectly, by saving them money or making them money, not just because their competitor did it. They should take their time and come up with really good, legitimate business justifications for what they are doing.

Question: How important is it to have a strategic plan? Do they normally cover all of the necessary points? If you were to write a strategic plan for others, what would be the highlights?

Answer: It depends on how big the project is. You don't need a strategic plan if you are just getting an e-mail account, but it's absolutely essential for a major project. If you have a long-term strategic plan, you will have difficulty with this technology because things are changing so rapidly. You have to make sure that the plan is flexible because the industry is so dynamic. You have to be thinking that as soon as you do something it's probably already out of date. You have to be ready with a new plan for what to do next. Your strategic plan has to be changing constantly if it's to be implemented and managed correctly.

Question: What are some of the mistakes that you see other companies making as they delve into the Internet? Why are they making them?

Answer: One of the most common mistakes people are making is that they make this huge effort to get it up there on the Net and they don't pay

(continued)

any follow-up attention. They then lose the benefits. A traditional product manufacturer wouldn't stop when he brings the product to market. The company continues to do sales and marketing, refining of the product, getting it into people's hands, and trying to improve it. People put a lot of effort into their strategy and Web site, and drop the ball on the follow-through. That's just Internet business suicide. If you are going to do business on the Internet, do not just put something up. Continue to do business with it.

Question: What has the Internet meant to the business of some of your clients?

Answer: In a lot of cases for our clients the Internet has had a very major impact on the way they do business. For example, First Union is on record in its annual report as saying they are going to change the way the bank is growing. Instead of building branches all over the country, they are going to build online banking. They are not going to make major bank acquisitions; they are just going to expand their business electronically.

Many other businesses we work with have developed whole new product lines or product groups. Or they have made their businesses more efficient by developing an intranet. For the most part, our clients are using the Internet to make more money.

Question: If you were new to the Internet/Web and were looking for a book to help you plan, coordinate, and execute an Internet strategy, what are some points you would want covered?

Answer: I would look for a book that would help people make the right business decisions when it comes to the Internet. They should look for a book that tells them what they should do in developing a strategy. The company may need to develop an RFP, and the book may need to tell them how to do that. This is where they can get input from a variety of vendors to help shape their project.

If they are new to the Internet and the Web they probably are going to need multiple books. Be sure to get a book about the Internet that helps them understand what it is all about. And if they don't already have Internet access, they should get it, even if it's a dial-up account, so they can get some hands-on experience.

Question: What are some factors companies should be looking for when selecting an ISP, Web site developer, and consulting firm?

Answer: In regards to an ISP, you need to recognize that this is a very dynamic business, and you need to be prepared that the company you work with today may not be in business tomorrow. If you aren't prepared to make changes like that, then pick a company that is likely to remain in the business, such as a large ISP. Then you need to ask questions such as, How well have they implemented their own infrastructure? You should get advice from others about how good the ISP is, from support to reliability to bandwidth and costs.

In picking a consultant or a Web company, I can't stress enough how important it is to get references. This is very similar to finding a good advertising agency. There is a subjective element to it, of course, but this is a highly technical field so it is much more important than the design. You definitely need someone who is strong in the technical domain. Look at examples of their work, get recommendations, and also try to get a feel for their capabilities in regards to their business background and experience. As I said earlier, this is a business where companies are going and coming every day. You want to be sure that the company will be around to finish the job.

They also really need to have a broad range of expertise. Graphic design. Strong technical people with regards to programming, people who understand Internet technology, marketing, and Internet security. Depending upon what your Internet strategy is, you may need more or less of each of these various elements, and you need to be cognizant of the fact that you may need to hire multiple firms to meet all your needs even though that makes the project more difficult to manage.

References

To get experience with current applications, visit the home page of the company that provides your Internet service or your browser software. There will often be pointers to plug-ins or other software that you can use. You should also visit the InterNIC at http://www.internic.net/ for a list of domain names already registered in the U.S., and their policy for resolving disputes.

CHAPTER 6

Architect the System

Chapter 5 has set the stage for the actual design of your Internet and/or Web site. Armed with a description of what you want to do, you can now identify the best way to get what you want. This step is also known as a *high-level design*, because it does not delve into the details of how specific devices are configured—a job covered in two later chapters.

Motivation

The reason to take the step is simple. You can't get there (i.e., the Internet/Web project) from here (still planning) without the design step. Organization and planning are fundamental to the success of your project, and this first step towards a technical layout is the crucial map by which the road will be built.

It should be noted that this will be more than a technology document. The architecture/high-level design document is a communications tool to let people who are involved in the project know what they are working together to accomplish. This will also help keep everyone focused. Too many companies stray from the objective, thus squandering time, resources, and effort.

As anyone following the Internet and Web industry knows, it is changing daily with new products, new software, and new technological advances coming forth at such a dizzying pace that no one can keep up. This document is important to help keep your team from being distracted by any new developments—by acting as a stake in the ground so that equipment can be ordered and devices configured. Otherwise, requirements revision can become an ongoing task.

The best design document will allow for technological change and improvements, but the process should not be stopped unless your team is convinced that the latest widget can impact your project in a positive fashion. The document also is necessary, since Project Team members will come to the project with their own history and their own perspectives about the program. For example, the nontechnical people involved in the project may not appreciate the importance of the LAN and router connection, whereas the technical staff may not understand the issues that arise when performing a corporate installation that impacts on many departments.

This is the stage where you synchronize, where you provide the details. When your family goes to the shopping mall, there often is a plan, such as when to meet at the food court, what to buy at what store, and the time and place to meet before leaving. Obviously a plan is needed here. If this step is accomplished well, much confusion, delay, and cost overruns can be prevented.

Dependencies

Technical people like to draw boxes, but they will be inclined to draw boxes for the network design before they truly understand what the system's requirements are. For example, browser/server tool compatibility and whether to use such tools as HTML 3.0, VRML, frames, and so on, should be taken into account. Make sure to be well underway to finishing Chapter 5 before you commit too much design to paper.

People also should resist the urge to call vendors other than those identified as *friendly resources*. If vendors are brought in too early, this makes you very vulnerable to vendor influence. While they will tell you a straight story, it will likely be slanted in their favor—that's how they earn their living. If you do need to solicit help because your project is particularly complex or unique, just be sure to listen to several vendors. By the end of the process, you should know which if any have the products or services you need most.

People with in-house computer experience should start thinking in more detail about their pieces of the project. The important thing is, while the groups are making advanced decisions they should communicate their ideas to the design team. Regardless of the size of the company, decisions may have been made to employ a certain device that is already available, such as computer hardware or routers, in order to reduce costs. This decision certainly needs to be explained to the design team early on.

Goal

This step should produce a written document.

Within a small company, you should insist upon five to ten pages of text and diagrams, excluding covers, table of contents, and references. This document has to explain how the pieces will work and how the system will function. Within a large company, this document could easily run over 30 pages, given that the system will have to do more things for more people.

The document will serve as the conceptual framework to be followed and help guide the various individuals or department or cross-departmental teams that become involved in the project. As we have explained earlier, this Internet/Web system will be built by teams working in parallel, and the products of these teams will interact in subtle or obvious ways. Having a document to guide everyone will help smooth these interactions and make them more effective.

Even though there will be individuals or teams working on the project, it's important that tasks aren't divided in such a way that groups don't talk to each other. People have to be linked and be in constant communication. Here again the Project Leader will have to keep everyone focused and on track. Of course, the Project Leader will have to track progress to see if the time lines laid out in your PERT chart can be met, or even the best design document will suffer as the various pieces come together late or are rushed and therefore subject to error or oversight.

People

Your core design team is already in place, and they should champion this technical document. The high-level design is theirs, and they should write the plan in conjunction with any outside resources that are deemed necessary. Because networking is very expensive and complicated, they have to enlist technical resources to get the deliverable item. There is no way an administrative type can put together a technical document.

There is another phenomenon that often surfaces in such situations: Upper-level management may begin driving the design. It is, after all, fun to draw boxes and talk about technology! Those who make the final decisions should be the ones with the most directly relevant experience—and that may not be upper management. The Internet's technology is markedly different than the legacy, proprietary networks on which so many careers have already been made. Let the designers be responsible for this step.

The design team also must not dumb down this document so that it is so light in detail as to be totally understood by every nontechnical person, just as a financial report should not be dumbed down so as to be understood by the technical staff. However, the document should be readable and not laden with acronyms and clichés. It should follow journalistic principals up front, answering the basic questions of who, what, when, where, why, and how. Then specific sections can be expanded as needed.

The document also must be complete and understandable by people who might come on-board for the project at a later date. You should anticipate personnel changes, for example, through turnover of transfer or resignation. If a key person leaves, the document should be able to help his or her replacement continue with the project.

Further, the document should allow for accountability. It will provide a written record of who signed up for what, and as things don't work you can fix the process, not just assign blame to the people or the technology. The sample design plan in the Appendix may help guide you.

Location

The document should be prepared where the people are. If you pick the right people in advance, you will already have anticipated the logistics involved. Is it better to have all the people in a central location? If not, how will you communicate with people off-site? By telephone? Fax? E-mail? Federal Express? Videoconferencing?

Your communications needs will have to deal with possible transfer of large files and major changes in scope or project design. Can a scattered design team meet these challenges with the infrastructure you have put at their disposal?

There must be a rapport among the team members in order to iron out differences and to address problems that inevitably will arise. There also will be a need for near instantaneous cooperation to deal with challenges. Otherwise the project process will drag out. Therefore, be sure your team has adequate means of communication. Here again, using the Internet and the Web provides an opportunity to communicate cheaply and effectively while serving as a training ground for people who are still unfamiliar with the Net.

Resources

There must be a task leader for the document, someone who can interface with the technical staff as well as managers. He or she will coordinate the document's production.

For each task in the document you need to assign a task leader, and each of these tasks may require different skill sets. You will need someone who both understands the technology and can write well to produce the document. Is this a realistic expectation for someone within your company, or do you need outside assistance? More about that in a moment.

Technical Writer

The first need is for a technical writer to prepare the document. By assigning a writer, you free your technical staff to concentrate on their individual strengths. The technical writer obviously needs to understand the technology; don't recruit someone who is lacking in that area. However, the writer also needs to be a wordsmith, someone who understands how to make a document readable. Design documents will also require illustrations, so graphics skills are a big plus.

Technical writers can be secured through temporary agencies. Be sure to identify what skill set you want this individual to have. A benefit from bringing someone from the outside is that your company gains additional insight and experience. This could help expand your horizons.

Be sure to sign the writer to a nondisclosure agreement. This NDA also should stipulate that the intellectual property, ideas, concepts, and designs remain your company's property and can't be reproduced or generated elsewhere. You don't want to pay a temp agency full rates to develop document formats or diagrams they will cut and paste into other sellable work.

Document Production Tools

A word processor should be chosen to which all design team members have access. This assures consistent standards. A drawing tool also is very important. Several different network design tools are available over the Internet, some of which are free for evaluation. The tools also should be able to generate industry conventions for network symbols (such as the cloud as the identifier for the Internet).

RFPs/RFIs

The design team can solicit outside ideas and proposals by submitting Requests for Proposals or Requests for Information. An RFP seeks solutions to a defined task at specific costs; an RFI seeks ideas about possible solutions to perhaps a nebulous set of problems or obstacles, and may not address price. Two factors determine whether an RFP or RFI is best for your company. One is time. This can be a slow process. The other is the size of your project. For larger networks, there may be eight different ways of doing something.

Bear in mind when writing RFPs or RFIs that the Internet is all about standards and open architecture. Key differences between RFP responses are prices and terms. You should be leery about proprietary solutions. If you choose a proprietary solution, be sure to ask: OK, let's say I stop buying from you tomorrow. Where do I get Piece A, Piece B, and Piece C to keep working what I've already bought from you? Get the company's response in writing.

Other Sources

The design team also may need access to outside resources and reference materials in order to gain access to *understanding* of the technology, its theory, and standards. This could include books and periodicals. A budget should be made available for the purchase of these documents, or reimbursement to staff for materials, books, or periodicals that they need to purchase on their own.

Other resources include the InterNIC, which has a repository of Internet resources that define the Internet. Prospective vendors also are likely to have Internet project white papers available or documentation to assist in specific areas of the project.

Duration

With experienced designers familiar with existing products, and no remarkable requirements, it should take no longer than five days to do the actual research and designing of the system; then five days to write the document, make revisions, and then publish it. You should allow team members and the technical writer up to three days to spend time online, at the library, reading magazines and books and talking with vendors.

Most system architectures for basic access will be apparent to experienced designers in a few days. If your designers take longer, ask for an explanation. If you are attempting a particularly difficult integration, such as Web-based commerce with existing proprietary computer systems, or trying to build a network for hundreds or thousands of people, it will take several weeks. And, of course, if the people you have working on the task are junior level, it will take longer.

The balance of the time should be spent creating a readable document. Be sure that is *socialized;* that is, shared among team members for editing, revisions, and discussion.

Security

The information contained in your design may be proprietary, could save other companies time and effort, and may assist outside hackers in the penetration of your defenses. While you need to share the design with enough outside interests to build it, do not share without reason. Such designs are usually proprietary to the corporation, and some aspects of the design (like those that provide security) might be known by even fewer.

We will visit the topic of designing a secure system in the following section.

TECHSOLV

If your business is contemplating incorporating the Internet into your business without any preplanning, a systems integrator with extensive Net experience suggests that you think again.

When asked why companies are making mistakes about the Internet, Kevin Yost, president of TechSolv (see Figure 6.1) in Raleigh, NC, responded: "They just don't have a plan. They simply plug in the Net like it

FIGURE 6.1   TechSolv, based in Raleigh, NC, focuses on Internet and Web system integration issues and strategy.

were a phone and hope that the need is justified. They know the Internet is important; they are just not sure how it fits in with their business model. Usually these mistakes are a result of poor planning, shortsightedness, or the lack of an Internet business strategy."

Mr. Yost warned further that companies often underestimate the changes in equipment and software that will be needed to successfully use the Internet. They often also do not realize all the potential the Internet and Web offer, taking a short-term view. In many cases, the result is that companies are upgrading or revising their Internet and Web capabilities within a few months, often at considerable expense.

Mr. Yost has been deeply involved in networking issues for more than a decade and has been among the pioneers who have successfully integrated the Internet and Web into businesses. He spent five years as a Network analyst for Northern Telecom, and also was a systems engineer for Apple Computers before launching his own business. TechSolv was incorporated in 1991.

The company also lives with the networking strategy it recommends and implements for others. TechSolv relies on ISDN connectivity to link its employees, and makes extensive use of videoconferencing. "We couldn't exist without the Net," Mr. Yost said.

TechSolv focuses on *Collective Interaction*, enabling companies with employees at different locations to Network their employees with Internet, videoconferencing and other tools. Mr. Yost urges his clients to plan their strategies and then find an experienced company to help implement those strategies.

Here is the Q&A with Mr. Yost:

Question: What factors and/or research should lead to a company's decision to develop an Internet strategy?

Answer: Virtually any company can justify the need for some type of Internet resources. By evaluation of the business case and market comparison of other companies in similar roles, an organization can develop a strategy that not only fits their needs but enables them to remain competitive in a technologically evolving marketplace.

Most companies don't have a strategic Internet plan. Every company has a different (frequently heterogeneous) environment. Without a needs/resource analysis, they are simply buying blind. You shouldn't just

(continued)

throw technology at a problem. First, determine the need and then intelligently implement using technology as the vehicle.

Question: Often in this startup process, there are many difficulties to be overcome, technical and otherwise. What are some of the most common? Did companies anticipate them? What were they able to do to overcome these obstacles? What lessons should companies learn from those?

Answer: Management justification is the most common (e.g., Do we really need this? What is the return on investment?). The Internet, and Internet connectivity, is essentially an intangible; management can't lay their hands on a T1 connection to the Internet and see what they have *bought* for $20,000 a year. This makes cost justification difficult. Also, the Internet is frequently a recurring cost and not a one-time purchase, which is difficult for an organization to absorb.

Technically, the implementation and overlay with existing resources to avoid duplication of hardware or effort is the most common difficulty. Sometimes the systems in use are so archaic or proprietary that Internet connectivity is simply impossible. Resistance to change and upgrades often prevents full implementations of necessary Internet resource access.

Existing systems often require:

▶ Additional resources (hardware, software, and personnel)
▶ Upgrades to existing systems to allow GUI interfaces
▶ RAM/hard drive space
▶ Application cost

In the Mac world most everything is free. In the Windows world (pre-95), everything costs, usually around $300 to $400 per seat for Chameleon. If you are using Windows 95, TCP/IP is included, so you can simply use Netscape for all your Internet needs.

Most companies do not anticipate the usage and abilities. They want the systems that they bought ten years ago to be able to support the Internet and not have to be upgraded. Some of these systems are still host-dumb terminal rather than client-server architectures (serial-based rather than LAN-based connectivity), and usually these systems do not support the Internet very well.

They expect to install the Internet and not do training (pretty common with many software packages/companies). Most companies also assume the Internet is e-mail and Web and are not familiar with the many uses of the Net (video, voice, etc.).

The lesson: Have a plan, plus get some help from someone who knows and has been there, done that.

Question: If these companies had the process to do over again, what are some things that they should/would do differently? What lessons were learned? What is some advice you would give others?

Answer: Many attempt to hold on to legacy systems and fit those into the Internet. Some work (mail usually); some don't (old hardware/software). I have seen a company that had over 75 dumb terminals attached to a dinosaur minicomputer running a text-based system that wanted to incorporate e-mail into its company. There is just no way to do this. They need to get with the '90s (client-server) and phase out their old systems. They don't like to hear this, although they usually know it needs to be done.

Many companies underestimate the need and necessity for everyone to have connectivity and access to the Internet. It is common for our organization to hear, Well, we just need e-mail for Bob and Betty; no one else needs access— only to find out two weeks later that really everyone in the company needs access. Obviously, this changes the way the Internet is implemented and frequently requires that the strategy be revised and/or hardware and software discarded.

Again, have someone who knows look things over. It is money well spent. Assuming that your in-house IS staff can develop and implement an Internet strategy is usually limiting. A systems integrator that has seen many different ways of doing the same thing (like setting up the Network) can offer a more global view and can recommend the best products and services for your needs.

Question: How important is it to have a strategic plan? Does it normally cover all of the necessary points? If you were to write a strategic plan for others, what would be the highlights?

Answer: Very important (read mandatory). Our ogranization is very thorough and ensures that we cover all the necessary points. The important things to note would include:

(continued)

▶ Integration with existing equipment
▶ Hardware needs
▶ Software needs
▶ Firewall needs
▶ Deployment
▶ Training
▶ Maintenance and support
▶ Any upgrades

Question: What are some mistakes that you see other companies making as they delve into the Internet? Why are they making them?
Answer: They just don't have a plan. They simply plug in several employees for e-mail, and the Internet spreads into a widespread necessity.

Frequently, companies underestimate their employees' needs for Internet access. They assume that e-mail for a select group will be enough, when actually virtually everyone in the company could benefit from Internet connectivity.

Many companies don't think long-term and end up investing in hardware/software/phone lines that will handle their needs for a quarter or two, but will have to be completely redesigned (and the old equipment phased out) when more people need access.

Usually these mistakes are a result of poor planning, shortsightedness or the lack of an Internet business strategy.

Question: What has the Internet/Web meant to your business?
Answer: Since our company specializes in a niche Internet market, we wouldn't exist were it not for the requirements of companies who need Internet implementation services.

Our organization is based upon a technology that we have trademarked called *Collective Interaction,* or the ability to work together even though you are in different physical locations. Our employees have Internet connections rather than offices, and we all share data and information in real time over the Internet using screen sharing and desktop videoconferencing to collaborate with each other. We have implemented this technology for many of our customers, and it has dramatically improved the way that they do business with their clientele.

We couldn't function without the Net.

Question: If you were new to the Internet/Web and looking for a book to help you plan/coordinate/execute an Internet strategy, what are some points you would want covered?
Answer:

- ▶ Integration with existing computer environment
- ▶ Internet uses other than e-mail and the Web
- ▶ Return on investment
- ▶ How to save/make money

Question: What are some factors companies should be looking for when selecting an ISP, Web-site developer, and consulting firm?
Answer: In picking an ISP, check for its reliability, longevity, connectivity, technical and customer support, as well as its clientele.

In picking a Web service provider, check for its server type, backup procedures, scripting capabilities, security, connectivity, support, and costs.

Issues

Designing an Internetwork system is a cross-functional activity. It blends the expertise of individuals skilled with computer networking, computer systems, graphics design, data center operations, and more. Getting everyone to contribute to a cohesive design document is quite a challenge, and the output may not be perfect. Some of the issues involved in getting it close are discussed in the following sections.

General Goals of the Design Document

If you ask ten people what a design document should contain, you are likely to get 11 different answers. To ease the process, we suggest you consider writing a sample document. A sample document could be designed to help you come to agreement on what is needed. It forms a reference point, a baseline for you to use. This can be employed to determine if you need more or less, because everybody will come at this project with different expectations, demands, specifications, and requirements. Also, a sample document could help prevent management from setting expectations that are too low, which could jeopardize the whole project. If expectations are set too high, you will end up with a nice, theoretical piece of work that ends up confusing and constraining the project.

The document also needs to be examined to ensure that it doesn't prevent design team members from working independently. If the design isn't right, you will come out of this with a system that doesn't meet your requirements, and down the road it will produce the project loop from hell.

The design document should answer the following questions:

▶ What is the right design for your company?
▶ What are the tests?
▶ Does it do what you need?
▶ Does it discuss general details—connection circuit types and computer interfaces—without providing too much specifics?
▶ If it fails to meet your objectives, are those failures considered minor by the people who submitted them?
▶ If it is designed to exceed your objectives, does the additional functionality justify the added incremental costs?
▶ Does the document tell people what they need to know to complete subsequent tasks?
▶ Can you hand the document to an employee or vendor, and will it give them enough information to make the necessary decisions?
▶ Does it speak to the process?
    ▶ How does the network work?
    ▶ How do people use it to retrieve information or exchange information?
    ▶ Does it address migration possibilities for growth?
    ▶ Where do people call for help?
    ▶ Does it assist in troubleshooting?
    ▶ Is there a help desk?
    ▶ How do you respond to questions from people seeking more information?
    ▶ Who reads the mail sent to the Web master?
▶ Does it explain how the system will grow with the company's needs?
▶ Does it become a tutorial on networking? (This is a tricky one—keep the tutorials in documents for users; make this short for the experts who need it.)

How to Organize the Design Document

When you sit down to a meal, you know it is nutritionally complete when you touch the four basic food groups. You also measure completeness by the number of courses (such as salad, soup, entree, dessert, cappuccino). Even though they are different dimensions by which to measure a meal, they both are correct.

A network design document also covers several different dimensions. To ensure that you've considered everything, you can *walk* each dimension and consider whether your design needs to account for each step. Some useful dimensions are discussed in the following sections.

OSI Reference Model

The International Standards Organization, a global collaboration for many types of engineering activities, defined one way in which computer networks could be decomposed into small elements. These elements are not physically realized separately—they are usually tightly integrated into the same box. By thinking of them as separate functions, it is easier to understand the similarities and differences in computer systems.

The Open Systems Interconnect (OSI) model has seven elements. The upper elements call on the services provided by the ones directly beneath. The network designer is almost always familiar with these, so it provides a useful framework with which to communicate. The layers and brief descriptions are provided in the following. By convention, the higher layers are listed first:

1. Applications Layer—The programs (like the World Wide Web browser or an e-mail client) that use the underlying computer network.
2. Presentation Layer—The standard used to convert text, images, voice, video, or other data types into a form that can be moved among different computers on a network. It is analogous to how two people need to speak the same language to communicate.
3. Session Layer—A way by which computers can remember conversations in progress, so they can be continued later if necessary. You implement a simple session layer when taking notes during a phone call, then putting the call on hold while you talk to someone else.

4. Transport Layer—This provides the exchange of information between computers of the desired reliability. For example, regular U.S. postal mail provides a no-guarantee mode of service, while U.S. registered mail provides a guarantee that your package will arrive.

5. Network Layer—Where universal addressing and package sizes are defined. Extending the analogy with the U.S. postal service, the network layer is where global mail addresses and zip codes would be defined, as well as guidelines for maximum package sizes.

6. Data Link Layer—Between computers, the data link layer is responsible for efficiently using the communications wires that extend directly between two or more devices, and for detecting information that was sent in error.

7. Physical Layer—Responsible for the encoding of information into a form suitable for transmission over wires or fiber optics. The physical layer also impacts the speed at which computers communicate.

OSI Model for Systems Management

Reflecting the increasing importance in global communications, the International Standards Organization also defined a reference model for the management of computer networks and systems. The five elements (in no particular order) are as follows:

▶ **Configuration:** The configuration aspect determines the system layout—both hardware physical location and interconnection, as well as logical settings of software parameters. It also includes such things as serial numbers and computer firmware levels.

▶ **Performance:** This area of management addresses the questions: How reliable is the system? What are the quality metrics? (i.e., How long will it take a packet to get to its destination? How many get there?) Is the system working as designed?

▶ **Fault:** Fault management considers the steps—automatic or manual—taken when the system behaves outside of normal parameters. It is usually achieved through a combination of monitoring activities and human procedures for repair.

▶ **Accounting:** In all systems, resources should be tracked. Computers and networks have a variety of important ones, like CPU utilization, disk access time, network bandwidth consumption, and so on. As noted earlier, it may also be necessary to provide more detailed information based on applications or user levels for billing or charge-back.

► **Security:** This is the perceived mother of all battles on the Internet. Doing a full security audit of your Internet connection is very important. This book cannot begin to discuss the threats and techniques used to prevent them; we just want to stress the importance of understanding your design's implications, and putting the procedures in place to detect when violations occur.

Evolution

While this document may represent your system for a snapshot in time, your project will evolve and perhaps be integrated, retired, or expanded. A good design document talks about how the network *grows*.

The document should tell everyone how the system works when the design is functional, and explain how additional functionality might be added incrementally. That way, reviewers can spot any inconsistencies. A good design will explain what the team has in mind in terms of future growth. Most people do design networks with the future in mind. If I buy a house without a yard, I'm going to have difficulty in building a garage. The design plan needs growth options. The mark of a good design will be one that knows how to include growth areas and exclude areas that can be ignored.

Design Methodology

Network design is somewhere between art and science. Despite the fact that computers and electronics are the products of a rigorous and detailed design process, and can be measured and observed with precision, many networks are assembled with intuition and educated guesswork. That's because the old maxim of garbage-in, garbage-out ensures that bad assumptions can make the most thorough of studies meaningless. As someone guiding the process, you should at least be aware of the techniques available.

Analytical Approach

While computers are excellent at evaluating equations, they often do not lend themselves to useful mathematical descriptions. The way information flows through them does not behave like the very tractable random systems that have been modeled and studied for decades. Furthermore, the options on modern networks tends to take them further from the idealized behavior suitable for description by solvable equations.

Computer Modeling and Simulation

The most accurate way to estimate modern computer network operation is with a detailed computer simulation. There are numerous products and services that can do detailed analysis, emulating the behavior of a proposed network over weeks of operation in just hours of running.

The drawbacks of simulation are in the cost-benefit analysis. Buying modeling software and building or buying the services are expensive and time-consuming, and the results are only as good as the assumptions that drive them. These efforts are often worthwhile for very large, expensive projects, but smaller efforts usually do without.

Rule-of-Thumb Design

Real Internet connections are usually constructed using a technique related to the preceding. The basic requirements dictate the general form of the network. Basic rules from the analytic approach are borrowed to estimate bandwidth requirements and buffer sizes. Then a healthy dose of practical experience is applied to adjust the values so that they work. This is why hands-on experience with products and working networks is such a critical skill set for this task. Yes, it is possible to design a perfect working network using the preceding techniques and no experience, but the authors have yet to see it. The problem is well recognized on the Web, to the point where service providers such as Pacific Bell provide guidance with *Transport Finder* at http://public.pacbell.net/whichone.html (see Figure 6.2). This short Web form is designed to estimate what speed connection will be required.

Outsourcing

Connecting your employees to the Web requires some infrastructure on your premises, but just putting up a Web site can be done with service providers' equipment and facilities. This design stage is where the decision is made. There are many factors to consider in outsourcing the Web hosting, as discussed in the following.

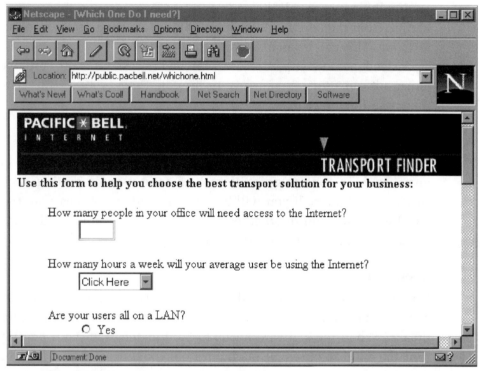

FIGURE 6.2   PacBell's Internet unit offers a Web page for estimating your Internet bandwidth needs.

Sophistication

Support for commerce, online ordering, and interactive applications that adjust for user needs or remember visitors can be complex endeavors. Interfacing with other information systems or sending faxes in response to Web queries can be especially challenging for small companies without a lot of experience. The more sophisticated the project and smaller the company, the more likely outsourcing will be the successful solution.

Switched Access

For some small offices, the bandwidth provided by dial-up service or Integrated Services Digital Network (ISDN) is suitable for their end users. Yet these services available from traditional telephone companies sometimes charge by the minute. Furthermore, sometimes there is no support for having the network call the end user—making it impossible to serve information from the end user's location without keeping up the connection all the time. This can be an expensive proposition.

Instead, some companies use switched access for their employees systems, but outsource a company to provide their Web hosting. This saves money in the long run.

Bundling

Sometimes a Web-hosting company will offer additional value-added services, such as content generation, automatic usage reporting, monitoring services, and more. If you will be obtaining other services from them, it is worthwhile to inquire whether a discount is available on the hosting. It might make that alternative the least costly.

Operations

While equipment costs are dropping, the cost—and difficulty level—of staffing an operations center are rising. What happens when your hardware breaks? When the software needs to be updated? Can your employees afford the time required to maintain your existing systems, let alone new ones? And do you have any particular factors—such as a high anticipated load or commerce support—that require special items you cannot provide in-house?

The design stage is where this option should be considered. Many companies find it ideal to allow an external firm with 7-day/24-hour operations support, especially if high availability is a requirement. Others just find it less expensive to pay a service provider several hundred dollars a month to host Web content than to assume the task internally.

References

OSI Reference Model is discussed in almost all computer network books available from most technical bookstores and some general ones as well. Use the design document in Appendix C as a starting point.

CHAPTER 7

Estimate Costs

Remember the old story about the man who promised a starving village he could make a tasty soup from a stone? Over time, he convinced people to contribute an item or two, and soon he had a quite tasty "stone" soup.

That's how Chuck Crews, president of Catalogue.com (see Figure 7.1) in Carboro, NC, describes the Web-site creation business. Mr. Crews, who is in the business of building Web sites and online catalogs, says that the Web technology is changing so quickly that his firm builds sites to individual specifications. "There is no plug-n-play on the Web," he said, granted that a company wants more than a storefront with a graphic or two and a few pages of text that never, or seldom, changes. "We have to build a lot of code."

Take an application from a company here for audio, an application from another company for virtual reality there, add some specific code writing for database management and suddenly a site is costing a company several thousand dollars.

Programming for dynamic database management, encryption, financial transactions, and other applications is where companies will spend most of their money. Once you have prepared your list of requirements, meet with Web service providers to get an estimate on what the costs will be.

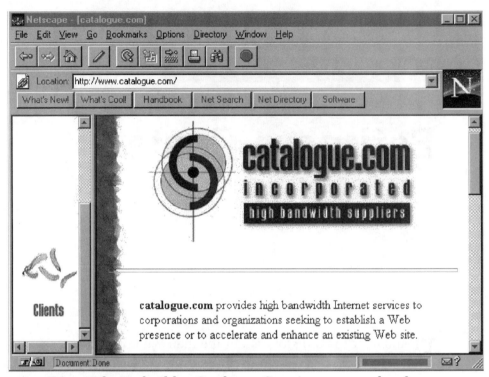

FIGURE 7.1   Web-site builder Catalogue.Com is an example of a company geared to custom designing sites based on a shopping list of requirements spelled out by its customers.

We suggest that if you want anything beyond the most basic site, you ignore one-price quotes for Web sites and content maintenance. There are many companies offering Web sites for $250, but options will be few and time spent on your site may be limited.

The same holds true in many ways to Internet access pricing. The cost of a T1 circuit at $20,000 per year doesn't begin to cover the expense of the entire connection. There are many options, much hardware, and other variables that have to be taken into account as the budget is prepared.

How to Use This Chapter

We want to point out that this chapter will not follow the specific format as followed in each of the others. Rather, this is a stand-alone document with various pieces to be pulled out for the appropriate steps of your project.

Goal

The purpose of this chapter is to help your company identify choices and opportunities, as well as to build its shopping list. The more homework you and your Project Team does before getting into actual negotiations with various vendors, the stronger hand you can play.

While we won't even chance at estimating total project costs, we believe that this information will help shape the basic queries that can refine estimates. For example, once you determine specific estimates on uses for your Internet connection (see forms to follow), you can use that information to get estimates on bandwidth needs and costs from Internet service providers.

On the other hand, we don't want to confuse the issue. You will see many options and many pieces of the Internet/Web project puzzle listed hereafter. But we hope you don't become like Curley of the Three Stooges, who once became so confused that he uttered: "I tried to think, but nuthin' happened!"

People

Your Project Team needs to address the information in this chapter point by point in order to determine specific costs and shape a budget. Consultants and vendors also should be asked to review your responses, particularly if you use this information as part of a Request for Information or Request for Proposal. They also represent the bulk of the resources needed, because there are no magical formulas to dictate your project's scope, needs, and price.

Issue One: Internet Price Overview

Price should not be the determining factor in selecting an Internet service provider unless all other factors (as cited earlier in the book) are even.

And as you can see based on Table 7.1, Internet prices vary greatly. This chart, compiled in 1996, tracks pricing information made by more

Table 7.1   **Price Survey/National ISPs**

Company	56k Install/Price	T1 Install/Price	Dial-Up Unlimited
Maloff Company survey	NA / $425	NA / $1,363	$25.80
National providers 3Q/'96	$1,534/ $660	$3,188 / $2,123	$22.22
National providers 1Q/'96	$1,828 / $656	$2,958 / $1,909	$21.83
AT&T	$3,800 / $595	$4,800 / $2,095	$19.95/$24.95*
BellSouth	$2,400 / $920+	$2,400 / $2,250+	$19.95
BBN Planet	$2,800 / $1,000	$4,000 / $2,975	NA
ComStar	NA / $275	NA / $2,995	NA
Diamond.Net	NA	$1,000 / $1,000(=)	NA
EarthLink	NA	NA	$19.95
Global Enterprises	$3,000 / $800	$2,500 / $2,000	NA
GTE	$675 / $630	$4,250 / $1,985	$19.95
Imagine	$1,000 / $380	$2,200 / $1,200	$15
InfiNet	$1,500 / $363	$1,500 / $1,500	$25
IBM	$2,000 / $1,000	$3,000 / $3,000	NA
IDT	NA	NA	$15.95
Internet OS	$3,000 / $350	$4,000 / $1,000	$29
MCI	NA / $1,500	NA / $2,300	$19.95/$24.95*
MindSpring	NS	NS	$19.95
Netcom	NA / $400	NA / $1,000	$19.95
Net99	NA	NA / $2,000	NA
Northwest	NA / $500	NA / $1,500	$25
OEM.Net	$500 / $150	$1,000 / $1,000	NA
PSI	$595 / $395	$2,000 / $2,295	NA
SprintLink	$750 / $966	$1,000 / $2,592	$19.95
UUNET	$1,000 / $750	$3,500 / $2,250	NA
Zocalo	$2,000 / $450	$6,000 / $1,750	NA
Zone	$495 / $395	$995 / $1,290	$35

CompuServe, America Online/ANS corporate prices are quoted by project only.
NA: Not applicable or available
NS: No service offered
(*): Higher price is for non-AT&T or non-MCI customers
(+): Includes local loop cost
(=): Three-year contract
For more information about The Maloff Company report, visit http://www.maloff.com.
Other prices based on survey by Internet Business Development, Inc. (http://www.ibd.com).
Other sources: The List (http://thelist.com); *BoardWatch* magazine.

than 20 of the larger United States-based ISPs, and deals with dedicated circuit port charges plus dial-up services (if offered). However, it should be noted that these are *list* prices. Various discounts are available from many ISPs (some of which are listed later in the chapter). Also, regional ISPs were not included in this survey. Other studies have found that their prices are somewhat lower than the national providers.

Issue Two: Internet Requirements

Not every company needs full T1 access to the Internet, so careful bandwidth estimation during the design phase can have a significant impact on your recurring line costs. T1 lines have dropped in price by remarkable amounts during the last several years, but the costs are still not negligible for many organizational budgets.

There are many key requirements though that should prevent you from cutting corners here. If you will serve dozens of simultaneous users, need a newsfeed, want to run real-time audio or video applications, or need to run certain special protocols that are sensitive to delay, a T1 link may be essential. Furthermore, if you plan to grow your connect speed in the next year or two, it is better to buy a router and CSU/DSU that can accommodate variable bit rates now, instead of a low-end device that has to be replaced before it is fully depreciated.

Issue Three: Internet Service Price Factors

The price study included earlier in this chapter indicates the wide disparity of prices across the United States, so it is impossible for us to specify that your Internet access will be *XXXX* dollars per year. It's simply not possible. Too many factors come into play.

For example, an ISP sales representative recently told one of the authors that a T1 could be obtained for three years for $1,000 a month even though the list price was more than twice that amount. Various other discounts were available as well, she said.

The point is this: The Internet has become a commodity and therefore is a buyer's market. Most ISPs, be they telephone company subsidiaries or independents, are so eager to make a sale that they will make a deal.

Your Project Team has defined the needs for your project, and that list includes much more than just bandwidth. Your ISPs also offer a wide variety of services that you may need.

The Internet shopping list therefore includes:

▶ Amount of bandwidth, 28.8 Kbps and up
▶ Type of service, which includes:
1. Dedicated 28.8 dial-up
2. Individual dial-up accounts
3. Dedicated 56K
4. Fractional T1 (using some of the 24 56K circuits)
5. Full T1
6. Measured-rate, or *burstable* T1 (fees based on usage)
7. Frame relay
8. ISDN (in 64K increments)
9. Megabits (ethernet)
10. (24 T1s)
11. SMDS
12. ATM
13. ASDL
14. Cable
15. Microwave
16. Wireless
▶ Primary DNS
▶ Secondary DNS
▶ E-mail boxes
▶ Newsfeed
▶ Browsers
▶ Customer support
▶ Backup links/redundancy
▶ Technical support

There are many optional items as well, such as:

▶ Remote LAN/WAN access
▶ Firewalls
▶ Security

▶ Hardware configuration
▶ Hardware installation
▶ Hardware maintenance up to corporate LAN and/or WAN
▶ Virtual private networks
▶ Network integration
▶ Intranet construction and implementation
▶ Consulting
▶ Training
▶ Seminars
▶ Service upgrade charges
▶ Web hosting
▶ Traffic reports

A number of discounts are available, so don't pay too much attention to list prices. Your company can simply ask the bidders for your project to match the lowest offer. Other negotiation points include:

▶ Installation fees
▶ One-year to multiyear contracts
▶ Combination of services
▶ Prepayment of fees
▶ Hardware
▶ Bulk individual accounts

Numerous types of organizations also can get discounts. Among them are:

▶ Nonprofits
▶ Government
▶ Educational
▶ Religious

Issue Four: Hardware Shopping List

The exact equipment needed for the Internet project will be determined by your requirements and your engineering plan. For example, if you have determined that ISDN bandwidth is sufficient to meet your demands, the connection will need a different device than those required for a leased-line or frame relay connection.

Prices indicated here also are for estimation purposes only. Few if any vendors now sell at list price, and all the equipment your company requires could be included in your Internet project's total package from some ISPs. (Many of the definitions for the acronyms cited in this section can be found in the Glossary.)

The shopping list for a leased-line connection may include:

- ▶ CSU/DSU (one for each end of the connection)
- ▶ Router
- ▶ Firewall (Options: none at all; software; or hardware and software)
- ▶ Servers for:
  1. World Wide Web
  2. News
  3. Mail
  4. FTP, other tools
- ▶ Channel Bank or *Drop-and-Insert*
- ▶ Dial-in modems

The capabilities and specifications that you need for your router will largely determine the specific choice and price. Prices start around $1,000.

CSU/DSUs are available in a range of prices and with varying capabilities. If your company starts with a connection at less than T1 speed, and thinks T1 capability might be needed at some point, the best choice is to buy CSU/DSUs capable of supporting T1s. The lower-priced CSU/DSUs may have to be replaced as your company's bandwidth needs increase. Prices are around $250 on the low end.

A Channel Bank and/or *Drop-and-Insert* most likely will be required if your company already has a T1 in place from a telephone company, and you wish to break off one or more of the 24 56K channels from the PBX in order to support data/Internet traffic. (Your telephone company or ISP representative can help you with more specific details.) Prices for channel banks range around $3,500. Drop-and-insert prices are between $1,700 and $3,000, depending upon specific needs.

Firewall systems for security have a drastic range in capabilities, configuration, and price. A security consultant or your ISP is best suited to help design your security system. Some ISPs offer *turnkey* firewall solutions up to $15,000 in price. On the other hand, packet filtering by your router or a software solution may be sufficient at no additional cost.

How many servers you require and what they will cost will be determined by your project plan. You do not necessarily need separate machines for each of the functions listed. Specific requirements for RAM, processing speed, and software for the needed applications will be determined by your Project Team.

The dial-in modems and the terminal server to which they would be linked are options if you chose to provide employees with remote access. Some routers also have terminal server capabilities. Stand-alone 28.8 modems now can be purchased for less than $200.

The shopping list for an ISDN solution includes:

▶ ISDN terminal adapter or ISDN router
▶ NT-1 (network termination device if not part of the ISDN TA)
▶ Firewall (Options: none at all; software; or hardware and software. See earlier references.)
▶ Servers for:
  1. World Wide Web
  2. News
  3. Mail
  4. FTP, other tools

Generally, ISDN terminal adapters are less expensive than the combination of a router and the CSU/DSUs. However, be sure to work with your consultant and/or ISP to map out a growth strategy best designed to fit your needs. For example, once your bandwidth needs have exceeded the 128K capability of an ISDN connection, you may have to replace the terminal adapter with a more expensive box.

Terminal adapters range widely in price from below $200 to $750 or more.

An NT-1 device recognizes your connection. It may be part of the TA. An NT-1 also can enable you to plug in regular analog phones. These can cost $200 or more.

Server needs will be determined by your specific requirements, as indicated earlier. Additional modems may be required if you permit dial-in access to your network by employees. You should be sure that your company works closely with a consultant or the ISP in order to map out the most economical and most effective ISDN strategy.

Other Options

ADSL and cable modems are rapidly coming on the scene. Both offer bandwidth capabilities, at least inbound, that exceed T1. However, ADSL and cable modems are still in the testing phase or being made available only in limited areas.

Also becoming more widely availability are wireless delivery and satellite services. Your telephone company or ISP should be able to provide information about the availability of these services, the configuration of each option and the likely costs.

The growing demand for videoconferencing, from simple desktop cameras and software to separate systems, differs vastly in capability, bandwidth requirements, and price. Again, particular vendors, telephone companies, and ISPs can help you determine if videoconferencing makes sense for your company and Internet project.

By late 1996, some videoconferencing systems utilizing the underlying TCP/IP Internet structure are to be on the market. One brand, from Compression Labs Incorporated, promises to utilize ISDN bandwidth and cost about $1,500 per desktop.

Buy? Rent? Lease?

Hardware is available for outright purchase, rental, and lease. Rather than buy equipment piecemeal, we suggest that you negotiate with your ISP, telephone company, and/or vendors for a package of hardware, software, Internet connectivity, and telephone services.

Service of the equipment should not be overlooked. Some ISPs will manage your equipment as part of a service package, or will do so for an additional charge. This certainly could benefit your IS department if it is unfamiliar with Internet and Web issues, or is pressed for resources.

Issue Five: Telephone Charges

Regardless of the medium of delivery your company chooses, there will have to be a link from your corporate Internet site to a public network and then to the Internet.

This could be through conventional phone lines, dedicated circuits, wireless, cellular, cable, microwave, or satellite. The prices for each vary widely, and with the passage of the 1996 telecommunications act some fees may no longer be tariffed, or regulated.

Planning with your vendors, telephone company, and ISPs is absolutely essential for exact prices to be determined and delivery schedules to be set. Otherwise you may be comparing apples to oranges in terms of service and price.

Landline access to the Internet using copper wires or fiber optics carries a variety of charges. The local telephone company will charge a fee for a dedicated circuit from its closest switching center to your office. This is called the *local loop*, and generally the prices are distance sensitive. Prices are based as well on the bandwidth required. T1 circuits generally cost several hundred dollars per month and do not include Internet charges.

The existence of so-called local bypass carriers enables you to order dedicated circuits from them without using the local telco. Often in those cases the monthly fees will be lower, because these carriers have their own networks and do not utilize the public, tariffed systems.

However, cost savings don't always occur. For example, Bell South's Internet subsidiary (www.bellsouth.net) will deliver Internet access to your firm in its nine-state region for one monthly fee. This covers all charges, including the Internet port charges.

ISDN service is now available in over 70 percent of the United States, and rates for service are determined for the most part by individual state utility commissions. Some companies charge a flat rate for the service. Others charge a monthly minimum plus a per-minute charge.

Frame relay, fractional-T1 (i.e., utilizing only selected channels of the circuit), ATM, and SMDS rates need to be obtained from the telephone companies. Discounts are often available, particularly if you chose to sign a long-term contract or chose to bundle a variety of services.

Issue Six: Web Services

The number of applications that could be used on your corporate Web site grows daily, and there are few if any signs that this amazing but confusing trend will slow down in the near future. Fortunately, Web sites can be designed to incorporate new features and add more services without having to be recreated from scratch. The Project Team should be very clear in defining the scope of the Web site, then meeting with a number of Web service companies in order to get specific price estimates.

Prices are impossible for the authors to estimate, because every company's goals are different and there are several factors that affect price. Those include:

▶ The services wanted
▶ How much your company can contribute to the site, from manpower to electronic content
▶ The time to design your site
▶ The time to create and program your site
▶ Extra fees for software development
▶ Fees for *off-the-shelf* application tools
▶ The size of the site
▶ The amount of traffic the site generates vs. flat rate
▶ Management of content
▶ Training
▶ Consulting
▶ Installation
▶ Server maintenance
▶ Programming
▶ On-corporate site hosting or off-site
▶ Secure server for financial transactions
▶ Your bandwidth needs
▶ Your server capacity needs
▶ Location of your server at the Web company or ISP company location

Issue Seven: Web Requirements

One of your Project Team's key tasks is to determine the specific applications your employees and/or customers will need from the site. Another is to estimate the demand that will be placed on the server. Your specifications will help determine the horsepower of your server(s), and the bandwidth required to feed queries to the site.

Issue Eight: Web Shopping List

What follows is, we admit, only a partial a list of specific features that all figure into the cost of your site:

- ▶ Cybermall, or electronic shopping mall, storefront
- ▶ Unique URL (address)
- ▶ Electronic commerce/financial transactions
- ▶ Shopping cart software
- ▶ Online catalogs
- ▶ Direct order procedures
- ▶ Dynamic databases
- ▶ Static databases
- ▶ Multimedia
- ▶ Telephony
- ▶ Audio
- ▶ Video
- ▶ FTP
- ▶ Forms
- ▶ Chat rooms
- ▶ VRML (virtual reality modeling language)
- ▶ Statistics
- ▶ Customer tracking
- ▶ E-mail response and forwarding
- ▶ Java applications
- ▶ Animation
- ▶ Security
- ▶ Shared server
- ▶ Private server

References

An essential site to visit is The List, at http://www.thelist.com/. There you will find a list of over 3,000 registered internet service providers, broken down by area and types of services. You should also plan to visit the sites of the vendors whose hardware is being considered, for updated product information and sometimes base pricing.

Once you have estimated the project's price, you must decide whether to continue unchanged, revise requirements and policy, or scrap the effort. We hope none of our readers will give up at this point. Although the costs can be surprising, there are many innovative companies on the Web right now, and having surfed quite a bit one gets the sense that in the long run, some of the business we now conduct in person will move irreversibly to that medium. Companies that tread there sooner rather than later will have the ultimate advantage.

On the other hand, nobody can spend more than their investors would reasonably allow. If you're over budget at this point, consider reworking the process with a reduced set of requirements. Consider eliminating interactive applications, newsfeeds, and other high-bandwidth applications that may be driving up costs. Also consider switched access approaches that can reduce telecommunications costs, or trying to negotiate a progressive rate for Web hosting. Designation of special corporate PCs for using a dial-up account can also provide employees access without breaking the bank.

CHAPTER 8

Design and Acquire Network

Many consumer communications technologies are somewhat *forgiving*. Plain, old telephone service is probably the best example: The wire you run for your extra in-house telephone extension needn't be the recommended size, can run past motors and sources of electrical noise, and might be wired backwards—and your phone will probably work. Some other types of consumer devices are as robust.

While the Internet has become much, much more user friendly since the earliest routers were deployed, it can still at times be a fragile entity. Minor mistakes in configuration files can disable large networks, and cost hours of frustration for already tired technicians. Your best weapon against such dangers is careful network planning. Improper network design can strand your computers from the Internet as effectively as a backhoe can cut a fiber optic cable.

Motivation

Why is there a separate track for this? Because it's a good dividing line for the infrastructure of the project. The issues around cabling, leased circuits, modems, and networks are somewhat different from those for installing software on client or server computers.

Companies that need to hire large staffs to handle all the workload often find it easier to secure people who want to do one job or another, not multiple tasks. The same challenge may be created here, since so much may have to be done. But at this point enough work to implement the design has been done to look for ways to organize it.

The team also needs to make sure that your Internet network can interface with the corporate network. For many companies, interconnection was never expected, and such issues as renumbering, protocol selection, software upgrades, and security design will arise.

Dependencies

High-level design is a prerequisite in order to make sure all the parts fit and the project works when the various pieces are assembled. You simply must have all the *parts* in place before the next phase, which is test and acceptance. Before filling out a shopping list of needed equipment and software, your Project Team should take time to review existing resources.

► Are some of the parts of this project available in-house, such as local area network and/or wide area network(s) capability or underutilized computers?
► How much of the existing network will need to be augmented or replaced?
► Is there spare bandwidth to the outside world through excess standard dial-up phone lines?
► If your firm has a dedicated high-speed T1 circuit for its voice telephone services, are there any unused 56K channels that could be utilized for Internet/data access? (Your IS department can answer that question.)
► Is Internet access already available in some fashion?

If you are constrained by having to use existing resources, or can benefit from their use, then your firm can accelerate some of the steps prescribed in the following sections.

The Project Team also needs to talk with various vendors who already work with the firm. What Internet experience do they have? Can you utilize existing hardware for this new project, or can it be traded in to vendors for credit? What discounts can the vendor make available?

Goal

The specific goal of this step is simple: Determine specifically all the parts, from hardware to browsers, that are needed to support Internet use and get them in-house with the best time/cost benefit possible.

The output that your team will generate is a detailed design document or road map. The result will be a set of properly designed devices and a network, as well as a lot of empty cardboard boxes.

People

One individual needs to be designated as the *task leader* for this step, and it may or may not be the same as the leader of the design team. Details to be worried about in this step also may not be the best use of the Project Leader's time, those activities including such things as writing purchase orders and running cable.

If your company has chosen to employ consultants, you should be able to hire installers at lower rates than high-end networking experts.

The leader of this phase of the project simply must have PC and networking expertise and is someone who knows how to push a project to completion. The leader also needs to be able to juggle multiple tasks to ensure that the network, Web, and all the other pieces come together as intended.

The company also will need an individual who knows how to select and configure routers as well as working with other Internet/Web pieces, such as mail servers and the Web server. If such an individual isn't available on staff, a consultant should be hired. Part of that consultant's task after getting the network deployed should be to train your company's staff on how to maintain or improve what has been built.

The key needs: specialized networking skills; hands-on experience with routers; hands-on experience with PCs.

Locations

Unlike in other phases, where team members could work from a central location, this step must be designed and implemented at every site where people will use the network.

This is a challenge for distributed companies.

If the corporate expertise is available at the main site, the Project Team should help develop a *dream team* to visit and inventory each site in determining each site's specific needs. Based on the dream team's information, the Project Team's document should outline plans for the installation of the network and the training of employees at the remote sites.

Resources

Vendors can get really involved with the project at this point. Numerous Internet service providers, Web production companies, telephone companies, and hardware/software companies are more than willing to offer ideas, suggestions, input, and to act as sounding boards. Of course, you must be aware that they are unlikely to have an unbiased view, particularly when talking about a competitor.

Short of preparing a formal Request for Information or Request for Proposal, you could meet with selected vendors and explain you ideas or possible plans. Ask them to shoot holes in it, make recommendations, or offer alternative views. If you take their views with a grain of salt, the process can be very helpful.

If you are buying equipment and software, the vendors most likely will provide people to be sure that the equipment meets your needs. They will configure and install equipment as necessary in many cases.

You also should seek technical and maintenance support of some kind and have it included in the contract. Be sure to ask for plans and ideas that do not lock you into a technological dead end or a plan that will require costly upgrades soon after the system is deployed. For example, a company exploring connectivity to the Internet wanted to pursue an ISDN option until it was explained to the managers that equipment would have to be swapped out quickly if bandwidth needs grew as expected. The company then opted for a frame relay network that could utilize routers and other equipment even as bandwidth was increased. ISDN equipment did not allow this option. It would have had to be replaced once basic ISDN bandwidth had been consumed.

We heartily suggest that you seek out experienced people from your vendors or from consulting firms to help you. Find people who have done similar installations at other sites, especially if you determine that your existing staff lacks the necessary experience. If you already have access to the Internet, you can find people through newsgroups. Your vendors also may have ideas or recommendations.

We reiterate the importance of developing more knowledge internally by getting you and members of your staff online so that you can get first-hand experience.

Depending upon the scale of your project, you also may need to consider outsourcing some duties. Vendors or consultants can point you to companies that can deliver technical support 7 days a week, 24 hours a day, as well as order taking and fulfillment and billing.

Duration

This is the longest pole in the project tent, taking anywhere from 45 to 60 days after the receipt of the order and the kind of connection that is required before installation occurs. Local telephone companies have their own install lead times, as do Internet service providers. The latter can take up to 45 days to deliver a T1 leased-line installation.

You can pay a premium in terms of human and physical resources if you choose to expedite an order. There will most likely be additional costs. There may also be cases in which insufficient facilities exist to install additional circuits. In such cases, reclaiming unused circuits or installing new wiring can be done, but it will take even longer than anticipated. Of course, you are reading this chapter in advance (as recommended), so you knew to begin this step as soon as possible after the design is finished.

Circuit ordering is a time-consuming process, and you should be careful. Data circuits are different than voice circuits. Here is where advice from vendors, the selected Internet service provider, and your own information systems staff is crucial.

Another possible delay could occur in the ordering of routers and other hardware due to the current high demand. Especially difficult to get are more complex, high-end routers.

Negotiations with Internet service providers, Web service providers, and other vendors also can be time-consuming. Additionally, your legal staff will want to review contracts before they are signed.

Security

We further suggest that you take steps to protect your intellectual property. Vendors should be required to sign nondisclosure agreements concerning the scope of your project, the network design, its configuration, and security details. (We also recommend that you use your own passwords and not inform the vendors, or change them once the installation is in place.) This step may add to the length of the contract process, because attorneys for the various parties involved may want to review the nondisclosure agreement's terms. Be sure to request and review the customer information policies of your providers. Most will not divulge any information to other companies about your plans, but if this is sensitive you should have it in writing.

Issues

Selecting vendors is a crucial step. You have to find companies that can deliver products and services on time, on budget, and then provide reliable service and ongoing technical support. Note that we do not go into detailed technical design issues here—a book of this length cannot give all the experience you need. Having hired the right talents full time or through consultants is critical to a good network design. Here are some other points to consider:

Beware the Prefab or Turnkey Install

There is no excuse for not doing your homework and turning over the project to someone else. This leaves you dangerously reliant on outside sources that are beyond your control. Your staff needs to be actively involved, at least in an oversight capacity.

MACRO*WORLD RESEARCH

Macro*World Research Corporation (see Figure 8.1) is in the business of tracking Wall Street, and since its founding in 1983 has developed a strong following. Publications and firms from *The Wall Street Journal* to *Computerized Investing* have praised the company for its accurate forecasts of the economy, stocks, and interest rates.

Now, Macro*World utilizes the Internet and its Web site to distribute its proprietary information to individuals and institutions. And according to its CEO, Doug Graham, the Internet has been a worthwhile investment.

"The Internet has had a dramatic, positive change in how we conduct our business," Mr. Graham said from his office in Winston-Salem, NC. "The strength of our company has always been its ability to design and develop innovative, personalized decision tools, financial analyses, and

(continued)

FIGURE 8.1   Macro*World utilizes its Web site to communicate financial information to its customers, private and corporate.

reports for investment-oriented individuals and institutions. The Internet has enabled us to unleash the power of our system and its derivative applications to a world of different users with different needs."

Mr. Graham stressed that the company faced many hurdles in moving from private data access and fax delivery to the Web and Internet. He suggests companies create a well-researched strategic plan, stick to objectives in order to avoid *mission creep*, and anticipate what impact the Internet and Web will have on all aspects of your company, not just the information services department.

The first discussion of an Internet strategy was triggered by the company's strategic audit in 1993. "In hindsight the essential and pervasive part the Internet would play in the company's strategy appears obvious because of how fast and far the Internet has developed," said Mr. Graham, a former Vice President of Research and Development at RJ Reynolds Industries. "In early 1993, however, it was not so obvious and some board members wondered if the refocusing of development efforts was appropriate at that juncture." But given Mr. Graham's background, he said the company's "long-range and strategic planning was perhaps more sharply honed than in most small technology development companies."

MWRC has specialized in developing and applying advanced financial analysis based on its proprietary forecasting engine, which has been in development and/or evolution since 1983. (In 1992, *The Wall Street Journal* reported that stock picks of Macro*World generated a 47.6-percent growth rate, and *Computerized Investing* said Macro*World has "a powerful system for investment analysis and economic forecasting.") Early customers used the system on their own PCs along with a small, integrated database of economic and financial data that enabled them to forecast economic and market indices, and construct optimal portfolios and perform asset allocation based on these forecasts. The firm's main database and analyses grew until by 1992 it was so large and sophisticated that the emphasis had shifted to providing institutional clients with customized reports, and individuals with personalized services. By 1993, the move to the Internet began.

What follows is the Q&A with Mr. Graham:

Question: What factors and/or research should lead to a company's decision to develop Internet and/or online strategy? What factors influenced your decisions?

Answer: The Internet decision should flow directly out of the company's strategic planning process, especially at the outset when performing a strategic audit.

A strategic audit of the firm's environment, its strengths and weaknesses, the threats and opportunities, should identify the observable impact the Internet is already having on each aspect of the firm's business. In addition, it should assess the potential uses of the Internet both by the company itself and by its competitors. This assessment should also consider the relevant resources that the firm and its competitors have in developing the Internet.

A company should not be misled into thinking of Internet development as a programming or systems issue. It is marketing skills and creativity that are most important. The technical skills will need to be acquired by all companies, since most of the languages (HTML, Java, etc.) are relatively new and a firm with a large programming staff is not necessarily better off (most of the programmers are probably fully employed, maintaining old legacy systems).

Any firm, no matter what product or service, from primary producer to retailer, should seriously examine the threats and the opportunities that the Internet affords. If a firm thinks there are none, then it better reexamine its strategic assumptions.

Question: Often in the startup process there are many difficulties to be overcome, technical and otherwise. What are some of the most common? Were you able to anticipate them? What were you able to do to overcome these obstacles? What lessons did you learn?

Answer: The surprises and delays we encountered in implementing our Internet strategy were, for the most part, not foreseeable. Most problems had to do with the complexity of our system; that is, the various flows of data, the editing and analyses performed, and the routing of different types of information to customers via different media and different times of day. In addition, feeding our Internet site and those of our clients with information all through the day and night, e-mail portfolio reviews to customers, feeding client's in-house intranet systems over dedicated T1s and frame relays, fax personalized financial reports, and modem data packets to online services and newspapers.

We did underestimate how long development would take, however. This is due in large part to the growth of the Internet. This growth meant

(continued)

that we could serve many more segments of users, which entailed adding functionality. The increased interactivity between users and our system, which is offered by the Internet, enabled us to add many features that we had contemplated but were never feasible.

The most useful input early in the project would have been a checklist of all the underlying hardware and software questions that would need to be answered, and some guidance in finding the answers or where to go for the answers. We stumbled over most of these one at a time, and it would have been far better had we known of these issues ahead of time.

The biggest unknown, especially for a highly interactive site that is moving a lot of information, centers around scalability; that is, what kind of hardware and server software is needed to handle an unknown but probably large level of customer usage. This was encountered even in selecting the T1 telecommunications lines. Expert opinions on our need varied from a single ISDN line to two T1 lines.

The initial Web server box chosen was a Pentium Pro 150, which has several satellite 586s that handle different database tasks, information flow from the rest of the M*W system, and various analytical operations, either automatically or upon a request from the Web server.

Companies exploring new Internet strategies today are in a better position to find help from consultants and others who have relevant experience than they were a few short years ago when every one was still learning.

Question: If you had the process to do over again, what are some things that you should/would do differently? What lessons were learned? What is some advice you would give others?

Answer: We were fortunate that our principal Internet efforts were driven by very specific, well-defined needs of some of our institutional clients. The Internet and intranet applications for our services involved primarily *add-ons,* or extensions, of our main system.

The only controllable factor in the process at that time was the development time, which tended to expand due to mission creep. The enthusiasm on our part and on the part of our clients resulted in numerous improvements, new embellishments, and enhancements that seemed insignificant at the time but on a cumulative basis added considerably to the overall development time.

There were no modifications that were not ultimately worthwhile, but in terms of deviations from original plans that could have been avoided, a rigid adherence to initial project specifications would have collapsed the time to initial site launch.

Question: How important is it to have a strategic plan? If you were to write a strategic plan, what would be some of the highlights?

Answer: The strategic plan is very important, because it ensures that at the senior management level there is understanding and agreement on the importance of the Internet and an overall view of how it will be dealt with. It is important that the plan not treat the Internet as simply a problem for the chief information officer; every functional area and every line of business needs to identify the threats and opportunities that the Internet affords.

The tenor of the firm's response should reflect its general stance in the industry; if it is a leader/innovator in the industry then it must obtain the core competencies it needs to ensure that it will be the industry leader in the use of the Internet. If the firm is a follower then it must determine what will be needed to at least stay in the game, or better yet, if the Internet can be used creatively to improve its competitive position.

The company must seriously consider the potential for the Internet:

▶ Alter how customers are reached and served
▶ Affect how operations are conducted
▶ Make reductions in the cost of doing business
▶ Improve employee productivity
▶ Hasten the pace of overall innovation

Key questions to be asked include:

▶ How can the Internet shift the competitive structure within the industry?
▶ What is the likely response of each of the firm's major competitors?
▶ Does the Internet provide an opportunity for the firm to make inroads into new market segments or another industry?
▶ Might the Internet provide an opening for new competitors to enter the firm's markets, either firms within the industry, new startup companies, or firms in another industry? (continued)

Each business unit should address these questions as well as each functional area: marketing, production, systems, personnel, purchasing, and so on.

Question: What are some mistakes that you see other companies making? Why are they making these mistakes?

Answer: Many companies do not view the Internet as a strategic issue, but leave it to individual functional areas to deal with as they wish. As each function and department struggles to find the Internet's role in its area, the company is suboptimizing its Internet efforts and will have wasted considerable time and money when it later realizes that a coordinated approach would have been more effective.

Some companies feel that by just dabbling in the Internet, they are avoiding making any large, costly mistakes. They think they can learn from the successes and failures of the industry's pioneers and then play catch-up later when the competitive paradigm for their industry on the Internet becomes better defined. When these halfhearted efforts yield meager results, the companies feel vindicated that the *market isn't there yet.*

Unfortunately, using the Internet effectively requires learning and experimenting, and the knowledge that a company gains will be cumulative and embodied within the corporation. That company's experience will not be revealed in trade articles or journals, and its competitors who are waiting on the sidelines will not learn anything. Because the interaction on the Internet is different from other media, a particular application or service on the Internet may *fail* not because the marketing concept is invalid, but because the execution of the concept has not yet been sufficiently refined.

Question: What has the Internet/Web meant to your business?

Answer: The Internet has had a dramatic, positive change in how we conduct our business. In order to fully utilize and leverage the proprietary M*W system and database, by 1992 the company was faced with the need to make major changes to the client software and to establish a direct dial-up access for individual customers and institutions.

It was not apparent in 1993 that the Internet would grow as fast as it did and become so quickly pervasive. However, the many advantages it potentially afforded the company made an Internet-based strategy imperative.

Offering our services via the Internet would mean huge benefits to our customers in accessing our worldwide financial and economic database, in conducting analyses, and in getting customized information at any time they wished. This also meshed well with our personalized e-mail and fax information services by providing them direct access and the ability to determine how and when they wished to receive information.

A better distribution process for our services was but one of the strategic impacts. Customer service changed, cost structures changed, operations were changed, personnel requirements and productivity were changed. Even the company's customer mix was changed. Large institutional clients could now be served efficiently in addition to individual investors. And a whole private label service for financial institutions was established.

The decision to scrap the previous upgrade plans and unify all of the services into one sophisticated Web site has, in fact, resulted in greater efficiencies and a flexibility not originally contemplated.

The strength of our company has always been its ability to design and develop innovative, personalized decision tools, financial analyses, and reports for investment-oriented individuals and institutions. The Internet has enabled us to unleash the power of our system and its derivative applications to a world of different users with different needs.

Question: If you were new to the Internet and were looking for a book, what would you want covered?

Answer: I would want a complete top-down approach to developing and implementing an Internet strategy.

First, guidance on what types of strategic issues should I be looking for with regard to the Internet, something that would broaden my concept, and those of my key executives and managers, of the different potentials of the Internet.

Second, how to go about identifying an overall development approach and the various resources my firm needs to consider in order to assist my various departments and business units in developing their applications for the Internet.

Third, guidance on technical hardware, software, and development staff issues that need to be addressed in developing and implementing.

(continued)

Question: What are some factors companies should be looking for when selecting ISP, site developer, and/or consulting firm?

Answer: The selection of our Internet service provider was complicated but relative to everything else it was fairly straightforward. Some of our major institutional clients arrange their own lines and support. Our job related to the main Internet site; finding out which ISPs in the area and nationally had the best reputations narrowed the field of candidates quickly. Because our services are multimedia we have split our initial T1 line between data lines and a few LD lines for our fax service; this makes it necessary that the ISP and long-distance provider have a good working relationship.

Most companies face a major decision related to the choice of doing their Internet-related software development in-house or farming it out. If the site is not highly interactive other than taking orders and providing customer service information, then it can make sense to use outside services. In our case, the information, analyses, and interactivity are far too complex to make outsourcing, except for graphic design, a feasible alternative.

Many vendors also promise turnkey solutions but fail to deliver. Be sure to screen the various companies. Ask for references, and be sure to check them. Be sure the vendors meet your specific needs rather than trying to substitute their own preferences.

There are many questions to be asked of the vendors as well:

▶ How will the connection and equipment be serviced and maintained? (More and more companies offer remote management and maintenance, some at no additional cost.)

▶ What kind of technical support will they offer? (Do they have people available around the clock through an 800 number or via e-mail? If your Internet connection is critical, you can't wait hours, or sometimes even minutes, to get assistance when you encounter a problem.)

▶ Can they help you train and set up your own technical support team that meets your goals and fits within your budget constraints? (As the Internet market becomes more competitive, training is offered as an incentive in many cases.)

► Do they offer training classes? (These may have to take place away from your corporate site, but again availability and price are negotiable.)

Your company should strive to become self-sufficient as quickly as possible, though. Reliance on others can be costly and takes the project out of your control.

Selecting Hardware

Various types of routers and other equipment are available from several different companies. The kind of equipment you need will be determined by the type of connection that you select. Some vendors may want to sell options and capabilities that you don't need, so be wary.

Your Project Team should be sure to check on reliability, availability, reputation, warranty and compatibility, as well as price. They should seek out people at other companies, who have dealt with similar projects, and seek their advice.

In keeping with the vendor-neutral goal of this book, we won't recommend specific manufacturers. But consultants, other Internet users, and Internet service providers can readily provide names, product suggestions, phone numbers, and points of contact.

Configuration Document

Be sure the detailed design phase produces a configuration document that details how to build your system. It should be as step-by-step as possible, allowing anyone skilled in this work to re-create your network from scratch. This guide can act as an insurance policy in the event key people leave your staff, or if you have to upgrade the project.

Question to Ask Prospective Internet Service Provider

Price should never be the primary concern. In most cases with ISPs, you get what you pay for. Quality and reliability cost money. Other points that you should stress include:

► ISP's compatibility with your project. Does it have the expertise to meet your bandwidth and other needs? (If you select ISDN, can the ISP handle

it, or is it part of a laundry list of product offerings with few, if any, installations having taken place?)

▶ Product packages. (What do you get for the price? Is there an installation
fee? Can that be waived? Does the contract include the cost of all telecommunications links? What, if any, hardware and software is included?)

▶ Support. (Where does the ISP's responsibility end and yours begin? A
growing trend is that the ISPs will support the connection and provide all
the equipment for the connection up to your company's network.)

▶ Functionality. (In its most basic form, just how reliable is their service?
Can they do everything they claim that they can?)

▶ Expandability. (What are the companies' growth plans? Can they add
bandwidth quickly? Are they exploring new technologies and tools?)

▶ Performance. (What is their *up time*? What is their bandwidth utilization?
What do they consider their peak loads? On the latter point, if your ISP's
backbone is averaging 50 percent or more in capacity utilization, beware
of traffic jams and slowdowns.)

▶ Support. (When, where, and how are people made available? If there is a
network problem, are senior Network Center Operations personnel on
call? Do they have *hot* spares in the event of equipment failure?)

▶ Warranties. (Some companies now guarantee bandwidth throughput and
network operability. Whatever they promise, get it in writing.)

▶ Reputation. (How is the company viewed within your community? Who
are the owners? How long have they been in business?)

▶ Bandwidth. (How is their network built? Is it redundant? Is excess bandwidth available? What are the growth plans?)

▶ Availability. (Can you get the services needed within the time frame allowed, or is the offering only *vaporware*? Be wary of companies that offer
services that will be available "the next quarter," as those deadlines are
likely to slide.)

▶ References. (This is crucial. Whatever strengths or weaknesses these companies have will be readily identified by customers.)

▶ Customers. (With whom else are these companies doing business?)

▶ Longevity. (What's their track record? Too many companies are here today,
gone tomorrow.)

▶ Usage reports. (Does the ISP offer monthly usage reports? Updates on network outages or problems?)

Note that no ISP can guarantee zero downtime or complete Internet reachability. The fact is, most of the infrastructure is not under their control! While a larger ISP can promise reachability to more sites, it doesn't matter if the particular site you need to reach on a Friday night is down. Having realistic expectations is very important in this business, and the service quality is very different than most people realize.

IP Address/Domain Name Registration

Except for the largest entities, IP addresses are provided by service providers due to issues of scaling the Internet. Be aware that if you change providers, your IP addresses will change. This can be a costly process, depending upon the number of machines you have attached to your network. If you contemplate changing ISPs, be sure to ask for what kind of support they will provide through any transition.

The ISP can attempt to register the name you want for your Web site and Internet address (such as widgets.com). However, you will be asked to make multiple selections in the event a name already has been taken. You also are responsible for making sure your name has been service-marked or trade-marked. You may also register the name yourself, ensuring that you are listed as the contact and possibly saving charges that some ISPs add.

References

For information on the Internet about Internet service providers, visit The List (www.thelist.com). Also, C-Net (www.cnet.com) publishes ratings on Internet service providers.

Magazines that cover Internet access issues include:

► *NetGuide*
► *Internet World*
► *RedHerring*
► *InformationWeek*
► *Inter@ctive Week*
► *Wired*

CHAPTER 9

Network Connection Testing and Acceptance

The telephone company installer was perplexed. He had followed all his directions regarding the installation of the customer's ISDN (integrated services digital network) telephone line, but something still was wrong. "I'm stumped," he told his customer, who was growing more impatient by the minute with the delays. "Everything is installed correctly, but I can't get any dial tone."

Unfortunately, the installer was unaware that there is no dial tone with a digital ISDN circuit. This anecdote goes back a while, but so does confidence in the companies that provide communications circuits. If a phone company employee were not adequately prepared for his or her job, imagine the risk of a company who depends on others to do its checking. The bottom line is that without a test and acceptance phase, you can expect trouble and delays.

When contracting with any outside vendor for any part of this project, make acceptance and test a prerequisite for payment when possible. The more complex and expensive the custom development, the more important this contingency is.

Your plan could call for separate contracts with each of the following:

▶ An Internet service provider
▶ A telephone company (long distance, local or both)

▶ A local circuit bypass carrier
▶ A Web site creator
▶ Hardware vendors
▶ Consultants

With that many spoons stirring the pot, you need to make sure that everyone is following the same recipe, and each has representatives available for help or guidance or problem resolution as the various pieces are assembled for testing. Murphy's Law applies just as well to the Internet and the Web as it does to any other business project, so test, test, test. Or as Ronald Reagan once said of arms talks with the Soviet Union: "Trust but verify."

Motivation

We make this an explicit step because too many companies learn the hard way that resources, money, and time have to be allotted for testing and installation. Some people assume everything magically arrives and works; experiences show lots of things can go wrong, often in subtle ways. One company had a slight misconfiguration of the routers that connected its LAN to the Internet, which allowed many—but not all—WWW sites to appear unreachable. For weeks, they assumed those locations were having trouble, until they realized the sites were the same places all the time. A little more checking and it was working—fully a month after the *installation* was complete. Test plans are valuable and often save time down the road.

Testing is also a time for doing contingency engineering. Sure, you may have planned everything in the previous step, down to the periods in the router configurations. When equipment arrives, you may receive a later software version, or a newer connector on a recently redesigned device. Often, the upgrades work to your long-term benefit—extending the time you need until the next upgrade. In the short term, you will need to cope with the unexpected, and the test phase gives you that opportunity.

It can also provide a little slack time: If there are delays in the ordering of equipment or acquisition of circuits, or there is difficulty getting the connection to the local phone company, some built-in excess time can be taken from this phase.

You also need to identify human resources needed and the amount of time that will be required, along with planning the soup-to-nuts installation and the final testing that defines the threshold for acceptance. Your Project Team needs to determine who decides when the Internet connection is working, how, and if it is acceptable. If you overlook any of these points, the mistake could end up costing you thousands of dollars and other consequences, such as project confusion, unmet expectations, and slipping deadlines.

Dependencies

Who tests what and who is responsible for which piece of the project will be determined by your Project Team's requirements and plan. Depending on how you will use your connection to the Internet, most or all of the following components will need to be available before you can complete this phase:

► Telephone circuit
► Internet connection
► Internet-related hardware
► Contracted-for throughput
► Hardware and software configuration
► Interoperability of connection with LAN or WAN
► Functioning of e-mail gateway
► DNS and secondary DNS
► IP number(s)
► Access to Internet newsgroups or other contracted-for services
► Rough measurement of throughput (with large file transfers)
► Access to sites of particular importance

The project, as you can see, resembles a puzzle. And even though your Project Team's plan anticipates that all pieces will fit nicely, some are being manufactured, or prefabricated if you will, elsewhere. That could lead to problems from a variety of resources.

You must complete the detailed network design phase and have ordered the equipment to start testing. It is possible, however, to begin testing the

clients and servers before this phase is complete. You can do limited testing of clients and servers with just a *stub* network connection between
them, which may allow you efficient use of your time while waiting for
long-lead network elements. Just do not consider the client and server testing complete until it's been done using your live connection. There are
some subtle problems that won't show up when you test them locally.

If you want to find more information on the Internet about installation
service details and what companies might provide, check out Yahoo's Web
site (http://www.yahoo.com). A search under the Internet section of Yahoo,
which contained the following words (Internet, installation, services),
yielded a wide variety of responses and pointed the authors toward a number of companies (see Figure 9.1).

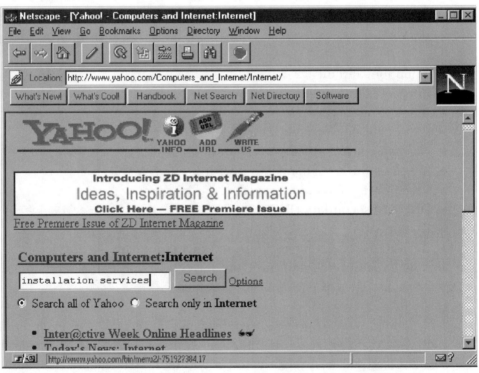

Figure 9.1   A search at Yahoo produced multiple leads for Installation services.

Goal

There should be two written outcomes from this step: The first is detailed engineering plans for the network and clients. The question comes up, Why weren't these detailed plans done before the machines were ordered? That is not practical because the manuals for the detailed configurations and software configurations won't be available until they are in-house. Even people who have some in-house find that the latest version or release has changed.

The other products that come out of this step are the test plan and results. The formal test plan describes the full range of functional and performance stresses that need to be done before the system is accepted. The test plan output represents a baseline for performance. As time progresses, if your service provider is later unable to provide the same throughput, you can reference your earlier tests.

In high-technology companies, test plans can be very elaborate, and test results can consume volumes of lab notebooks. If your needs are more modest, your test results may be a short list of checkmarks and some numbers on throughput and delay. It may seem pretty minor, but if you suspect problems down the road, having a baseline performance measurement will be invaluable.

People

The important thing to stress at this stage is continuity. When this step is completed the network is operational, and your client and server testing will depend on its continued availability. You'll need to begin some level of monitoring, and if it stops working you'll need some resources to fix it.

The best way to help support and maintain your connection and service is to involve the people who will be running the network and/or the PC network in this test. So when you are picking people to participate, ask who is going to fix the system when it breaks, as it inevitably will, and draft them for the testing phase. Also include the people who helped design it. They will probably need to explain why things were done, and contribute to the test plans based on their designs.

The total number of people who will be involved depends upon the size of the network and the number of clients. Large companies (100 + PCs) may need to add support people just to work on Internet applications. Smaller companies should consider how busy their current support staff already is, and determine if hours are available or if outsourcing will be necessary.

The use of external support, such as vendors, that will not be around to support the products should be considered carefully. Unless they are going to provide rigorous and thorough documentation about what they do, losing their intellectual capital about how problems were solved will cost you considerable time and money later. The exception is if you contract with a vendor for continuing maintenance and support.

The architect doesn't have to work in the building when it is done, but you certainly need to have someone who knows where all the wires are.

Location

You go where the work is, so count on covering every site that ultimately will be connected in the original design. Most companies will order sites in terms of requirements priority. They will put headquarters or sites with immediate needs at the front of the list. In an ideal world you definitely want to work from the Internet connection out, the core of the network first then add satellite sites.

The same testing procedure should be followed at each location to make sure every connection is in order and all sites linked on that particular LAN are reachable as designed. As sites are added later, be sure that the proper safeguards are in place to prevent your entire network from coming down.

Resources

Depending upon the Internet service provider you have chosen, a wide variety of services may be available at little or no additional costs. Some ISPs even now offer all the equipment needed, plus installation and maintenance of your Internet connection up to your local area network. If so, they can be of assistance in making sure your network is properly linked to the outside world.

A liaison definitely needs to be established between your service provider and your staff, however, so that they can mutually resolve any problems. The service provider may simply notify your company that there is a problem on your side of the *demarc,* or demarcation point, where its responsibility ends and yours begins. The demarc can be where the telecommunications circuit is installed in your facility, or it can be at the LAN connection of a router.

The ISP also should assist you in ordering the telephone circuits needed from your local phone company. A technician from that company will install the circuit and then turn it over to you and the service provider. You should be sure to get a point of contact with the phone company for any future problems.

If you choose to order equipment directly (and some ISPs won't allow you to do that) from the vendor, be sure that online or some type of telephone technical support is available. Invariably questions will come up.

Since many machines are available to act as Web servers, and the variety of server software sets is growing, be sure your own staff is asking questions of the ISP and Internet hardware vendors about compatibility and reliability.

There have been efforts started to define baseline performance guarantees or metrics by which your service provider can be evaluated. At the time of this writing, no results were available, primarily because it is a very difficult problem. The subtle ways in which systems can malfunction make thorough testing nearly impossible—you would have to use all the capacity of your network just to tell if it was working! Hopefully as part of another phase of your ongoing Internet project, good metrics will be defined and measurement tools will be available.

Duration

We suggest a minimum of ten days for testing.

Automobile and airplane builders, even soap manufacturers, don't release products without building and thoroughly testing prototypes. You need to do the same with your Internet/Web project, making sure everything works as planned before releasing it *live* for general consumption.

There are legitimate dangers in underestimating the problems and delays you will face. Problems will occur and will range from software bugs to noisy phone connections.

If problems arise, there could be additional ordering or circuit reordering or software configuration changes or server patches. Remember, the network has to be up before you can really test.

Additionally, if you've been following the plan until now, many people in your company are probably excited about using the Internet. If the service is deployed before it's ready, problems will arise and people will be frustrated. Early frustration will lead to a slower adoption—as people regain their trust. If you go to a new restaurant and the service is bad, how anxious are you to return? Make sure you allow adequate testing time.

One other reason to extend the testing duration: Parallel to this step, your servers may be arriving, and their installation may begin. It's okay if they are using the network as a *beta* test. They are taking advantage of your connectivity, but your users are not expecting availability yet. This stresses the network without leading the users astray.

Security

The test phase can actually be a dangerous time from a security standpoint. Imagine this common scenario: It's early afternoon, and after a long morning, the hardware is in place, configured, and *should* work—but it doesn't. What do you do? Well, you start eliminating possible problems. You remove configuration information like filters. You disable firewalls. You lessen security. Then you find an unrelated problem, fix it, and it's already late evening, so you go home. All those security measures designed into the system have been omitted for a night. Maybe you'll remember to put them back in tomorrow. Maybe.

The fact is, the testing phase is a vulnerable time. A little bit of sloppiness is okay; too much is unrecoverable. It's partly due to the way vendors ship products with the spigots wide open—and it's up to you to close them until you're comfortable. Again, this is where testing your security measures in the test plan is critical. You'll have to have a process that prevents the network from passing until it is safe. And safety should include not just a one-time test, but should be tested after all equipment is powered down and then back up. Devices often take on completely different personalities when they wake up than what they had before sleeping.

PC TRAVEL

When judging a Web site, David Lea of PC Travel (see Figure 9.2) minces no words: "In the arena of strategy, it's not how pretty a site is; it's: Does the site accomplish its mission?" For his company's site, that means selling thousands of airline tickets every month online.

His advice to companies contemplating an Internet/Web strategy? Plan and learn more about the Internet. Companies that do so will have a better opportunity at success similar to what PCTravel has enjoyed.

"About 20 percent of our users who register online, and we have about 150,000, buy tickets," Mr. Lea said. "We add about 5,000 users per week. Our challenge is to increase the awareness of our site and therefore the usage. We are exploring ways of using the Internet and the Web to heighten that awareness." (continued)

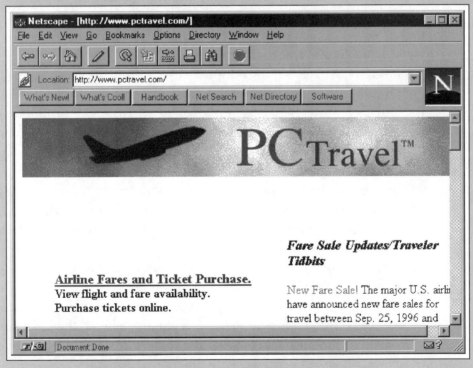

FIGURE 9.2   PC Travel home page.

Mr. Lea, who is former Vice President of Marketing and part owner of the Raleigh-based travel firm, has traveled around the United States speaking about the potential of the Internet and the Web. He is a popular speaker because of his no-nonsense approach and the success of PC-Travel's online and Internet/Web airline ticket sales strategy.

PCTravel is easy to use, is available 24 hours a day, 7 days a week, offers access to databases that show what seats are available when, and then allow people to order through an encrypted process. "Convenience by far is the number-one reason people use us," Mr. Lea said. "Second is price. They can research prices and sometimes we offer specials."

PCTravel was launched in 1993 and began offering an Internet gateway as it became popular in 1994. "Online travel reservations and ordering has been around ten years with EAASY SABRE (a subsidiary of American Airlines)," Mr. Lea said. "What is new is the widespread availability to the Internet and people who can use their access to make travel arrangements."

What follows is the Q&A with Mr. Lea:

Question: What factors and/or research should lead to a company's decision to develop an Internet strategy?

Answer: PCTravel was developed as an online service to tap into the growing online market, and not as an Internet service. This market was thought to be primarily consumer oriented, which complimented what we were doing with our telemarketing of airline tickets to the consumer arena. At the time we released PCTravel, the Internet was almost unheard of and certainly not as a commercial medium.

We got into the Internet as a way for users to connect to our service for no phone costs. We were marketing to a nationwide audience as a BBS with the obvious problem that user phone calls were billed to them. The Internet provided an opportunity for connecting to our service without extra phone charges. And we had a vague idea that the Internet was a growing medium with more potential users.

Question: Often in this startup process, there are many difficulties to be overcome, technical and otherwise. What are some of the most common? Were you able to anticipate them? What were you able to do to overcome those obstacles? What lessons did you learn?

Answer: Getting on the Internet was particularly frustrating at that time. Unlike today, there were no canned approaches; each was unique. It was hard for us to determine what exactly was needed and why. Since TCP/IP and UNIX were foreign to everything we were doing, that was another learning process. Nearly every problem was unanticipated, as connecting was like stepping back 15 years in the networking business where everything seemed to be decided on the fly.

We overcame the problems with perseverance and help from providers. Like all similar efforts, you pick up bits and pieces from each step and they finally fit together.

Question: If you had the process to do over again, what are some things that you should/would do differently? What lessons were learned? What is some advice you would give others?

Answer: If we had it to do over we would have done much more planning up front and not done so much on the fly. We did not create a detailed plan and then work to execute the plan. Today it is much easier, more of a cookie-cutter approach but planning is a must. There is no substitute for it.

Question: How important is it to have a strategic plan? If you were to write a strategic plan, what would be some of the highlights?

Answer: We did not have a formal strategic plan—we did things as we encountered them. As a lesson, more planning is essential; however, there is a trap here. The Internet is an evolving medium, changing faster than any other in the world. A key part of any plan has to be how to adapt to the change that is absolutely going to occur. Part of the difficulty and the potential downside of a strategic plan for Internet-related activity is the problem of accurately predicting the operating environment, so planning must have a great flexibility quotient.

Question: What are some mistakes that you see other companies making as they delve into the Internet? Why are they making them?

Answer: Most mistakes I see are the result of not understanding the medium; the reluctance to *get hands dirty* with the Internet to better see how an Internet presence can benefit the company. What is unfortunate is that learning the medium is as simple as getting on and playing around. Then you are just like everyone else.

The most common mistake is turning marketing issues over to technical skills. Because someone can design a Web page does not make them a marketeer, probably just the opposite. There seems to be a great failure to

(continued)

put yourself in the user's shoes to understand why or what they get from your Web site. Additional mistakes include basic spelling, grammar, phrasing, etc.

Question: What has Internet/Web access meant to your business?

Answer: Today we are a Web business only. Being privately held we do not publish financial statistics, but we have grown in two years from nothing to more than 250,000 visitors a month. We sell hundreds of thousands of tickets monthly with an average sale approaching $300. Growth averages about 20 percent per month.

Question: If you were new to the Internet/Web and were looking for a book to help you plan/coordinate/execute an Internet strategy, what are some points you would want covered?

Answer: If I were new to the Internet I would want to have something explained to me in terms I could relate to, and would not assume I was technoliterate. I would want to have some basic steps to follow and I would like a checklist of things to watch for that would indicate I was getting off track. Almost a workbook approach.

Question: What are some factors companies should be looking for when selecting an ISP, Web site developer, and/or consulting firm?

Answer: How do you evaluate someone? You ask, What have you done? To me, the first thing I would do is ask to see URLs of sites these companies have done, and then check to see how well those sites conveyed the intent of that entity. That's also taking advantage of the Internet. In the arena of strategy, it's not how pretty a Web site is. It's: Does the site accomplish its mission?

In terms of access providers, you have to try their service and see what their experiences with others have been. When considering consultants, check out the pedigree. What is their experience? How do they operate?

Issues

For companies that develop technical products, testing and test plans are commonplace. For others, it is unfamiliar territory, with unusual, tedious practices. Understanding a little more about the nature of testing will make this step seem more reasonable, and understanding the special aspects related to the Internet will help prevent mistakes.

What Is an Engineering Plan?

In theory, an engineering plan should give somebody enough detail to build a completely new system if the original system is lost due to some sort of disaster, be it natural or unnatural. The devil is in the details. If you lose a computer, or a network device loses its network configuration information, the plan is the place where the needed information is found, not scrawled in a notebook or buried in the recesses of someone's mind. If that notebook is tied to an equipment rack and is lost in a fire, then you are in trouble. Re-creating the plan from scratch can be difficult, especially if the creator or creators have left your company.

In practice, it is so difficult to maintain a current engineering plan, and the risk of catastrophic loss is usually so small that few people do this. In the computer business, perhaps you should consider a different plan or terms, such as a *soft* engineering document. Why does this have to be a printed document and copied 100 times? Imagine it as a diskette or a tape that's easily updated, dynamic, and completely transportable off premises. It begins to take on the properties that make it maintainable while still serving the original purpose, so when you insist on an engineering plan specify it in different terms: The document contains all the information aggregated on how to build the network, and is available in multiple copies. At least one hardcopy is needed, but make sure you know where the electronic copies are, and that they are kept updated.

Testing Primer

Systems testing is a complex field of study, primarily because modern systems can be extremely complicated. Systems such as the public switched telephone network, the space shuttle, and new generations of microprocessors are based on millions of lines of computer instructions. Due to the high cost of failure, these systems undergo rigorous quality assurance programs, with large resources and time. Even so, the telephone network has suffered several localized outages in the last few years due to software coding mistakes. Years ago, a major (unmanned) rocket was lost due to a single incorrect punctuation mark. More recently, a minor arithmetic error was revealed in a popular microprocessor, forcing a recall of some PC motherboards. These are just the stories that make the press.

Why aren't these mistakes found? Part of the reason is in the very reason computers have become so useful: They contain memory. Like the human equivalent, digital memory assumes a given set of recollections about the past behavior of the system. Larger memories remember more histories. A complete test plan examines the behavior for every possible system history, but as the number of histories grows, completeness becomes impossible. Systems do not run fast enough to examine every possible state. Consider a personal computer with a small main memory of 8MB. To write the number of possible states that represents, you would have to write the numeral "1" followed by a *million zeroes*. That's a small main memory, and does not include the state that can be kept on the hard disk.

So how do designers cope? One means is by performing *verification* instead of testing. System verification attempts to prove a system will operate correctly by examining its design, rather than its behavior. Having your design performed by skilled individuals and reviewed was a manual means of verification. The formal computer modeling discussed in Chapter 6 was another means of verification—albeit almost always not worth the effort. Verification is usually done, but not formally.

The primary problem with verification is that it tests intent, not implementation. What if there is a material defect in your devices? Verification may tell you *it should work*, but only testing will reveal flaws. Testing is necessary—and the way to make it tractable is through *divide and conquer*. The testing must be broken into smaller problems that can be tested individually. When the pieces are tested, assembled, and tested again, it usually provides enough confidence that the system as a whole is working. The following sections explore some of the ways testing is reduced from a very, very large problem to several smaller ones.

Unit vs. System Test

The fundamental way in which testing is made practical is by separating unit and system testing. Unit testing seeks to examine a single device—a router, a modem, a LAN hub. System testing examines their operations together. If system testing covers all of them, why bother with unit tests? The range of behavior to which a specific device can be subjected is usually far greater in a unit test. For example, under normal operation of the components just listed, a modem would never be put into *loopback* mode, where signals are sent back to the other side. Under unit testing, that particular operation would be performed before the three devices are connected.

In practice, some unit testing is always done. Making a separate place for it in the testing plans just highlights the need to test parts individually, as well as together.

Black-Box vs. White-Box Testing

Most people are familiar with the distinction between these two methods. If you have ever cooked a food item or repaired a device and asked people to sample it without telling them what you did, that is *black-box testing*. You solicited feedback without revealing information about your changes. If you did the same thing and told samplers what you did before the test, you performed *white-box testing*. The former attempts to hide the bias of the subjective testers, while the latter gives them clues as to what to examine.

Black-box testing can be good in that it forces you to throw away preconceived notions about what might be wrong. This forces a more scientific approach. People are less likely to assume that some functions are going to work. White-box testing may let you do a more thorough examination of some things, but may keep all aspects of the system from being tested.

Both methods are quite useful in testing networks and computers. For example, you will probably want to offer some of your operations folks a chance to *break the firewall*—encouraging them to find ways to get around the security measures designed into the system. For this initial test, do not reveal anything about the firewall, so their imaginations will not be constrained with what they think will work.

As a second phase, do white-box testing. Reveal what mechanisms have been put in place, and let them test those specifically. Chances are, they were not all checked during black-box testing. To obtain more thorough coverage, both techniques may be used together.

Boundary Testing

It's possible to test a system under normal usage conditions indefinitely without detecting a failure. When it's placed in operation, some operating threshold may exceed normal values—and the system may stop working as expected. *Boundary* testing seeks to stress a system in ways it will not normally see, to ensure the unexpected does not happen in the real world.

Your Internet connection should be subjected to some moderate forms of boundary testing. Following is a short list of parameters that could be varied outside normal ranges of operation to see how the system reacts:

► High load
► Oversized packets
► Continuous traffic
► Unspecified TCP or UDP port numbers
► Invalid or unused IP addresses

Written Test Results

You are going to need a baseline. Without a quantitative description of how quickly things are working, there is no way to substantiate claims that data sending and retrieval are slower than expected, or the system is not as responsive. This baseline will be needed especially if there is a problem with the Internet service provider or another vendor, or with warranty service. To simply say it's not as fast as yesterday will not suffice, particularly in the extreme event that you consider legal action.

The Internet also provides a very different quality of service option than regular telephone service. A phone either completes your call or doesn't; there is no in-between. The Internet is fundamentally different. Sometimes data is transferred quickly, sometimes slowly; sometimes in bursts and sometimes not at all. Having as quantitative an assessment initially of that performance as you can lets you identify true service degradation or improvements. Under typical office conditions and on the humanly noticeable scale, computer behaviors are generally deterministic. That's not true for the Internet.

Outsourcing and Consultants

You set the standards and performance levels, not the vendor or the consultant. This should be understood from the beginning and put in writing.

Don't you feel uncomfortable when someone on the outside who doesn't have as vested an interest in your company as you does tells you something is working and you know it's not? You want to hear that everything is working as expected from your employees. The end result is to make the consultants' work more valued. They are going to show full-time employees how to spot problems, measure acceptance, and perhaps show ways to improve performance beyond the specifications.

If the company chooses to outsource PC support, LAN support, or any piece of the project, these pieces of the project also should be thoroughly tested during the trial phase. Be sure to test their help desk support (e-mail or voice mail or both), or ask for a *hot spare* (preconfigured equipment) switch to be made.

Each vendor, from your Internet service provider to any consultant, should be required to provide you with regular, written reports on progress, product updates, problems, or anticipated problems.

Monthly statistics from the Internet service provider should cover network uptime and the network throughput, or capacity, for which you have contracted. Your agreements with vendors also should cover problem reporting procedures, problem resolution and escalation, and response time for onsite equipment repairs.

Further, you should bear in mind that telephony hardware and Internet and Web software are constantly changing and evolving. You need constant communication from your vendors about new services, upgrades, and new products.

References

Visiting the various Web sites of the Internet service providers you are considering should tell you what services are offered and for what price. You then should ask to see contracts to ensure that promised services are covered in those documents. Sales representatives may promise more than they can deliver.

The same holds true for the hardware and software vendors. If they offer *free* maintenance or software upgrades, you should be sure to get it in writing.

The Internet Society's home page (http://www.isoc.org) and the MIT-maintained WWW3 directory (http://www.w3.org) contain a wealth of information and can point you to more sources.

Newsgroups abound concerning Internet service providers and vendors. There, some refined *truth in advertising* can be found by word of mouth, but you should be aware that some people have an ax to grind. Be sure to have an open mind when viewing these complaints and/or compliments.

CHAPTER 10

Design and Acquire Clients and Servers

Whether your company has one or 100 employees, you can promote it as powerfully as a 10,000-person company via the World Wide Web—*if* you have the right infrastructure and content. The Web can help level the playing field of competition, making you appear as polished as your information kiosk. The Web can also be a double-edged sword: If your site appears amateurish, it doesn't matter how large or good or professional your staff really is. That starts to become apparent in the selection of your Web server.

Motivation

There are several reasons the design of your client and software systems warrants a discrete step, first of which has to do with competition. Right now, the fight for your dollars is fierce. Software for the Internet and the World Wide Web began as freeware, and many excellent packages continue in that tradition. Supported by the engineering community, students, and even some companies, you can find public-domain software for e-mail, news, WWW browsers and servers, and a lot more. This has made the traditional software vendors furiously competitive about adding new features and maintaining low prices in the battle for your desktop.

Likewise, the competition for hardware is similarly strong. PC prices are plummeting, fueled in part by the rapid pace of processor development, oversupply of memory components, and effective cost reductions in other pieces. PC and UNIX system vendors with products targeted for servers are also vying for your dollars, with clever schemes to increase capabilities and availability while keeping costs low. In fact, many high-end manufacturers of fault-tolerant computers also want to make inroads into the WWW server market.

Even service providers are bidding for the chance to host your data and provide your connection to the Internet. As dedicated connections become commodities in the Internet world, vendors will compete with value-added services such as Web hosting. Many will offer package prices to lure new customers.

This can be a tremendous opportunity—or a large trap. Desperation breeds both good and bad deals. While your network connections are being obtained, you have time for a careful selection process of software and hardware. This will be necessary to separate the good deals from the bad.

Another important reason is compatibility. Just because the WWW is based on standards does not mean everything interoperates. For example, a major telecommunications company was developing Internet access and marketing on two separate tracks. The network people did not talk to the marketing people, and no one had been assigned to oversee all Internet-related efforts. The result was chaos.

Only after the Web site had been designed did the team working on the network portion discover that one of the Web browsers it was considering did not support some of the higher-end applications that were designed into the Web site. Thank goodness this fact was discovered in time so that the Web-ordering process could be redirected. Otherwise the cost would have been high both in negative publicity (imagine the reaction if its own customers could not utilize some of the site's tools while noncustomers could!) and browsers that might either have to be thrown out or modified and upgraded.

Applications compatibility is a complex topic, full of subtleties that even professionals often miss. Allowing time for a good design will help minimize the number and severity of problems that arise down the road.

Dependencies

Not everyone involved in your project will need to perform this step. If you plan to use the Web only to host information about your company, it can often be economically realized through outsourcing. While having access to the Web ensures your employees share the same view of your marketing as your customers, and allows them e-mail and other communication, not every company will have those requirements, so make sure this chapter is appropriate for your plan.

If you do need to provide servers, make sure the high-level system design is finished and relatively stable before proceeding. Remember that while the Internet is based on standards, there are still several from which to choose. Just because you have a client, a network, and a server for the Web does not necessarily mean that they will interoperate. You should not jump to this task unless you have done considerable work on the network and client. And you can't move on till the testing of the servers is complete.

Goal

The goal is to come up with particular hardware and software for your clients and servers. Not just any hardware and software, of course, but those that do what you need at minimum cost over the entire project life cycle. The costs of the hardware and software are usually much less than the costs of supporting them. Furthermore, if you need to replace them before full depreciation, their effective cost is much higher. You cannot know with certainty that your selections are ideal, but you should keep in mind the long term when your purchases are made.

This phase is really complete when you start breaking open the cellophane shrink wrap on the box containing the computer and the software.

People

People who can order servers and create relationships with your vendors are the same ones who have done that for the client software and hardware. In fact you may end up dealing with the same companies, so use the same purchasing agents.

The people who evaluate and select the particular vendors, however, may be different. In the computer industry the skills used for network operations are often different from those used in PC help desk support and server administration. The former typically understand routers, packets, and wiring; while the latter deal with Windows-based PC software configuration, NT, or UNIX system issues. It's important to find people with good server experience. As your system becomes critical to how you do business, maintaining availability is important for both good customer appreciation and low maintenance costs. Spending time now to get the right integration will save money later.

You should look for people who have maintained PCs and servers in the past, not just selected them. What information they really need to know comes from running it, not just material contained in glossy brochures. There should be some willingness to consider a range of options that are available. Many people who live in the country think every house should have a barn and a silo, but there is a wide range of variance here. There definitely needs to be a team leader for this portion of the project, but drawing on the people who will maintain the server for help in evaluating them keeps them involved in the process, and helps them understand the decisions later on. Depending upon the size of your organization or the size of your network or your servers, this could be a one-person task or a small team of three or four people.

Location

This phase need not be done where the servers will be located. The expertise to select and evaluate can be separate from the place where they are installed. Keep in mind it is sometimes easier to get support from a vendor that is in your backyard, however, and the team will want to consider where the servers will be located in selecting the company that will provide them.

Resources

If you believe the pace of development on the Internet is fast, then try to keep up with developments on the Web (see Figure 10.1). More and more

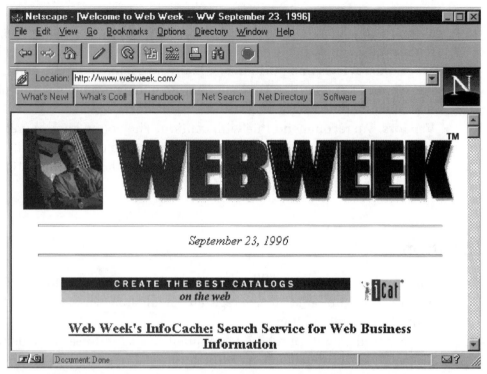

FIGURE 10.1   For information about the latest Web trends, visit www.webweek.com.

applications, or applets, are becoming available each week. More and more competitors are vying for attention.

Given the turmoil and rapid change, consultant expertise could be particularly valuable to you in this area. Many times, the experience needed to evaluate servers will not be located in-house, let alone other Web developments. If that's true for you, there are several external resources to consider:

▶ **Consultants:** The most directly beneficial is the external consultant. You should be sure to get a list of clients and references, complete with URLs, and it is essential to check them out online. Try them out on numerous occasions and at different times during the day. If you already have e-mail access, don't be shy about sending mail to Webmaster@foo.com (or whatever reference is listed) and asking for people's experiences. Most people on the Web tell it like it is.

▶ **Newsgroups:** Almost every type of protocol and almost every product has at least one related bulletin board or newsgroup available. Checking on them can be beneficial.

▶ **Magazine reviews and periodicals:** Many magazine reporters and freelance authors spend their time summarizing their products with stories that often include useful charts and screen shots.

▶ **Vendors:** We recommend this with caution. They often know a great deal about the products in the industry, but they can be biased as well. You should ask them for white papers, and then read those with a critical eye. You also should ask them for references.

Duration

Twenty days should be sufficient to make the server selection for the average site. Few sites are truly average—most fall above or below—and the exceptions may require longer.

Few readers will purchase large quantities of end-user PCs just for this project. If so, we urge you to consult additional references to aid in that decision, and add several weeks to this step. The issues around software compatibility and support costs are far too complex to fit in this book. If you already have many PCs and plan to reuse them, your client hardware selection is complete.

Some sites may already have client software selected—for use with internal network applications. You may already use an internal e-mail package, or a Web browser, and there may be technical or political reasons why you cannot change. If not, this is a good opportunity to reevaluate your software selections. The large number of public-domain packages, and the reduction in software and support costs that comes with choosing one set of clients for both internal and external use, often make this a wise measure. If you have many internal applications that you want to reevaluate, add another week or two to this step.

Most companies try to leverage existing hardware for their servers. If you already have hardware in place dedicated for this task, there's very little additional time. If you need to acquire hardware, you may wish to add another two weeks. Evaluating all the system options is a long process, and an important one for your plan.

Server software may become obvious at this point—especially if you have chosen to align your client software selection with that of a particular company (or vice versa). While there is generally good compatibility between clients and servers from different vendors, support is often easiest if you use the products from the same company. Better pricing may also be available—depending on how much you are spending. Ideally, you would treat these as separate choices, but in practice server and client software often go hand in hand.

If you have been keeping a running total and realize the large duration of this project, you should find some consolation in the fact that this takes drastically less time than constructing an equivalent complete client-server application using most proprietary solutions.

Security

Your selection of client hardware and software is barely a secret. While it may signal your general plans to other companies, it's not the heart of your Internet strategy, and it is not difficult to figure out: Most browsers identify themselves to WWW servers at each request (that's how electronic surveys are conducted that count the relative number of clients of each type).

You selection of e-mail, news, WWW, and other servers is somewhat more proprietary, possibly signaling your plans of scaling your presence on the Web. The exact details of your configuration could save your competition some time and effort, but these days such basic efforts are relatively easy to acquire—tune into any news group discussion on servers. If you outsource some of your hosting activities, the design of those systems is going to be somewhat available to anyone who interviews the same hosting service.

The significant source of proprietary information for this task comes with the design of customized integration of Internet and WWW servers into your company's back-end databases. These efforts—your foray into electronic commerce—are highly sensitive. The actual design may have cost your company considerable money, and the knowledge of it could spur your competition into a catch-up effort. If you have a lot of customized designs planned for your servers, keep the design work confidential, adhering to the general practice of requesting NDAs with your vendors and sharing the word with your employees.

We will return to security as an aspect of your Internet applications design in the next section.

Issues

If you have managed any programming efforts in the past, you appreciate how complex they can be. Developers are faced with a staggering array of products with which to design, compile, test, and manage their applications. Vendor options (an often ill-defined problem description), platform options, and their own experiences influence their selection—choices your company has to live with possibly for years. Following are some things you'll want to be aware of to make the choices as good as possible.

Selecting Client and Server Software

First, ask yourself some basic questions. What is your existing platform? Do you anticipate any changes in the near future? There may not be software available for your existing platform, or it may not have sufficient memory or processing power to drive high-end applications. And if a systems upgrade is anticipated soon, you will be much better offer to blend this upgrade with your Internet project in order to reduce costs and confusion.

Also, you must ask if the existing platform supports all the functions as described in your requirements document. If not, changes are needed in either the platform or your system design.

Further, is it your intent to pay for software? How is the licensing structured, by site or by individual PC? Making a checklist of the current capabilities of each package is highly recommended; it was not reasonable to include one in this book, since it would be out of date before printing.

Given the Internet battle between major vendors, it's important to ask what software is most compatible with your project. Are there certain capabilities that are necessary for your users that are supported only by particular vendors? Are there other features that steer you toward one or the other? The various Web extensions available are dividing the WWW into subsets, and this must be considered when choosing among the assorted browsers on the market.

When choosing among the providers, do a costs/benefits analysis. Which needs are met? Which are not?

Be sure to check out various resources for information about the various products. Your vendors may be able to provide information. There also are various books, periodicals, and magazines that can be reviewed. Newsgroups also can be monitored.

When mulling final decisions, be sure to ask the following questions:

▶ What kind of support is available? (What is the help desk situation? Is on-line documentation available, and is it up to date?)

▶ Is the product evolving and growing? (Example: Will upgrades be offered free of charge?)

▶ What is its reputation for reliability? (Has the software been sufficiently tested through several *beta* versions?)

Obtaining evaluation copies of most browser software should be straightforward. If you have unanswered questions, get them in-house and begin experimenting with them. Visit sites your employees are likely to frequent. Run them alongside other key applications. Try to simulate actual usage conditions as closely as possible.

Evaluating Web Hosting Services

Web hosting sites are often in different leagues, and you want to place yourself in the right league. The major-league hosting services provide a full range of capabilities. They will help design your graphics, integrate the server with legacy databases, provide comprehensive usage statistics and demographics, and dedicate resources to you if necessary to ensure responsiveness and capacity. The major leaguers also will charge you a premium.

The minor-league Web hosting houses typically require you to share systems with other people. They also won't have as extensive integration capabilities or capacity planning support. Their prices will be much more competitive.

The third tier contains companies that have a 56K line into their basement, and a Windows NT; and they will host your page.

You need to understand how the services and system architecture will help you achieve your short-, medium-, and long-term requirements. Ask pointed questions, and walk away if the situation doesn't feel right.

Visit their site using your dial-up copy to the Internet. Were they reachable every time you tried? Was their site as responsive as others you visited? Do other customers use them for intricate back-end integration, forms, or e-mail? Do their customers have their own *vanity* URLs, or do they have to use the hosting service's name?

Back-End Interfaces

One of the most exciting trends in information systems development is the use of the WWW browser as a front end for legacy databases. Customer reach is expanded, errors are reduced, and new capabilities are supported without the expensive and time-consuming need to rewrite custom applications for every supported PC platform. If the trend continues, the Internet and intranet may encompass nearly every interface to databases and order entry systems in existence.

Such efforts do not exist without a strong link between the open world of TCP/IP and that of existing systems. There are in fact several technologies that compete with and complement each other in that space. Following are some of the associated development issues.

Applications Programming Interface (API)

If your Web server needs to process forms-based information or otherwise customize its response to users, software needs to be written to handle requests. This software is called by the server application itself through the *Applications Programming Interface*, or API. It defines a critical interface between the server and the software, which makes your application unique.

There is one standard API supported by all server software vendors: the *Common Gateway Interface* (CGI). Using CGI, you can ensure portability of your application from one vendor to another. Some vendors' APIs give you more flexibility or speed, and may drive your selection. If this is so, be careful to understand the impact on switching down the road. Some of the APIs are proprietary to the vendors, and are not likely to be duplicated—possibly locking you into your selection or make switching costly.

Server Programming Language

Writing software to process WWW server information—or even information from other applications such as e-mail—can make your Web site useful and engaging. There are numerous choices for the language in which it is written: PERL, C, Java, and so on. Questions that need to be considered for this selection include:

▶ Does the language need to be portable? Is there a likelihood of switching server platforms?
▶ How important is speed? Does the application need to be optimized by a compiler (like C), or is it sufficient to interpret it (like PERL or Java)?
▶ Is the application too complex to economically rewrite in another language?
▶ Can a balance be reached—writing some of the application in a compiled language for speed, with other parts in an interpreted language such as PERL?
▶ Is the choice driven by the development staff's preferences? Or are their sound technical reasons guiding the choice?

Database

Highly interactive WWW applications maintain a database of user-specific information, and adapt to the preferences and behaviors of the user. The term *database* refers generically to a set of information stored with some organization that makes access possible. There are several approaches to that: flat ASCII files, Open Database Compliant (ODBC) interfaces, Structured Query Language (SQL) interfaces, etc. All have various strengths and weaknesses. Among the questions to consider are:

▶ How scalable does the system have to be? How many users may be expected? How soon?
▶ Does the database have to be shared with other applications? Might it have to be distributed across multiple servers?
▶ How much cost can be allocated to the database? (Some industrial-strength products are quite expensive.)
▶ Is there any in-house experience with a particular database product? (Running a single one can reduce the equipment requirements and lower operations costs.)

Availability

If your back-end application is important enough to warrant a high-availability solution, now is the time to consider what it will be. There are several approaches—some provide graceful failure recovery mechanism—making problems often undetected by users. Others may involve a little more manual intervention. Whether you are considering a spare machine or a fully redundant, load-sharing, fallback server, consider how your options fit with your needs.

Outsourcing

If you have ever thought about leasing a car, then you already know that sometimes ownership isn't the best solution. In the case of a car, leasing can insure you against obsolescence, reduce your capital expenditures, and may offer improved maintenance.

The same is true for Web hosting. Once you have developed your content and signed a contract to lease space on another company's server, it becomes that firm's responsibility to provide the following:

▶ Adequate bandwidth to meet customer demand
▶ Adequate CPU power on the server to satisfy demand
▶ Maintenance and support
▶ Hardware and software upgrades

Your company can focus on the content side and then ask that the Web host company provide additional services, such as audio, video, or other applications. It is your responsibility to include the basic support for those services in the code of your site, but the other company is paid to run those applications as users order them.

Before making the decision about outsourcing, you need to collect your requirements and assumptions, and evaluate the options that are available to you based upon those documents. Then consider the following questions:

1. Do you have a dedicated or switched access connection? Typically sites want to be available 24 hours/7 days on the Web, and unless you have a dedicated service it won't be economical to run your own Web server.

2. How important is availability? Check your requirements document. If your site goes down for an hour or two a day, do you miss hundreds of hits? Do you risk losing viewers that gave up on you and visited a competitor's site instead?

3. What's your expected server load? Are you the next Disney Web site, or are you going to feel lucky with one hit per day? Typically the Web hosting services can provide some capacity planning support.

4. How much internal operation support will you get or do you have? Some companies grossly underestimate the man hours required to keep a server going. If you don't have the budget or resources to maintain your own servers, consider outsourcing.

5. What reporting do you need? Total Web hits? Total hits by requesting domain? Hits per day or per week?

6. How integrated are your services? Will your Web customers need to access internal databases? Providing those links from a hosted service can be difficult to coordinate and to keep secure. You should consider running this kind of server operation yourself.

7. How many types of servers do you need? The Web is exploding with capabilities, from real-time voice and video, to hypertext and virtual worlds. The more protocols you need to support, the less likely your Web hosting service will be able to keep up. Again, you need to consider doing it yourself (and don't underestimate the size of the job!), or find a Web hosting company that is at the forefront of Web technology and services and intends to stay there.

8. How concerned are you about security? Do you want to serve and protect? Often Web sites aren't inherently targets for eavesdropping, because most Web sites put up basic information to make it readily available. But there are risks, as the U.S. Justice Department discovered recently when its site was broken into and altered. For the most part, dangers arise when the Web sites do more.

9. Do you want to support credit-card transactions? There is a small potential for intercepting credit-card information exchanged over unsecured servers. The relative probability of this kind of eavesdropping vs. someone going through its garbage has been and will continue to be hotly debated. A site that supports secure credit transactions is much more involved, from software applications to fees (payments to credit-card companies for

the privilege of using their cards). It may be best to utilize Web servers of a company that already has the process in place and can fulfill the demands you have.

10.   Is server integration into your network a concern? If your Web servers provide *front ends* to other sensitive systems, then an attacker may try to compromise their security with your open Web site.

11.   Content modification: What if your competitor replaced your price list with one reading ten times as much? How quickly would you catch it before some of your potential customers did? Controlling right access to your servers is extremely important.

12.   Are you concerned about access to your corporate LAN? Many sites that use Web servers for both internal and external access also use firewalls as insulation layers between the two. A misconfigured server may enable somebody from the outside to get through your firewall and snoop around on the inside. You should pay careful attention during the server design process to your security requirements. Use your Project Team and/or consultants, and make sure they can explain in layman terms how people can attack your server or your resources through your server. Only those people will be able to adequately explain how they can protect you.

13.   How many more protocols and servers can your network and computer system support? In some companies the addition of another protocol means the addition of another computer system.

14.   Do you prefer segmented servers or individual servers? Even if you do not have a Web site, you will need machines to provide e-mail services and access to news groups, and permit the use of other services such as FTP and gopher. Some companies prefer that each protocol or service have its own box. The other extreme is having almost every protocol running on the same box. As that box runs out of capacity you add another configured the same way. There are pros and cons to each method. On the one extreme, a set of identically configured systems is easier to maintain and scale. But none of the servers would be optimized for any single protocol. Making the decision requires a deeper understanding of the disk drives, CPUs, and network utilization of each protocol.

15.   Do you prefer vendor loyalty to diversification? You already have had to pick a vendor for your internal computer platforms and some of your client software. Should your servers be based on the same choices? There are two clear benefits to doing so. First, there are potential cost advan-

tages. Many vendors base quantity discounts on total dollars, so money spent on client software or clients' PCs can count toward total discounts or total savings. Second, there is improved support benefit. You have fewer help desks to mess with, and you will leverage your experiences with your client software and systems for use with your servers.

16. Do you really need high-end servers? This is an extremely competitive market with many choices and many capabilities. Therefore, in many instances the particular choice for a server may be clearly inappropriate for use with clients. For example, Sun and Silicon Graphics are going to make the best large-scale servers you can get, but you certainly don't need to put one on everybody's desktop. But you need to know what the capabilities of the Web service companies are that you are considering. If they have numerous clients running high-end applications, you need to be sure they can adequately support what your company will be doing. The main issue depends on the size and sophistication of the server that is needed for your uses. Larger, high-availability, expandable servers may force you to pick a higher-priced Web service company that can meet your needs.

Prices

Prices for servers and Web hosting services vary widely. Bear in mind that you will need at least one machine at your location to host a working version of your Web site unless you completely outsource all aspects of the site's creation and maintenance. Many companies choose to maintain the original Web site data on a server at the corporate site, and then FTP any changes or retrieve any information from the off-campus site where the Web information is made available to the public.

The costs of a server and the type of Internet connection you will need depend on several factors:

▶ Do you want to host the site, or serve as a mirror with little traffic expected as a result?
▶ Do you want to create and support high-end graphical and multimedia functions?
▶ Do you want separate servers for each of the functions mentioned earlier in this chapter, or do you want a megaserver?
▶ What kind of emergency backup system do you want?

▶ Do you want a firewall consisting of a software set running on your server, or do you want a separate box?

Once your Project Team has discussed the preceding points, we recommend that you talk with various Web site hosting companies and PC vendors to determine the specifications for your Web server(s), and to recommend courses of action.

Prices for Web sites vary widely, from $50 or less a month for up to 10 megabytes of space on a server that is shared with other clients, to several hundred dollars monthly for a private server with redundant and high-speed bandwidth connections plus financial transaction support.

Some companies also charge premiums if traffic on your site exceeds so many megabytes of transfer per month. You should be sure that there is a cap on the transfer fees, or you open your company up to expenses that exceed your budget.

Security

Frequent Internet users have a heightened awareness of applications layer security. They've been prompted by an e-mail client to enter a user name and password. They have also been prompted by Web browsers for passwords, and have been warned that transactions were unsecure. They've initiated file transfers using *anonymous* FTP with the well-known password *guest*.

What do the above examples have in common? At some point in the application, the user is prompted for information—if it's not correct, the application stops. The similarities end there. Almost every current Internet application uses a slightly different method to achieve data privacy or integrity. While work is underway to provide a unifying framework, we must live with a variety in the meantime, and that means difficulty.

Designing security for your applications is very challenging because each one is different. It requires maintaining multiple databases, and educating users about each one separately. If you have any kind of sensitive data in your plans—such as end-user credit-card numbers or even corporate proprietary information—you'll need a thorough security audit to understand the implications. The Internet can be quite secure, but your piece must be designed to provide it.

References

One of the best starting points on the Web is the W3 consortium, http://www.w3.org/, where many of the WWW standards are discussed. For information about specific vendors and their services, visit Cnet Central at http://www.cnet.com/, or The List at http://www.thelist.com/. A variety of magazines offer regular reviews of companies that provide Web services and the software they or you can use. Check out any of the following:

- *OnLine Access*
- *NetGuide*
- *WebWeek*
- *Internet World*
- *PC Computing*
- *PCMagazine*
- *MacWorld*
- *MacUser*

CHAPTER 11

Install and Test Clients and Servers

Suppose you have just installed a new phone system. Calls are automatically routed to the proper destination, presented with menu options for frequently requested information, transferred to a free customer service representative, and logged for planning purposes. While these systems are installed every day, they are still fairly complex. Would you announce your new capabilities to the world before testing them?

The answer is hopefully no, and the reason is basic—mistakes happen. Calls are accidentally placed on hold, forwarded, or dropped. The fix is often quick—a simply programming error that takes a minute to alter once detected. But once your customers have a bad experience, it becomes part of their association with you. It does not matter if the voice system works flawlessly from that point on, your company lost that important call.

The complexity of Internet services can be orders of magnitude higher than voice systems. Even though they are installed every day, minor programming mistakes are common, and the results are often not discovered for days. A thorough testing plan helps ensure you do not turn it over to the world before it's ready for prime time.

Motivation

The motivation for this step is clear: to make sure your Web site delivers whatever product it is supposed to do—easily, quickly, and reliably—before your employees or prospective customers are given access. They will expect the site to work immediately, especially if information or products offered through the site are critical to them in some fashion.

In order to prepare adequately, we suggest that the Project Team compile written documents that encompass a rigorous test of every aspect of your server and Web site. Unfortunately, not every company adequately tests its site or server. The results can be embarrassing, if not disastrous (see Figure 11.1).

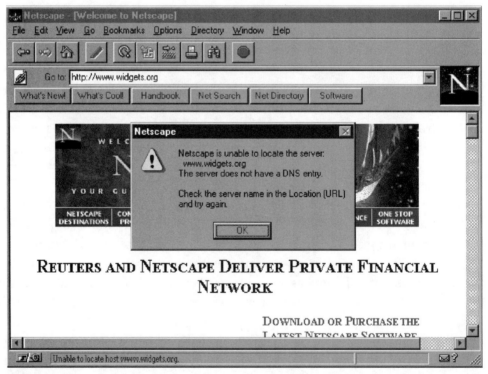

FIGURE 11.1   What your company wants to avoid at all times is a message like this, which indicates a link is *broken*, or the site you wanted to direct people to no longer exists or has been moved to another location.

For example, a software firm decided to use the Web to make copies of its two new products available. Both products had been tested extensively, and polling of potential users via the Internet had disclosed the product would be popular.

One problem: The server where the Web site was put online was simply unable to deal with the demands placed upon it. As a result, the server kept crashing and had to be rebooted. And even when the server was operating properly it operated slower than molasses flows in a New England winter.

As one would expect, user response was not at all favorable. So even though the products worked and were very popular, the company suffered a black eye because its gateway simply couldn't meet demand.

Also, as pointed out in Chapter 8, your company is likely to have contracts with multiple vendors for this project. If any of those fails in the tasks it was assigned, the results can be disastrous for your Web site.

It is simply not sufficient to bring up your Web server, post your information, and then show your employees how pretty it is. Nor would you want to pay vendors for unacceptable work. Testing can also be a contingency for payment in some cases, giving you a little more leverage in obtaining quick results.

Dependencies

By this point you have the server hardware and software in-house. Ideally you have the network connection in-house as well. A lot of work with servers goes faster with Internet access. Downloading software, operating system patches, and sampling content all go quicker on the Internet.

Even if your company has chosen to have another company develop and maintain the Web site, the following points still apply. The same is true if your company has a development server that will be linked only to another server off site.

If you have decided to support high-end applications on the Web, such as financial transactions, all the background programming must be complete. Interfaces with your internal databases (such as for real-time inventory control) and with external services (such as credit-card authorization through a third party) should be ready for testing both separately and collectively, as designed.

Content for the site, from promotional company materials to photos and inventory listings for a catalog, should be underway by now—or it will not be completely ready when the testing phase is complete. Using some of the content under production is convenient and can help identify problems down the road, but is not mandatory for this step.

The server will be linked to your network connection that is in the process of being tested, or already has been. Your key corporate staff will need access to the server site to monitor progress and test it themselves before giving their blessing for unveiling it to general, corporatewide use or access by the public.

Your company also may want to provide services other than Web access off servers, such as FTP and gopher. The content and the application software for each offered service must be checked off the Project Team's master list and tested as well.

This also is the final opportunity to confirm that your customers have the tools needed on their end to be able to access your information. For example, if your company is offering special applications that require plug-ins, such as Portable Document Format, Java, or Shockwave, be sure that customers can get access to browsers or the necessary tools that can handle them. Otherwise they are missing out on a feature that may be crucial (see Figure 11.2).

Other factors included as part of the project will directly impact your server. As cited in Chapter 9, these include:

- Telephone circuit
- Internet connection
- Internet-related hardware
- Bandwidth
- Interoperability of your system with your corporate LAN or WAN
- Functioning of e-mail gateway
- DNS and secondary DNS
- Web browser functionality
- Firewall/security operability
- Desktop access and clients
- Antiviral software

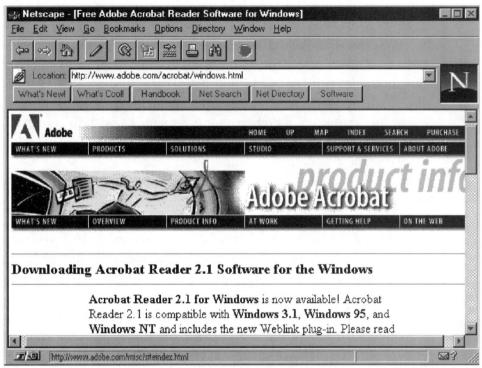

FIGURE 11.2   If your site wants to make information available in regular format rather than converting to HTML, Adobe's Acrobat Reader offers an alternative. The reader is available through FTP at: http://www.adobe.com/Software/Acrobat.

Goal

The objectives of this step include the production and use of a test plan for the Web server similar to that developed for the Internet connection in Chapter 9, along with a *soft* configuration method. Your Project Team's planning for the Web should have provided enough detail to determine what applications will run on the server, what expected demand might be, and what horsepower the server will need to meet all these expectations.

Second, this step should include the drafting of a test plan by the Project Team, which will rigorously pound on every aspect of the site: response time; reliability of links; reliability of special applications, such as ordering software and forms or gathering e-mail responses from customers and users. All must work as your team specified.

People

The Web master selected to oversee the project is the key person. This could be a new hiree, someone trained internally, or someone working for your firm as an outside consultant. Regardless of the site's complexity, one person is responsible for building the puzzle and making sure each piece fits. In this context, the Web master is concerned with the technical operation of the server—in some companies, it refers to the individual who maintains the content.

People involved in programming various pieces and providing the content also should be involved. They know how the site should appear, how it should work, and whether colors appear as they should.

As discussed before, no part of this project exists in a vacuum. Therefore, the Web master and the people supporting him have to be communicating with the people responsible for the company's Internet connection and the corporate LAN/WAN.

Problems inevitably will occur, so people across departments will have to cooperate to determine what is causing them and then implement the proper solutions.

If your Information Systems department and Web people are communicating with each other, they also will talk about bandwidth demands, server capacity, and reliability as the project moves past the testing phase. Once you are *live*, you want a team of people to respond, not individuals pointing fingers.

A point of contact from the Web service provider also needs to be in this loop if your company has chosen this route. That person's input in the testing phase is crucial in order to make sure the service provider is meeting its obligations, from server capacity to bandwidth throughput and system reliability.

Project Team members need to monitor the site's progress to make sure all corporate objectives are being met.

Location

The testing will take place wherever your company will have its servers. This could be onsite or at a site maintained by another firm. If the people involved in the testing process have Internet access, they should visit the sites and try all applications just as other Internet users will.

Remember, access to the site can be limited in a variety of ways, so having people test the site from a variety of locations and using a number of different browsers at different modem speeds would be helpful.

Resources

Your testers obviously have to have Web browsers and Internet access in order to visit. Your team needs to make sure that various browsers are used so as to reflect the usage patterns of your prospective customers. Testers also need modems or access devices (such as ISDN terminal adapters or dedicated high-speed connections) that vary in speed and capability, as indicated earlier.

To test the responsiveness and capacity of the server, we suggest you enlist testers who will hit the site simultaneously, using a variety of access methods.

It is important that responses from your testers be gathered and studied in order to determine what changes, if any, need to be made. Some additional resources may be needed, such as an individual or team that is designated to gather e-mail, 800 phone calls, and Web-page responses; and forward the relevant data to the Project Team. Your Web master also should provide logs that are kept by the server, and if the Web site is at a remote location you will need reports from that company as well.

Duration

Ten days.

You likely already have used the servers to test the network connection and some of the client functions. In fact the whole process is *test as you go*. You turn something on, such as a software feature, and you try it right away to see if it works. Bugs are usually identified through the performance of the various tasks that will be required of the server and the site.

Your internal and beta testing, however, can do only so much. The real proof comes from feedback of people on the Internet and the Web. Your expectations for this phase or test should be limited to having things work well enough to solicit a response from the rest of the world. Sometimes your first performance on the Web is not flawless.

Security

The testing phase security issues follow those of the client and server design phases, with one possible addition. If you begin to use actual content for your server testing, be certain that it is not too early for the world to see it. As soon as your server is available on the Internet, people will find it—even if you do not market it heavily. Don't place anything on the WWW that you are not ready to share. See the previous chapter for more details on security.

INDELIBLE BLUE

Buck Bohac and Katy Ansardi had a dream when they founded Indelible Blue (see Figure 11.3) in January 1993: Start a business that would meet the need of IBM customers who were having difficulty getting OS2 system software and accessories.

Three years later, Mr. Bohac and Ms. Ansardi have a successful venture in Raleigh, NC, with sales of more than $10 million in 1995. And much of that business is coming from its online strategy of employing the Internet as well as the World Wide Web. Indelible Blue used the Internet aggressively to promote its business and to take orders electronically before the Web was developed. In 1995 the company put up its Web site, and by March of 1996 6 percent of its sales could be directly traced to its Web site, according to Deborah Kania, who is Director of Sales and Marketing. Ms. Kania expects that percentage will increase substantially once the company has implemented secure online transactions.

Ms. Kania also said many other sales were generated through traditional means after leads were generated by Indelible Blue's Web site.

The firm now has a direct connection to the Internet, a full-time Web master, and space leased on an Internet service provider's server. That could change in the future, dependent upon growth, Ms. Kania added.

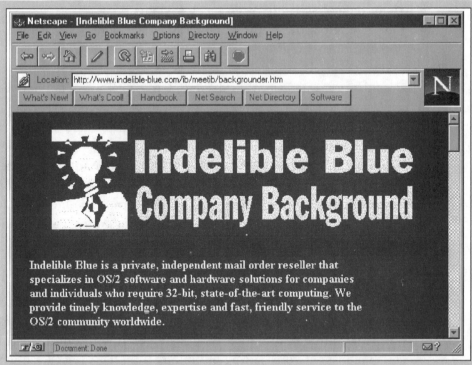

Figure 11.3   Indelible Blue's home page.

Here is the Q&A with Ms. Kania:

Question: What factors and/or research should lead to a company's decision to develop an Internet strategy?

Answer: Will the Internet benefit my type of customers? And how? This is the most basic question a company should ask. It will help to have some knowledge of the Net's power and the company's market to answer this question. We decided to use the Internet as a market and public relations tool, and are expanding it to help our internal business processes.

Since the Net can help companies in a variety of ways beyond providing information, a company should determine how the Net fits with a company's overall business plan, not just the marketing plan. We initially used the Web to have a presence and have since made it a place for extensive information, links to our *market community,* a way to for customers to place orders and provide feedback. We are also going to use the Web as an internal tool that has many benefits: (continued)

- ▶ Tie into databases and order entry systems
- ▶ Have a single browser interface for our sales staff to access information and place orders

Organizations also should do some homework to get beyond all of the hype. Attend seminars, visit competitive sites, read trade journals, talk to pioneering companies who adopted the Web earlier, talk to ISPs and consultants.

Question: Often in this startup process, there are many difficulties to be overcome, technical and otherwise. What are some of the most common? Did your company anticipate them? What were they able to do to overcome these obstacles? What lessons should companies learn from those?

Answer: Among the common difficulties:

- ▶ Keeping up with Net technology and staying on the front line, because customers see all kinds of sites and yours should, at minimum, incorporate what the majority of sites provide (i.e., lots of information, entertainment, interactivity, search engine, shopping cart that calls database if your selling online, mailing list server for e-mail notification, comments/feedback mechanism, etc.)
- ▶ Determine if your needs warrant space on an ISP server, or having your own server. Having your own server requires you to have full-time folks as well.
- ▶ Build flexibly. Technology changes at lightning speed, so don't hang your hat on any one hardware or software technology.
- ▶ Realistic expectations based on a plan! Of course, it is hard to gauge early on, so be patient!

Question: If these companies had the process to do over again, what are some things that they should/would do differently? What lessons were learned? What is some advice you would give others?

Answer: Map out what should be done and accomplished on the Internet. Marketing and IS should actively communicate the possibilities regularly!

Question: How important is it to have a strategic plan? Does it normally cover all of the necessary points? If you were to write a strategic plan for others, what would be the highlights?

Answer: It is interesting to make a Web plan. It is very dynamic! But it is important to have a set of goals, objectives, and measures like you would plan for other marketing activities. The Net should be integrated with other plans within a company. Since we are a smaller business, we did not do a formal plan at the beginning. Now we are planning for future implementations.

Necessary points:

1. Objective/goals
2. Nature of market
3. Capabilities of technology
4. Who the key players are in plan
5. Make or outsource decision
6. Determine required investment/resources to build
7. Determine required investment/resources to maintain
8. Identify appropriate measures/expectations

Question: What are some mistakes that you see other companies making as they delve into the Internet? Why are they making them?

Answer: A fair number of companies have remarked, Now that I have a Web site, what do I do? Maybe these folks left it solely up to the ISP or the Web master, without even a short plan. they didn't do their homework to know enough about the Net to have realistic expectations. Others that are disappointed with the results, did they have the right expectations?

Just being on the Net isn't enough. You have to do it right. And commit to the long haul!

Question: What has the Internet access meant to your business? Can you share any numbers in terms of sales and additional revenues? Return on investment? Did you establish a separate budget for the Internet plan?

Answer: As a technology business, it was an easy decision to make. We have about 25 percent of our mail-order revenues we can now actually attribute to the Web. It has also opened our business and opportunities to the global market. (Our customers are typical of the current Internet user, so our results are what we expected.) We have not yet established ROI or separate budget (it straddles marketing and IS budgets).

(continued)

Question: If you were new to the Internet/Web and looking for a book to help you plan/coordinate/execute an Internet strategy, what are some points you would want covered?
Answer:

▶ Overview of technologies and why they are important
▶ Demographics and growth data
▶ Case studies with numbers/ROI; examples of sites and what they are trying to accomplish with their sites (i.e., inform, sell, support retail outlets)
▶ The additional benefit of intranet
▶ Workshop to build a plan

Question: What are some factors companies should be looking for when selecting an ISP, Web site developer, and consulting firm?
Answer:

▶ Expertise and guidance
▶ References
▶ Responsiveness

Issues

These issues are very similar to those outlined in Chapter 9, because your company needs the same types of written documentation.

Writing the Engineering Plan

Having the design of the Web site and the configuration of a Web server residing only in the memory of the Web master is outright dangerous. Your company should have a plan written that provides enough detail to rebuild a server and Web site if the originals are lost for some reason. While the same would ideally be true for client configurations, in practice they are sufficiently basic as to be practically self-documenting.

Maintaining an engineering plan can be time-consuming, but it is necessary. This doesn't have to be a hard-copy document. Rather, it could be an electronic one that resides on another sever and is made readily accessible to all developers involved in the project. Keeping the document current should be part of their job responsibilities.

What Makes Up the Test Plan?

When your company picked its software client and established its network, most likely the Project Team tested the chosen brand of browser and the network access to various places in the world. However, when a Web site is made available, your company probably wants it to be accessible to and viewable by everyone on the Net. Not everyone is using your brand of client, so you have to consider whether you have to test for other clients. Given the dominance of Microsoft and Netscape browsers, these both probably need to be tested.

For e-mail access, testing for various types can be quite unwieldy. There are many mail and gateway packages, and it's very difficult to test them all. Hopefully your choice of software has provided you with compatibility for all mail systems.

We suggest that early on you create some simple HTML content for testing purposes, rather than your actual production pages. Your team should be sure to load raw, test information first and label the Web site as being *under construction* if any part of the Web site is going to be made public before it is officially unveiled.

So how does your company measure the success of the Web site from the first toe-in-the-water tests previously described to full-scale testing of all site content and tools? Through the test plan document that should be linked with your requirements plan.

We reiterate that your Project Team must adopt a methodology that works and that really examines what you want to measure. It should include a simple checklist of items, and procedures for checking every one of your requirements. That checklist should include items such as:

▶ Response times to various loads, from light to heavy
▶ Reaching specified capacity for simultaneous *hits*, or *views*
▶ Functionality of every link, both internally and externally
▶ Operation of response mechanisms to customers, such as mail reflectors or notices sent to your own staff for personal replies via e-mail, phone, fax, or mail

► Effectiveness of site search engine
► Actual page width
► Screen resolution
► Operation of scroll bars (or elevators)
► Working links from thumbnail images to larger images
► Functionality of every application or plug-in, such as:
   1. Frames
   2. Java
   3. WYSIWG (what you see is what you get) editing
   4. Database access
   5. Tables
   6. Animation
   7. VRML (virtual reality modeling language)
   8. Shockwave
   9. Banners
► How the screen is viewed by various browsers
► How the colors appear
► How content will be loaded
► How content will be managed
► Tests for posting of new information to ensure old information is overwritten or removed
► Root access is provided to key people responsible for content maintenance
► Functionality of forms and each specification for the forms are met
► Operability of versions of the site for different viewers, such as *text only*
► Verification that DNS is set up correctly
► Verification that the Web site is reachable from the Internet
► Ensure that all log files for recording statistics are operational
► Be sure that gateways to other services, such as the one for credit-card verification, are secure
► Be sure that other services, such as FTP, work
► Review of all multimedia applications, from loading to delivery. Those applications include, but aren't limited to:
   1. Audio
   2. Video
   3. Telephony

4. Interactive features such as chat
5. Videoconferencing
▶ Verification of all security features

How the testing is actually conducted and measured will be up to your Web master and technical staff affiliated with the project. But they should report the results to you in readable English.

We also recommend that the testing plan be revisited routinely so that if problems do occur, chances are your staff discovers them first, not customers.

Security concerns should be addressed by vendors, too, if your company has contracted with them to provide those services. You should ask for test data that confirms their service is as good as promised before your site is unveiled.

As said in Chapter 9, the test results correlate most strongly to the original system requirements, and must be done in that context. You can get completely carried away with looking at how things work, but in the end if they don't meet your needs you haven't done a good job.

Written Test Results

Speed of response and capacity of the server can be measured, and should be. However, what your company wants in those terms needs to be documented in the requirements planning, and then used as a baseline for the testing program.

These hard numbers can be used to hold accountable your Web master, your Web team, and the various vendors involved in the project. Without the numbers, you will be left with subjective complaints.

While speed of access across the Internet will vary, depending upon the amount of traffic, your Web site should be able to handle all the traffic it was designed to. The server and its programming are much more controllable than the Internet at large, so if something fails the fingers of blame point at your company.

Test results should be documented, shared, and reviewed. If there are problems, these should be corrected and tested again, with the new results being posted to those who need to know. And the tests should be conducted periodically even after the project has gone public in order to document the baseline of the site's performance.

Outsourcing and Consultants

As said in Chapter 9, your company sets the standards, expectations, and performance levels—not the vendors, service providers, or the consultants. This should be understood from the beginning, and put in writing in order to hold accountable everyone involved for deeds and deliverables.

If you have chosen to have your Web site created and/or maintained by an outside company, every one of that company's responsibilities should be examined. This could include a test of its disaster recovery plan and its escalation procedures in the event of outages or equipment failures.

Each vendor, from your Web site creator and maintenance company, should provide you with regular written reports on progress, product updates, problems, or anticipated problems.

Monthly statistics from the Web hosting company should cover server uptime, server response time, and sever usage. Some companies charge monthly fees based on the amount of data transfer. If so, statistics verifying that billing ought to be mandatory.

To help address your security concerns, we suggest that you consider retaining a consultant to review your site and to test the various security features. Ask this person or company to *hack* away and to report back on any weak spots that are found, as well as written suggestions for improvement or correction. This may be costly, since technical consultants charge $150 or so per hour. But an investment now may save more money later.

References

A number of Web sites (see Figure 11.4) can be used to evaluate your page design and functionality. They include:

▶ WWW Consortium's Arena Trial Browser (http://www.w3.org/hypertext/WWW/Arena)
▶ Browser Caps (http://www.pragmaticain.com/bc/)
▶ Kinder Gentler Validator (http://ugweb.cs.ualberta.ca/~gerald/validate/)

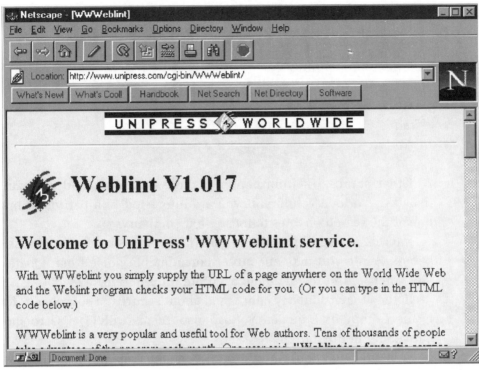

FIGURE 11.4   UniPress offers an HTML rating product, Weblint.

▶ Web Techs (http://www.webtechs.com/html-val-save)

▶ Digital (http://www.research.digital.com/nsl/formtest/home.html)

▶ Weblint (http://www.unipress.com/cgi-bin/WWWeblint)

▶ WWW Viewer Test Page (http://www-dsed.llnl.gov/documents/WWWtest.html)

A number of periodicals pay close attention to Web server applications and hardware issues. Among them are:

▶ *PC Computing*

▶ *WebWeek*

▶ *Information Week*

▶ *PC Magazine*

▶ *Mac World*

▶ *PC Guide*

▶ *NetGuide*

- *Internet World*
- *LAN Times*
- *PC Week*
- *Data Communications*
- *Network World*
- *Communications Week*
- *Wired*
- *PC Today*

Other sources of information include Web sites and magazines published by various vendors. If you are interested in a particular brand, use one of the search engines to locate that company.

Internet newsgroups also are good places to seek information, as stressed before. While you may encounter considerable *noise* from debates, generally you can find relevant and accurate information.

If you are particularly concerned about security, a source of information is the Computer Emergency Response Team (CERT) at Carnegie-Mellon University in Pittsburgh.

Web sites that contain information about Web applications and servers include:

- C/Net (www.cnet.com)
- NewsPage (www.newspage.com)
- Yahoo (www.yahoo.com)
- Inside the Internet (www.cobb.com)
- Internet Business Report (www.jup.com)
- Internet Week (www.phillips.com:3200/)

12

Generate Content

In real estate, the crucial selling point is location, location, location. On the World Wide Web, your location is mostly transparent. The crucial selling point is content, content, content.

Whether you are posting information for internal or external use, people will not visit your Web site it if is filled with day-old news of no interest or importance. With every Web site effectively next door to yours, giving away fresh pastries of information, you will not attract anyone with stale morsels of news. Your site will function best if it has the best, the latest, the freshest information relevant to your business and your customers.

Consider, for example, the explosion of sports sites on the Internet. The best offer the latest scores, information on trades and other transactions, game stories, and commentary. The breadth of information far exceeds what can be found in any traditional newspaper sports section or magazine. Rather than left behind by their electronic competitors, many of these same newspapers and magazines now offer Web sites themselves.

The sites offer data, audio, and video. Some even offer *cybercasts* of audio play by play over the Internet.

Here are screen shots (Figures 12.1 through 12.3) from a couple of the better Web sports pages, as we see them.

The *Indianapolis Star/News*, meanwhile, has its own Web site, with specific sections set aside for hardy basketball fans. Indiana University, Purdue University, and the Indiana Pacers all have die-hard fans, so *The Star/News* set up a special Indiana's Game section, with stories about each team. The site also pays particular interest to auto racing, since the Indianapolis Motor Speedway plays host to The Indianapolis 500 and The Brickyard 400, arguably the most prestigious races of their type each year.

That kind of targeting and knowledge of its customers led *The Star/News* to develop an effective, popular Web site with people visiting from all over the world.

FIGURE 12.1 ESPN, the 24-hour sports network, has developed one of the Web's most popular and comprehensive Web sites in terms of content and types of features.

FIGURE 12.2 The Fox Network, trying not to be outdone by ESPN, offers its own virtual newspaper sports section.

Motivation

So why should you and your Project Team spend a specific amount of time planning your Web site? As indicated by the sites mentioned earlier, good content doesn't just happen. Compelling Web sites are the result of many person hours and creative input and often revisions.

Making sure that your debut on the Web receives positive response from your users and customers, as well as rave reviews from peers and Web professionals, requires a solid plan for the creation and loading of your content. That's what this chapter is about.

Why would you want positive if not rave reviews? To generate traffic you have to generate interest. Even more, in the world of automotive repair

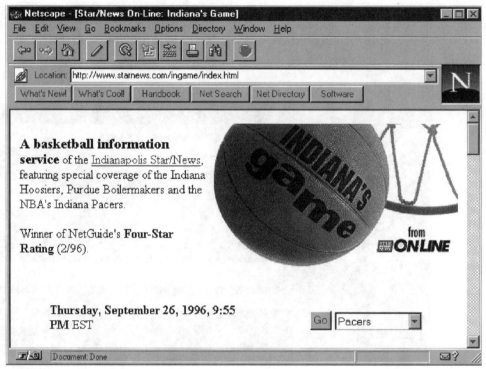

FIGURE 12.3   The *Indianapolis Star/News* pays particular attention to the needs of its readers, who are Indiana Hoosier, Indiana Pacer, and Purdue University basketball fans.

you advertise, you market, you direct market; but in the long run word of mouth is important to help sustain your business. On the Internet, word of mouth means people link to you from their Web sites, and people won't link to you unless you have information, entertainment, or preferably both. Consider this your first automotive repair, and you want to make sure it works right the first time.

Your Web information will also be subject to editorial review unlike anything experienced by your marketing brochures. Numerous sites that compile their own Best Sites or Worst Sites lists would love to list you as an extreme example of either.

Dependencies

This step is contingent upon your desire to publish on the Web. For some organizations this will prove inappropriate and/or not necessary. On the other hand, even if you outsource your Web hosting, you'll either want to generate your own content, or at least understand the process your vendor uses.

If you chose this step, the design must be finished before you begin the phase. The design is going to determine the scope of your Web's capability; that is, how many graphics it supports, how much content it can hold, whether it supports transactions, how frequently the content can be changed, and so on. Not knowing these before you build the content will definitely lead to rework down the road, delays, and additional expense.

In addition, your Web can't debut until your content is prepared. If you want to avoid Under Construction graphics at every hyperlink, then this step needs to be done in advance. Plays don't start before the scenery is finished, and your Web site shouldn't go online before the first version of the content (graphics, text, and other formats) is prepared.

Finally, you should definitely begin this step soon after design issues are resolved. Content generation can be a laborious process for many companies. First of all, the creation of compelling multimedia presentations is often new. Even experienced designers take a little time to adjust to the tools and technologies of the WWW. Also, getting people to provide the information they want to publish and sign off on it can be somewhat frustrating too. People are busy, and while this can ultimately reduce the time spent handling individual queries, it does take away from their immediate tasks. While full executive support will help mitigate this effect, be prepared to feel like you're imposing on people when you ask the for information to publish.

Goal

Your Project Team's goal at this stage is to produce and output a collection of multimedia information. It is self-documenting. You don't need to write a report about what it has. You instead create a collection of files that are consistent and coherent and then are transferred to your server.

Unlike the designs of your system, this information can change on a regular basis. It's therefore even more important that you have an archival system in mind so that new revisions can be generated and loaded.

Depending on whether your server is run by someone else or internally, your content might be loaded over the network or by a tape or diskette. While network loading can be faster, having a tape provides a backup for disaster recovery. The creation of the first version of the tape is really your first goal. Since this step is repeated throughout the life of the Web, subsequent tapes become your subsequent goals.

There is another result of this step: definition of a process. Fresh content demands a procedure by which somebody maintains your information. Ideally, you will document this procedure—but that's somewhat optimistic. Many companies maintain their content in an *ad hoc* way—perhaps just leaving it to the Web master's whim. That's okay—until your Web master takes a new job for 50 percent more money. People do need to understand their roles in developing content—use whatever practice works in your company to communicate that fact.

People

To date, everyone we have talked about either knew your business or knew the technology or both. And while your Web builders have to understand the technology, they also require one other skill that no one else needed to this point: graphics design.

Creating compelling and informative images and, if needed, audio takes a set of special skills. These may not be available internally. It's not enough that somebody knows Image Editor or some basic drawing package in order to do a good design. Web design also has to consider technical factors. The number of colors shown on a given page can be limited on some computers by the number of bits per pixel, or the display characteristics. The size of an image or audio file is limited by the speed of the modem.

Even the layout of the Web site and the efficiency by which a person can find the needed information depends significantly on how the site is constructed. Finding a graphic artist with Web design experience can make a tremendous difference between a successful site and a functioning site that may not meet basic needs and desires.

Finding good designers has become challenging due to the demand. If you look outside your company, as many people will, make sure to get references—specific URLs designed by the person or persons who will be doing your site. Try to find someone with a style that suits your corporate image—don't expect a cartoonist to find a style that supports your serious issues.

Sending your graphics designers for training to enhance their Web skills can be a very positive decision—investing in your own employee, someone who already understands your graphics and your people. Be sure any training you select is accomplished on tools that you will have available. There are some wonderfully powerful, high-end electronic production tools on which you can be trained, but if your company cannot afford them in-house it only serves to frustrate.

Location

This can be done anywhere. Just like a remote server can be loaded on the network, your server run in-house can have graphics designed anywhere in the world. Like all consulting work, it may be easier to enlist the services of a local company, but there's nothing to prevent you to turning to out-of-town, out-of-state, or out-of-country vendors.

Resources

Graphics designers use a variety of specialized tools, both hardware and software. Among the former, scanners, digital cameras, video digitizers, and graphics tablets are but just a few. Sometimes these can be rented, but since the graphics production is an ongoing effort and many of these items are decreasing in price, it's often more reasonable to purchase the equipment.

These tools also can be used for various other needs within the company for production of standard marketing materials, and so on. The equipment also may be rented on hourly rates from local office-supply stores.

Graphic artist applications also come in many varieties. Basic painting and drawing packages are the low end, while sophisticated, three-dimension modeling and animation packages are at the high end. In between there are programs that convert graphics from one program to another, transform or morph images, and read images from scanners, photos, and video cameras.

A basic set of tools may be found in shareware packages, but there are some graphics capabilities for which you must still pay. Of course, for every image tool there may be a corresponding tool for dealing with audio or video.

At the heart of all Web pages is HTML. This humanly readable set of commands, as opposed to a binary data stream that can't be interpreted, manually instructs browsers how to lay out pages. This also specifies hyperlinks to other sites. If the HTML is wrong, the page will either look bad or will be broken and thus not be viewable. Fortunately there are a growing number of tools on the Web that will check or compose HTML documents. Some will give you a what-you-see-is-what-you-get (wysiwyg) editor so that you can create your HTML files without the tedious, manual authoring process. These tend to be very worthwhile in the time they save and the mistakes they correct.

There is even some online help for Web authoring. Some sites on the Net will read any Web site you specify and locate HTML errors. If you don't run one of these for your site, someone else may. Because Web development is a repeated task, the time you save in the long run by using the automated test tools can be significant.

Some Web sites (see Figure 12.4) where information can be found about Web authoring include:

▶ http://www.w3.org/
▶ http://www.Webtechniques.com/
▶ http://www.netsurf.com/
▶ http://www.javaworld.com/

There are a great many kindhearted people on the Web, so also available on the Web are a number of graphics resources (images and audio snippets) available for a small fee or no fee.

Of course, you need some sort of network access in order to retrieve these, and be careful not to overuse them! After a point, users recognize copied graphics and common audio clips. A site thus can become a digital cliché.

FIGURE 12.4   One of the hottest set of applications for the Web is Java. *Java World* magazine is available at http://www.javaworld.com.

Duration

Typically, you should allow at least 30 days for this step—more or less depending on how much information you publish. The big time consumer is gathering the information from various departments that you want to put on the Web. The technical component of authoring can be easily expedited with the tools we have listed previously. What slows the process down is getting people to tell you what they want on the Net while they are keeping up with their other responsibilities. Here is where having visibility at the highest company layers is going to payoff. Make sure that your president/CEO/whoever makes this project a priority, and insist that people cooperate.

Consider getting everyone who needs to contribute information for the Web together at least once, so you can efficiently communicate what it is you need and they can appreciate the magnitude and the complexity of your task. Don't just show up at their office doors and expect them to give you exactly what you need at the hour you want it.

Initially, you should allow 50 percent to 75 percent of your total time to be spent collecting the information. You should allocate the remainder to putting it into digital form. Make sure the finished product is not too light on information. It's okay to have a few Under Construction logos on your server, but resist the urge to have every link point to one. If people do not find something useful on their first visit, they are less likely to return.

Security

The intellectual property investment for a Web site can be very high. A unique concept coupled with many hours of work are as valuable as a major marketing blitz for a soft drink company. Those campaigns are guarded with very tight security, and your Web content may deserve the same.

With the intersection of marketing and technical communities, the problems often arise with what is *not* said. Have marketing people explain when information is to be guarded before release on the Web server. If it is important to time its dissemination with other events, make that need clear. Meanwhile, the technical people should explain how easy it is to replicate content in flawless digital form, and how tracking its retrieval does not exactly track its use. Start the dialogue between the two camps to avoid misunderstandings down the road.

Additionally, ensure you have intellectual property agreements in place that protect your custom development work. You do not want an external design-house leveraging for other customers the hours spent on your products.

ALLEN MARKETING

Cliff Allen, president of Allen Marketing Group in Raleigh, NC, has helped numerous companies develop an Internet/World Wide Web strategy (see Figure 12.5). And a consistent problem he has seen is the failure of these companies to integrate their Internet/Web efforts into their traditional marketing plans. He also suggests incorporating a feedback mechanism (such as e-mail) into sites so that hosting companies can interact with their visitors. Such mechanisms can serve as lead generators for additional business.

Mr. Allen recommends that companies pursue a deliberative policy, taking care to address problems before they can be created. Firms also need to develop a better understanding of the Net, its capabilities, and its limitations. (continued)

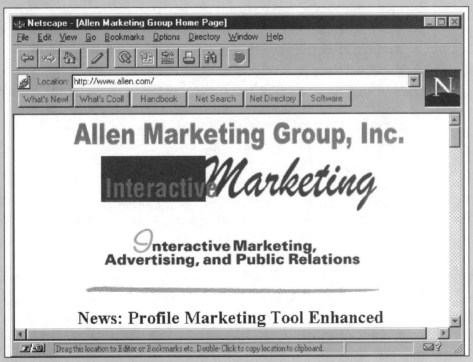

Figure 12.5   Allen Marketing home page.

Among Allen Marketing's clients are John Wiley & Sons, the Nash Bridges television show on CBS, and Business Telecom, Inc., one of America's 15 largest long-distance telephone carriers.

Before entering the Internet/Web business in 1994, Allen Marketing Group was a traditional advertising and public relations company. Seeing the Internet as an opportunity, however, Allen was among the early adopters of the Internet and quickly expanded the offerings of his firm.

Here is the Q&A with Mr. Allen:

Question: What factors and/or research should lead to a company's decision to develop an Internet strategy?

Answer: A company's marketing management should consider a variety of factors related to the online marketing environment and their traditional marketing activities, including:

▶ Do the demographic characteristics of existing customers match the demographics of a significant portion of Internet users?

▶ Do focus group meetings (either in person or online) indicate that the company's target market is interested in gathering information about the company's products, or buying products, via the Internet?

▶ Is the company committed to making changes in the sales and order-processing process to take advantage of the marketing effort?

▶ Will there be problems with the existing sales and distribution channels if an Internet channel is added?

Question: Often in this startup process, there are many difficulties to be overcome, technical and otherwise. What are some of the most common? Did companies anticipate them? What were they able to do to overcome these obstacles? What lessons should companies learn from those?

Answer: Most of the difficulties we have seen companies face have been related to integrating their Internet marketing activities into their traditional marketing communications activities. In other words, many of the companies with an early Internet presence did not understand the importance of traditional marketing (i.e., print-based advertising and direct mail) in generating traffic to their Web sites.

The second most difficult challenge for many companies has been to understand how the traditional marketing concept of *reach and frequency* should be handled in the online world.

The easiest approach for companies to use in maintaining contact with people who have visited their Web site is to use an e-mail list server to distribute a newsletter each month, promoting the new material, products, and so on.

Question: If these companies had the process to do over again, what are some things that they should/would do differently? What lessons were learned? What is some advice you would give others?

Answer: I think that many of the early companies with Web sites would like to have had more knowledge about how the Internet market was going to respond to their Web marketing efforts. Specifically, companies have learned that Web sites—like brochures, advertisements, trade-show booths, and so on—need to make a significant impact on the audience and deliver a consistent marketing message.

Fortunately, many of those companies have the experience with the Internet market to understand what is required to be successful, so the companies that gained that early experience will turn out to be the most successful.

Question: How important is it to have a strategic plan? Does it normally cover all of the necessary points? If you were to write a strategic plan for others, what would be the highlights?

Answer: The ideal Internet marketing plan dovetails nicely with the company's overall marketing plan. As with any other marketing communications and sales plan, it should include:

- ▶ Goals to be accomplished
- ▶ Objective measurements used to determine when success has been achieved
- ▶ Projects related to marketing message
- ▶ Projects related to the technical implementation
- ▶ Schedules for all members of the team to follow

Question: What has the Internet access meant to your business?

(continued)

Answer: As an Internet marketing firm, we have experienced tremendous growth in both clients and the number of exceptional contacts throughout the world.

Question: If you were new to the Internet/Web and looking for a book to help you plan/coordinate/execute an Internet strategy, what are some points you would want covered?

Answer: There are two types of books that are needed for companies looking to become involved with the Internet. First, senior marketing management should read books describing how sound management and marketing principles are applied to this new form of electronic media.

Second, managers should have an understanding of the technical aspects of using the Internet.

Question: What are some factors companies should be looking for when selecting an ISP, Web site developer, and consulting firm?

Answer: An Internet consulting firm should have experience with companies near your size and general industry. The backgrounds of the principals should include experience in your industry, as well as computer and data communications experience.

A Web site development company should have experience developing Web sites similar in graphic appeal and ease of navigation to what you are looking for. They should also have experience working with advertising agencies and marketing communications departments of companies similar to yours.

An ISP should be selected on the basis of bandwidth available, percent of time systems are accessible on the Internet, and the quality and depth of technical support.

Issues

By the time you reach this step, you are in the home stretch. Your servers are nearly ready for prime time and your content is being generated. Still, there are some issues that could threaten your project's overall success—ones related to an important aspect: what the customer sees.

Cutting-Edge Sites

First of all, we want to convey a sense of how creative and interesting some WWW sites are. You don't want to jump in too far behind your competition, or you will forever be catching up. For examples of sites that use a wide variety of features, from real-time inventory tracking and stock quotes to high-end multimedia applications and home banking, here's a short list. Remember: These are not meant to intimidate you, but to motivate your design team to excellence.

► Federal Express (www.fedex.com)
► Sharper Image catalog (www.sharperimage.com)
► Avis rental cars (www.avis.com)
► *USA Today* (www.usatoday.com)
► PointCast (www.pointcast.com)
► Time Warner (www.pathfinder.com)
► Encyclopedia Britanica (www.eb.com)
► *Slate* magazine (www.slate.com)
► NationsBank (www.nationsbank.com)
► Quote.com (www.quote.com)
► Fidelity Investments (www.fid-inv.com)
► Prudential Securities (www.prusec.com)
► First Union bank (www.firstunion.com)
► Wells Fargo bank (www.wellsfargo.com)
► Cable News Network (www.cnn.com)
► Politics Now (www.politicsnow.com)
► *Washington Post* (www.washingtonpost.com)
► *New York Times* (www.nytimes.com)
► *Wall Street Journal* (www.wsj.com)
► Dow Jones News/Retrieval (www.bis.dowjones.com)
► *Los Angeles Times* (www.latimes.com)
► *Washington Times* (www.washtimes.com)
► Computer Network (www.cnet.com)
► AT&T's Lead Story (www.leadstory.com)
► Pizza Hut (www.pizzahut.com)
► Coldwell Banker Real Estate (www.coldwellbanker.com)
► Rush Limbaugh Tie Collection (www.rushties.com)

▶ Security and Exchange Commission (www.sec.gov)
▶ PC Travel (airline tickets) (www.pctravel.com)

If these are not representative of your competition, search for them. With about 50 percent of U.S. companies on the WWW, chances are they are out there. There are numerous search engines on the Internet to help you find subjects by keyword or topic; here are just a few:

▶ http://www.altavista.digital.com
▶ http://www.lycos.com
▶ http://www.yahoo.com
▶ http://www.search.com
▶ http://Webcrawler.com
▶ http://www.excite.com
▶ http://www.hotbot.com

Developing Your Style Guide

While ideally your corporate publications department would author a Web publishing style guide, that's a practice even some of the large companies eschew. Mainly it's a time constraint—taking time away from the production of actual content. It can also be a little stifling to creativity, forcing creative minds to think within defined boundaries.

We think you will have a corporate style guide, whether or not it is written. That's mainly because you do not want every page on your Web to look different. Don't use different fonts, with different backgrounds, different icons. It's too disorienting to the users, and does not convey a strong corporate image. There will be an implicit guide; here is a laundry list of issues to consider as it is developed:

▶ Visual Style—Choice of fonts, colors, layout
▶ Navigation—Consistent use of quick links; availability of a site map
▶ Search—Providing a search engine with both quick and detailed query forms
▶ Multiple Browser Support—Optimizing for popular graphical browsers, or text browsers (especially with respect to multimedia file formats, HTML extensions, and downloadable applications based on Java or Active-X)

► Average Page Size—Keeping average graphic file size small for users with slow links (or if your visitors tend to be other companies with high-speed connections, allowing larger images and files)

► Multiple Formats—Making download files available in multiple formats (i.e., PostScript, text, HTML, etc.)

► Multiple Languages—Supporting international customers

► Cross-Marketing—When to link to other sites; when to encourage other sites to link to you

► Copyright Issues—Proper use of corporate logos and copyright notice

As you can see, the list is quite long. Writing out the style guide will make it easier to develop content in the future, and easier to communicate your requirements to future design resources. Following is just one example of how multiple language sites can be created (see Figure 12.6).

FIGURE 12.6   Accent Soft's Web site offers its users access to multiple-language versions of its Web site. That makes sense, given Accent Soft's business: Web sites built in a number of different languages.

External Web Design Houses

Web design becomes a very attractive task for considering external design houses. The special set of skills required may simply not be present in some small companies. They also often use their own tools, saving more time and money.

Another plus is that you can typically view their work directly. When you interview prospective design houses, simply ask for references and URLs to their work. You immediately discover what kind of work they have done in the past. (You also should find out what their employee turnover rate is, as turnover could adversely affect your project.)

On the downside, Web design typically is a recurring task, and this could be a cash drain on some companies. Therefore if cost is an issue, try to create a Web site with text not embedded in the graphics so that you can change the information while reusing the look and feel of the site.

Some Web hosting services will also do Web design, and this can be a tremendous advantage. They instantly know what capabilities the Web server will provide, and they also can simplify the task of loading content.

But there could be a downside to letting your Web host provide your graphics. The better hosts know the technology, but the best Web designer knows your business and graphics. You may find a company that has done many Web sites for companies or organizations like yours, and you may want to use them down the road. That could be difficult, splitting away from your Web hosting arrangement.

References

There are numerous texts dedicated to HTML and WWW page design; we recommend you visit the store where you acquired this book and select one that suits your needs. Be sure to couple it with liberal browsing of other Web sites to understand what the competition is doing.

CHAPTER 13

Turn Over to Operations

As the headlines surrounding the 16-hour outage of America Online in the summer of 1996 indicated, electronic, online, and Internet commerce has become mission-critical for thousands of companies and millions of individuals around the globe.

Smart executives were immediately questioning if their firms had the on-hand expertise to deal with a problem such as AOL experienced. Sadly, many companies do not, relying on vendors, contractors, or consultants. That lack of self-reliance can be reason for concern.

But solutions are not easy or cheap. The relative newness of the Internet combined with its ever increasing popularity has led to a considerable shortfall on qualified technical personnel who can effectively maintain and manage Internet and Web services. People who are available are expensive, and technical consultants charge $150 per hour or more in many cases. Chances are, your company lacks the internal expertise to handle the intricacies of a TCP/IP or HTML world.

Whether you will try to find them outside or groom them internally, the technical people at your company need to be a part of using the Internet and the Web. They need to have a say in the repair goals and a sense of involvement; they don't need to have heaps of standards thrown on them, such as how long they can wait before responding to a query, the standards for responsiveness. They need to be a part of establishing the procedures. This chapter will talk about how those procedures are developed.

Motivation

An earlier chapter noted how designers like to draw boxes—and we won't recant. In fact, it's also fair to say that drawing new boxes is more interesting to most technical people than, say, continually erasing and redrawing other peoples' boxes. Or creating instructions for others on how to draw boxes. Or defining standards for how to evaluate boxes. So now that you have involved talented technical people to create your Internet infrastructure, don't expect them to become 7 day/24 hour maintenance technicians, or develop detailed operations procedures. It just won't happen.

Ordinarily, hand-off to operations would be considered a project milestone instead of a task. On some sunny Monday morning, all incoming trouble requests are forwarded to the help desk; pager schedules become active; all those involved in the design distance themselves from daily issues. In reality, completing the hand-off from design to operations is one of the biggest challenges in your project. The large amount of specialized knowledge can dissipate onto other interesting tasks, like employees flocking to newly restocked vending machines. Keeping enough continuity to ensure smooth operations is a challenge deserving of its own task.

Dependencies

This step assumes that you have installed some new infrastructure in support of this project. Companies that simply rely on external Web hosting may not need to develop operations procedures beyond deciding how to contact your provider to load new content or report problems.

It's critical that you have an infrastructure mostly in place before you define your procedures. Some companies can anticipate their needs, or leverage their experience enough to develop nearly complete instructions for how to operate their services—but those examples are rare. Most borrow small device-oriented procedures where possible, and develop their in-house procedures on the fly. This lets them be based more on experience than predictions.

Of course, we recommend that you not review the success of this project until this critical step is complete. Most importantly, control your desire to market your presence until operations procedures are well underway. Creating customer expectations is dangerous if you do not deliver.

Goal

The primary goal is to have trained people ready to run your service with the level of quality you desire. There need to be several people, unless your organization does not believe in vacations or sick days. They need to be motivated and feel they have the tools and knowledge to do a good job.

While trained personnel are necessary, it is not sufficient. Turnover is especially high in the Internet and Web business, and there are no signs of this abating. You will also need to create a series of procedures, slides, and booklets that instruct operations personnel how to maintain your system. Before concluding this task, we hope that some will be in place—but we won't pretend they will be complete. Definitions of the tasks that need to be written, and some handle on how they will be done, are often enough.

People

The operations personnel you choose may be existing tech support people, or may be looking for a career change into an entry-level technical position. They need to be conscientious, detail oriented, and fairly good at dealing with people. Being patient and methodical to work out problems over the phone is especially important.

In terms of the instructors, you will need to count on the people who designed your service to convey system-specific information. They will have to make some presentations, and provide some documentation and recommendations for how to run things. However, it's a poor use of their time to count on them for basic technical training. Computer skills and simple networking theory are often economically and effectively taught through hands-on training courses.

Junior people will listen to anyone who has a clue; but they can tell when a person is clueless, so adequate screening of companies chosen to provide instruction or guidance is absolutely critical. You also don't want teachers or instructors who will mislead or misguide your technical staff. That could lead to disastrous consequences when problems occur.

Location

Operations people always function better with an understanding of the entire system. If your company is geographically distributed, consider holding training at or near the headquarters, and making a time at the hub or operations center part of the training plan.

The ability to visualize all parts of the system can greatly enhance some people's ability to work with problems. If that's not possible, or if your company isn't geographically distributed, then clearly you will want to have the training at the most central, cost-effective location.

Resources

Everything that was true for training your users applies for training your technical staff, but this must be deeper because the technical staff will be employing special tools of their trade. You will want to make sure they spend time hands-on with as much of the equipment as they will actually be using. This includes the actual network components and the troubleshooting tools to help conquer difficult problems.

This is where use of a training center can have another strong advantage, because there are hands-on troubleshooting courses that can put a network analyzer available for each pair of students. That's rarely the case in the organization itself, where a much higher equipment-to-student ratio is the norm.

Some equipment vendors will provide routers, CSU/DSUs, and other hardware as part of their own instruction courses. But training on one brand doesn't necessarily apply to another, so bear that in mind as you move through the acquisition process.

For more information about training, please refer to the same section in Chapter 2.

Duration

Operations training is ongoing just as it is for the rest of your staff. Employee turnover, the continual introduction of new capabilities, and refinement of skills necessitate that this task never really stops. However, a midsize company of several hundred people should plan on three weeks of training per full-time operations staff member without prior experience before they step up to their jobs. You want them to be proficient and able to deal with a battery of tests (hypothetical or real situations), testing out in the 75–80 percent range or higher. Smaller companies or ones with more in-house expertise may do with less.

Isn't that a lot of time, you ask? Yes.

Won't that be expensive, given that technical training can run several hundred dollars per day, let alone the production time lost from normal duties? Yes.

This also may require shifting of job responsibilities and cross-training. However, this step is essential, and the necessary funds, staff time, and resources must be dedicated if you are to sufficiently train your staff.

But look at it in perspective. If you have somebody whose full-time job is to monitor and/or maintain your Internet access and they have never done this before, then three weeks of full-time training is the rough equivalent of a single, college class accounting for time spent doing homework, projects, and exercises. The complexity of the Internet easily rivals that of introductory chemistry or calculus. There is just so much for a full-time operations person to know. Even in those classes it is often difficult to attain a 90-percent to 95-percent comprehension level, so by all means, think. If you are bringing in someone cold and expect them to do a good job it will take at least three weeks to get them prepared.

In practice, most people have a little prior experience that can be applied. And unless you are a large company, Internet maintenance is not a full-time job, anyway.

There is another reason to allow more time. From the day your Internet system is operational, you can expect that the designated support staff will have to provide some level of ongoing support in addition to their learning responsibilities. For example, Murphy's Law struck Internet startup company Interpath in Raleigh, NC, on the day it was to go online on April 1, 1994. Everything was operational, from T1 backbone connection to phone lines, when the nearly 50-line phone rotary went dead. Unknown to the company, a change had been ordered regarding the local telephone circuits, and Interpath's technical staff—strongly qualified in all Internet matters—was left wringing its hands while waiting for help from the phone company. But they did know enough to determine what the problem was and to get corrective measures started. If that time had been allocated to lessons, the training schedule would easily have slipped.

SAS INSTITUTE

SAS Institute, a global leader in software design for 20 years, has moved quickly and aggressively to incorporate the Internet, World Wide Web, and intranet into its business (see Figure 13.1). And the company, which is based in Cary, NC, continues to look for new ways to utilize the Internet, from distributing its products electronically to improving internal communications.

According to SAS, a coordinated Internet strategy enabled the company to not only help itself internally, but also meet the needs of customers. "The ability to share information in real time among distant groups of sales, marketing, research, and development organizations is what allows SAS Institute to move its products and services forward at the pace our customers require," said Mr. Curt Yeo, program manager for Web strategy at SAS.

SAS, which focuses on data management tools, was among the first companies with a corporate Web site that went online in 1994. Now, SAS maintains an internal Web site as well, plus an intranet that links its 4,500 employees, global offices, subsidiaries, and distributors. And corporate usage has been so strong that Mr. Yeo said: "Usage of the Web is almost a requirement if you want to figure out what is going on."

The success of its various Net projects and the growing acceptance of the Internet as a medium for commerce have led SAS to explore using them for sales and delivery of goods and services beyond the books it already sells online. SAS also has changed its marketing strategies from

Security

For large service providers, procedures are gold. A good set of trained employees and written procedures makes the difference between barely meeting requirements and exceeding customer expectations. Written procedures are guarded, but in reality the transfer of people is unstoppable.

Your company's procedures will probably not be as closely guarded. While they do represent effort and work, the variations in operations tend to be much more substantial than the variations in designs—making their protection of little value. Of course, if you choose to guard yours tightly, you need to communicate this desire in your training.

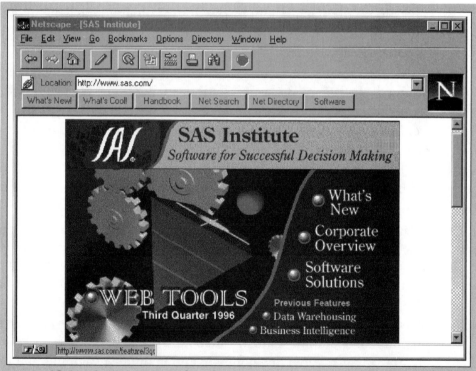

FIGURE 13.1 SAS Institute has both an internal and external Web site, and maintains an intranet in addition to its global Internet link.

more conventional means to a polished presentation on the Web. Ultimately, SAS also hopes to *Web enable* its products so customers can use them via the Web and Internet. (continued)

"Customers' expectations also have been affected by the Internet in general," Mr. Yeo said, "so SAS has had to rethink the way we have traditionally architected our software, and find ways of embracing those new perceptions while maintaining a revenue stream to support our efforts." At the same time, however, he said the Internet also is opening new markets for SAS.

SAS, a privately held company directed by President and Chief Executive Officer Jim Goodnight, focuses on data access, data management, data analysis, and data presentation tools. The company had one product when launched in 1976, but now features nearly 30.

What follows is the Q&A with SAS Institute. Respondents were Mr. Yeo and Mr. Chip Kelley, program manager for Web enablement:

Question: What factors and/or research should lead to a company's decision to develop an Internet and/or online strategy? What factors influenced your decisions?

Answer: SAS Institute has always used the most cost-effective methods available to ensure wide distribution of internal information. With the availability of intranet technologies, we were able to capitalize on our sophisticated internal global network to securely deliver confidential company information to all of our employees around the world. The ability to share information in real time among distant groups of sales, marketing, research, and development organizations is what allows SAS Institute to move its products and services forward at the pace our customers require.

Question: Often in this startup process, there are many difficulties to be overcome, technical and otherwise. What are some of the most common? Were you able to anticipate them? What were you able to do to overcome these obstacles? What lessons did you learn?

Answer: Probably the best lesson in our movement from centralized, mainframe operations to distributed network operations is the need to decentralize the content development and maintenance of internal information systems. There is a need for centralized control of execution and storage space, but the delivery of current information can be maintained only by the owners of the data.

Question: If you had the process to do over again, what are some things that you should/would do differently? What lessons were learned? What is some advice you would give others?

Answer: The decision to use static Web pages was the path of least resistance when our intranet was first being developed. Dynamically generated Web pages offer more program control over content, and are now looking like the better choice, especially considering the huge volume of information that is being generated and maintained on our internal site. Conversion is not impossible, but it is nonetheless a daunting task.

Question: How important is it to have a strategic plan? If you were to write a strategic plan, what would be some of the highlights?

Answer: A strategic plan is a cornerstone to any endeavor that has the potential magnitude of an intranet for a company the size of SAS Institute. Even more important, however, is executive buy-in at the earliest stages of the process. The last thing you want is to enter into the process of developing an intranet as a skunkworks project.

Question: What are some mistakes that you see other companies making as they delve into the Internet? Why are they making them?

Answer: Shifting to the external Internet, SAS Institute has taken a very conservative approach to the delivery of information from our Web site. The advantage of that approach is that we tend to reach the broadest community of interested Web users, and we are able to deliver *substance* to the World Wide Web. It is our opinion that using the WWW to deliver hype and *fluff* is a disservice to the intelligence of the Web community, and we try to avoid including either in our content.

Question: What has the Internet/Web meant to your business?

Answer: The Web presents a shift in users' expectations, and in methods associated with the processes that our software is designed to support. Web users perceive interaction with software products as relatively inexpensive transactions that can be performed on inexpensive processors using inexpensive software. Those expectations are causing us to rethink the way we have traditionally architected our software, and find ways of embracing those new perceptions while maintaining a revenue stream to support our efforts.

Those same perceptions, however, are allowing us to address the needs of an entirely new community of users that have never before been exposed to the power of our products. SAS Institute is moving quickly to address this change in our market, and will continue to reinvent the SAS System to meet the needs of our users. (continued)

Question: If you were new to the Internet/Web and were looking for a book to help you plan/coordinate/execute an Internet strategy, what are some points you would want covered?

Answer: What is important when establishing a presence on the Internet is determining who your audience is, and what you want them to do with the information that you are making available to them.

Question: What are some factors companies should be looking for when selecting an ISP, Web site developer, and/or consulting firm?

Answer:

1. Select an ISP that can grow bandwidth with the needs of your site.
2. Select a Web site developer that understands your business model and can deliver the necessary creative and technical resources to accomplish your goals.
3. Select a consulting firm with enough experienced resources to cover all aspects of your project within a desirable time frame.

Issues

We'll leave general training issues to Chapter 2, and concentrate in this section on issues specific to operations training and procedures definition.

Procedures List

Here are some procedures we think will be highest on your list to create or train. This list is by no means complete—the specific list will be highly dependent on your company's needs. We'll categorize them according to whether you need them during normal operations or under special circumstances.

Maintenance Procedures

▶ System tape backups and restores
▶ Basic availability testing

- ► System resource monitoring (disk, CPU utilization, bandwidth)
- ► Security sudits
- ► New user
- ► New computer (client or server)
- ► Accounting reporting

Problem Procedures

- ► Application not working on client
- ► Application not working on server
- ► System slow
- ► Passwords forgotten/changed
- ► Site unreachable

Scheduled Downtime

Your system isn't live yet, is it? It's not supposed to be. You are supposed to have procedures defined first. Before you cut the ribbon officially, you should define you maintenance window. Your system may target 100 percent uptime, but that can only be approached with a recurring time allocated for system upgrades and preventive procedures. Devise a standard mechanism for alerting users—internal and external—of impending downtime. That might be some e-mail, a place on the home page, or a spot on a bulletin board. Get in the practice of providing reasonable warning, or people will not count on having access.

You'll also want to allow some time so your operations staff can train on the live system. Live training is very valuable—and also extends the system testing discussed in earlier chapters.

Employee User Manuals

This last and important section discusses a point you may not have considered up until now. While your employees have hopefully received general training on how the Internet can be used for their jobs, they don't have any specific information on using the service in your company. These questions belong in a User Guide or manual that you provide.

We haven't mentioned it as a specific task until now because it usually depends highly on developing operations procedures—which we have just finished covering. We also believe that these procedures don't usually exist as stand-alone, but should be integrated into existing PC procedures. Further, we realize that if procedures don't already exist, they well may not be written for this in particular.

If you haven't documented PC procedures to date, it's time to rethink your approach. Internet applications often rely on configuration information that cannot be inferred by experienced users (as is true with many stand-alone applications). Furthermore, inexperienced users can literally bring down part of your network or system by using information they guess! We recommend you have a one- or two-page startup sheet so that users who want to get their applications going without waiting for help can do so. Such a startup sheet should include:

▶ Supported software sources
▶ IP address assignment
▶ standard install directories
▶ E-mail account conventions
▶ Where to get help

Once users are bootstrapped, you can point them toward more complete information kept on your internal Web. This makes it far easier to keep help information updated, and gives your users online experience.

References

See the Chapter 2 section for a list of training-related references.

CHAPTER 14

Market Your Presence

I f you've promoted yourself with magazines, newspapers, or broadcast, you realize what a unique culture and language they pose. You need to understand them at technical levels—to understand the time constraints, legal issues, resolution, compatibility issues, and so on. You need to understand the business issues: how deals are made. And you need to understand the marketing issues: who is out there at what times, and how to reach them.

Move over radio, TV, and print: The Internet is the new medium. And instead of limited interactivity (like radio call-ins), it allows full activity. Include the fact that standards, scope, and market are all rapidly changing, and you'll appreciate why marketing deserves its own chapter.

Motivation

With literally hundreds of Web sites coming online each week, your company must be concerned about cutting through the clutter and making sure that your Internet presence receives the exposure necessary to ensure a successful launch.

At the risk of overusing a cliché, just building it doesn't ensure people will come. If nobody knows your site exists, no one will use it. If you look at the tremendous amount of information on the Web, it is almost like several libraries full of data; and where would someone be without the card catalog or the index to help them find the information they want? They would be lost, or frustrated, and give up.

In business, lost leads mean lost sales.

Exacerbating the problem is the Web's phenomenal growth. As of mid-1996 there were more Web pages (30 million plus) than Web users (20 million plus), according to various estimates. And the trend of Web growth shows no sign of abating, so the clutter will be getting thicker. You simply must let people know the site is there and what they can do with it in order to attract users, viewers, and customers.

There are many examples of Web sites that have been designed well, promoted well, and therefore successful in terms of generating interest and traffic. An example is PointCast (www.pointcast.com). PointCast (see Figure 14.1) is a combination screen saver, Web browser, and personalized news service that hit the Internet early in 1996. It drew millions of users, heavy media attention, and extensive advertising support.

The site is unique in its combination of services and cutting-edge technology. PointCast also works very well, is simple to install, and it's free. When the product was released, it received widespread attention from the traditional media as well as Internet-related publications. And the resulting hype helped trigger an onrush of customers.

What does the success of PointCast have to do with your site? Use the following as a litmus test for your site and see if it passes. If so, the chances that your site can cut through the clutter will be enhanced.

Web site success factors include:

- ► Not only new but different
- ► Interesting content
- ► Offers a wide range of services
- ► Can appeal to narrow bands of users with specific services or products
- ► Offers a new concept, such as personalized service in your particular field
- ► Heavily promoted in advance through conventional media and your company's existing marketing efforts
- ► Able to meet the demand for access at its unveiling
- ► Fast
- ► Reliable

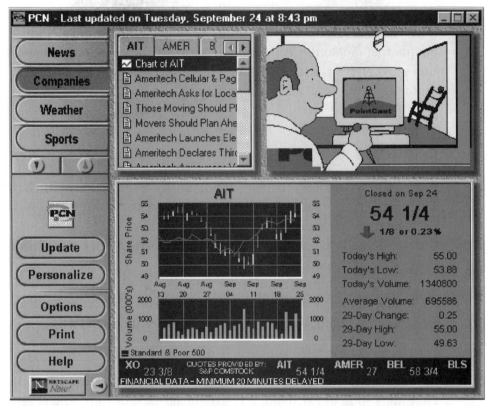

FIGURE 14.1   PointCast offers personalized news and information to millions of people over the Internet. It is a free, advertising-supported service.

► Easy to use
► Constantly updated with valuable information, new products, or new special features
► Encourages interaction with users

The importance of the marketing step may tend to be very obvious to people who are familiar with ways of promoting services over the Internet. But by making this part of the plan we are creating one important effect: synchronization.

To get to this point you may have had several tasks executed in parallel, each one of varying lengths. To move forward, you want to be careful not to advertise before you are ready. It's like putting an ad in the paper stating that your restaurant is open before the tables and chairs arrive. At the same time you don't want to wait too long. In some organizations the technical people that create the Web don't give the sales or marketers a good indication of when it's ready. This step will help coordinate all the efforts exerted up to this point with all the benefits of being on the Net.

Dependencies

Before you go to market, most—if not all—of your Web site has to be ready. There are some capabilities that might not be known until the last minute, but you certainly want to make sure the names you advertise are the ones that are actually being used. Your Project Team simply must have most of the preliminary work done at this point.

All other applications of your Internet project should be operable as well, such as an Internet connection of some kind, individual or e-mail gateways, and an operable Web server for design, beta testing, and experimentation.

But planning for marketing your presence should have begun as soon as the basic concept was in place. Your Project Team should be working with your marketing department, advertising agency, or individuals responsible for publicity so that items with long lead times (business cards, brochures, traditional advertising) can include your new Web and e-mail addresses.

You had better make sure your domain name and what your Web site can do are ready when the long lead items are ready and your customers as well as the public become aware of what you are doing.

In terms of waiting for this step to be done, the only task that depends on marketing has to do with getting people on your site and actually using it. The next steps really depend upon this being done; otherwise people will not know about it, let alone use it and provide feedback for measuring its success—or failure.

Goal

There is little in the way of a single, identifiable output from this task. In fact, it is the generation of many scattered references to your site. You can measure the success of this step not by the tight organization or system that results, but rather the wide dispersion of news, publicity, and information about your site and the amount of response.

We are going to list later myriad ways of marketing, and your goal should be to market yourself in as many ways as you reasonably can.

People

The persons responsible for marketing at your company should have been involved in the project from the start. If not, then you need to get them involved immediately. You should be aware, however, that the paradigms and methods that traditionally apply to advertising and marketing don't necessarily apply to the Internet and the Web. Therefore, two distinct sets of skills and orientation are needed.

The goal of the people who are well versed in the traditional forms of marketing is to make sure that references to the Web site and Internet presence are included in all traditional media. You also want people who know how to market in cyberspace.

They must understand the Internet directories, the Web presence, and how people use both. They must know how to utilize search engines in order to increase the likelihood that people looking for products or services offered by your company will in fact find your firm. They must understand the relationship between the directories and the Web. They must know how to go about securing advertising or *hot links* on other people's Web sites. Further, they must understand Netiquette and where not to market your site.

They also will be aware of how to help your company market your presence internally through every day interactions, from phone calls to letters and faxes, with existing customers, prospects, and corporate peers.

The second set of skills is more difficult to find these days, and if this ability is not available in-house your team needs to look for external resources. Possible sources include advertising agencies, consultants, and Web site creation firms.

If you must go outside, be sure you get and verify references for anyone who is willing to perform these kinds of services. Find out what other companies they have advertised, how they did so, and search for that company on the Web. You should make sure their clients are as easy to find as you want your company to be.

(The case studies included with this book also offer insight and tips about marketing your products and services. See in particular The Maloff Company, TriNet Services, and Allen Marketing Group.)

Location

Planning for this stage of your project should take place where the people tasked with this assignment are located. Of course, your Project Team needs to be in close communication so that marketing and implementation plans are coordinated.

The planning can be done anywhere, since you are communicating the results of the project and aren't working on the physical output that might be linked to a specific location.

However, if your company has numerous locations or has close affiliation with distributors and agents, your team probably will be dealing with local marketers who know how to target your customers and what sales tactics work best in their respective areas. These people need to be included in the information loop.

Resources

Getting the word out doesn't take much more than a pen and a terminal with which to access the Web. The primary need is knowledge of the Internet and the Web. Given that the goal is to disseminate information, the tools for doing so will be the written letter, the telephone, the press release, e-mail, and access to some of the online Web sites. A little legwork will also prove useful; you may find some travel for face-to-face meetings unavoidable.

Duration

With a little planning early in the project, there is probably no more than five days' worth of effort. The key is making sure that those long lead-time items were started in advance. These are not five consecutive days—phone tag and people's busy schedules will drag this out considerably. Otherwise you can create entries on Web directories, and send e-mail to sites that may want to reference you, in a matter of hours.

However, the advertising and promotion efforts should closely track with the project. As your Internet and Web plans evolve, so should the marketing plans.

Security

Marketing plans are often closely guarded secrets. If your competitors know your plans in advance, they can probe their weaknesses, mount a defensive response earlier, or simply *borrow* from them. You will definitely want to guard your plans until they are implemented. Those with prior experience will have to communicate to the technical folks how information releases are to be timed, and why.

Issues

We divide the marketing discussion into those issues around existing marketing media and techniques, and those that are unique to the Web.

Traditional Marketing Techniques

A friend of the authors once said that he realized the Internet and Web had reached the mainstream when he saw a Web address on a perfume company's billboard that was placed in the New York subway system.

We assume you are already familiar with the traditional means of marketing your company. The challenge is how to integrate your Web site and Internet connection into your standard marketing, publicity, and advertising.

Many companies include their home page URL in print and electronic ads. From that basic beginning they make available individual e-mail addresses and other online capabilities your company may offer. This consumes less space and also protects you against reprinting charges as names and details change.

We also suggest that the Web and Internet provide your company with opportunities to reach new customers, to expand your market share, and to permit your company to sell products globally. Therefore you might want to consider launching an integrated marketing campaign that focuses on your strategy. Following are some points for that strategy.

Media Announcements

As the Internet and Web have exploded in growth, so has the interest of the media. If your company has a good story to tell, the media will want to hear about it.

Especially interested are the various electronic services that focus on the Internet and the Web. These include:

▶ The Computer Network (www.cnet.com)
▶ Individual (www.individual.com)
▶ Cowles Media Group (www.simbanet,com)
▶ *Inter@ctive Week* (www.interactive-week.com)
▶ Infoseek (www.infoseek.com)
▶ Ziff-Davis Net (www.zdnet.com or www.anchordesk.com)

Many newspapers, television stations, and magazines now have reporters and editors scouring the Internet and the Web for story ideas. The people responsible for promoting your site should be sure to contact local as well as national media.

Magazines that focus on the Internet, the Web, and computers are obvious choices. Business-related magazines and newspapers also are keenly interested in new products, new methods, and novel approaches to online commerce. Many of the niche publications, which cover specific segments of industry, also are interested in news about your company.

Your marketing team should have a list of media outlets to approach, and then brief each in detail on specifics of your Web site, your products, and your goals. Press packets should include your URL, your e-mail address, and an explanation of how your site works and why it is unique or why you feel the site is deserving of attention. Screen shots of your Web site would be helpful.

Be sure at least one person is designated as the point of contact to respond to press queries. Obviously this person needs to understand all aspects of your project, and be able to explain clearly and succinctly the salient points.

Various services also will post news releases about your firm electronically or via fax—for a fee.

Existing Customers

If your Internet and Web project will have any impact on your existing customers, then you should notify them immediately. This can be done conventionally, of course, and provides a great opportunity to brief them about how the project might help your company meet their needs.

For example, if you are publishing a catalog on the Web that will enable your customers to order directly from you online, explain to them how the process will work.

An adequate explanation of your project will include details about how this new service affects your relationship, particularly if it is designed to lower costs, increase responsiveness, and improve customer relations.

We encourage you to include some of your existing customers among your beta users as you try to work the bugs out of your system. Ask them for feedback and suggestions about what works and what doesn't. This will help you be better prepared when the electronic doors open to your new service, and your clients will be less likely to be offended, caught unawares, or irritated if a promised service doesn't perform as expected.

Mining your existing client base is the least costly way to improve your bottom line. The fact that you have embraced a new technology also may impress your clients, particularly if they have been asking for the services you now can provide.

Normal Channels

Here is a short laundry list of places to list your electronic contact information; please add to it as appropriate.

► E-mail and Web addresses on all corporate letterhead
► E-mail and Web addresses on all business cards and catalogues
► E-mail and Web addresses on your annual reports, press releases, and product literature
► References to your Web site and e-mail gateway on voice mail or answering services

▶ Mention of your Web site and e-mail access on all marketing give-aways, from hats to T-shirts and pencils

▶ References to your Web site and e-mail in all conventional advertising, from newspapers to TV and radio spots to billboards

Internet–Specific Marketing

There are several ways to market your organization that the Internet enables, because of the interactive nature and multimedia support. Some of them are listed in the following sections.

Web Directories

For electronic marketing, your Project Team or designated individuals should start by registering your site with the various Web directories and search engines.

If no one on your team is knowledgeable about how to do this, it might be wise to retain a consultant or Web creation firm that is. For a modest fee, they will find sites appropriate for your business and post the appropriate news or information to those sites.

We suggest that you visit the home page of your Internet service provider or your browser provider, and look for a list of the directories. Each should be contacted via phone or e-mail and asked if you can add your Web site to their list, or asked for a pointer from their sites to yours. Some directories locate in catalog sites on their own. An example is Web Crawler, which crawls the Internet in search of information, as the name applies. They are also generically referred to as *spiders*, pun intended.

However, you should never assume that all the various Web search engines will find your site the day after it goes online. Each follows different schedules, and each has different capabilities. Contacting each is the best way to ensure getting the exposure and publicity you want (see Figure 14.2).

Some of the top search engines include:

▶ AltaVista (http:www.altavista.digital.com)
▶ Web Crawler (http:Webcrawler.com)
▶ Lycos (http:www.lycos.com)
▶ C/Net (http:www.search.com)
▶ Yahoo (http://www.yahoo.com)

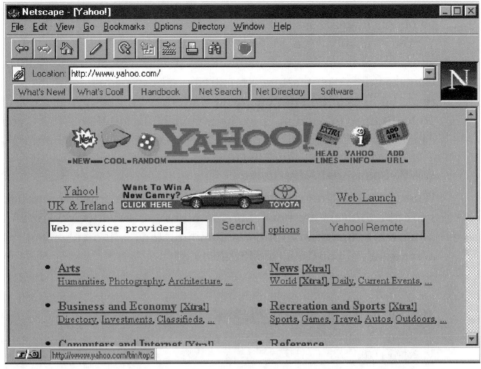

FIGURE 14.2 Yahoo has a wide variety of categories listed in its directory. As users visit each category they can delve deeper into more specific topics.

▶ Netlocator (http://nln.com)
▶ InfoSeek (http://guide.infoseek.com)
▶ Excite (http://www.excite.com)
▶ Hotbot (http://www.hotbot.com)

Directed Cross-Marketing

Internet directories are not the only sources of hyperlinks out there. Every organization that has a Web site has them as well, and most of them value keeping a set of links to other sites of interest. If you have, for example, important information or guidance for selecting the best cheese to go with wines, then Ernest and Julio Gallo may be interested in having a link to you from their site. You may have something of interest to say to their visitors and customers.

Again, this is where a consultant or a Web site creation company might be of considerable assistance.

You probably want to send e-mail to the Web masters at other related sites and let them know about your site. We also recommend that you be extremely brief. Web masters are extremely busy people, and if they have to read 100 lines to find out what you want they may skip your message. Write 10 to 20 lines maximum, give them your URL, tell them where you are located and why your site is unique or of interest. Let them go from there.

WWW-Sponsored Advertising

Where a polite letter fails, cash often succeeds. A growing number of Web sites free to users are now charging money to advertisers. For a rate from hundreds to many thousands each month, they will display your logo with a hyperlink to your site (see Figure 14.3).

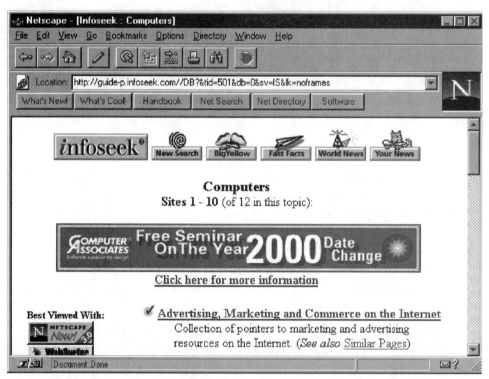

FIGURE 14.3   Infoseek sells advertising on its home page, and these advertising banners change as site visitors seek information on the Web.

As of this writing, there are very popular Web directories that will for a fee let you put your logo on their site hyperlinked to your own site. In some cases the logo always appears in a predetermined place. In others it appears only if people search for information or topics related to your site.

The latter approach is more targeted and perhaps less costly, but the former approach may give you statistics on what kind of searches or what people were looking for when they came to your site.

These so-called banner ads are a growing means of attracting interest and business on the Internet and the Web. The market for this kind of advertising is growing, with some studies forecasting between $2 billion and $5 billion by the year 2000, and from $200 million to $300 million in 1996. Rates vary widely, as do how firms are charged (per month, per week, or per *hit* or visit).

Among the more popular sites for advertisers are the search engine and electronic media sites mentioned earlier in this chapter.

E-Mail Signature Files

Almost every major e-mail client will allow you to attach a "signature" of your choice (see Figure 14.4). This signature can be automatically attached to every piece of e-mail you and your employees send. Although they are all text, they can include a great deal of information that can be beneficial to your firm.

These signatures should include phone, e-mail, fax number, a memorable quote, and even a text-based rendition of your corporate logo. You should be sure to encourage your employees to add the URL for your company. Some e-mail clients embedded in browsers can automatically create hyperlinks from these references.

```
Rick R. Smith,

President,                                President,
Internet Business Development, Inc.       Internet Association of the
                                          Carolinas
4917 Royal Troon Drive                    160 Wind Chime Court Suite B
Raleigh, N.C. 27604                       Raleigh, N.C. 27615-6459
(919) 250-0090                            (919) 846-7858
Fax: (919) 250-0741                       http://www.iac.org/iac
```

FIGURE 14.4 Eudora's mail program allows its users to write a *signature* that can be automatically attached to every piece of e-mail sent.

Newsgroups and Mailing Lists

If you have a product or a service, chances are there is a mailing list devoted to discussing it, or something related to it (see Figure 14.5). There may be several. Many people form strong impressions about companies both from the contributions of company employees and the word-of-mouth advertising or comments by other users. It can be vital that you maintain your reputation through these forums. Many niche networking companies make or break their reputations on these lists. One good spokesperson giving your company's perspective on issues in a professional, timely fashion leaves a strong, positive impression on the Internet's psyche.

You can also sponsor some mailing lists on the Internet. Many well-respected individuals spend large portions of their time compiling information for distribution via e-mail, or moderating discussion groups. A growing number will accept a token stipend in exchange for prominent mention of your business. If there is a discussion list or newsgroup related to your business, you may be able to offer sponsorship. Beware that sponsorship is not always appropriate: Some lists pride themselves on vendor neutrality.

Likewise, your company may want to host a discussion group or mailing list on a particular topic. But you should be prepared for frank discussions. The customers don't always have nice things to say about the sponsors, and their candid remarks can be very helpful. If such a group is started, you also should insist that your company respond to questions or issues that are poised there. Silence can be interpreted as a noncaring atti-

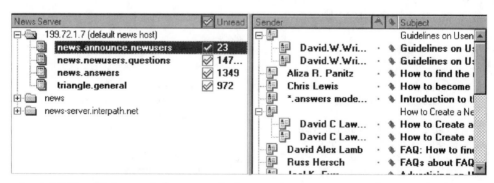

FIGURE 14.5   Netscape's browser helps sorts newsgroups into various categories. As of summer 1996 there were more than 16,000 newsgroups, and hundreds more are created each week.

tude on the part of your corporate management, or acknowledgment that the posted criticisms are valid.

Other Innovative Approaches

There are a growing number of interactive protocols on the Internet, such as messaging, chat reflectors, video and videoconference reflectors, audio, white boards, and games. If it is appropriate, your company could operate an interactive system for topics of interest. This can project a very positive image to the Web, because you are giving people a forum to express themselves.

Some pioneers have turned interactive Web technologies into engaging user games. While perhaps the gaming value is low, they create habitual users to whom new marketing information can be sent. Even without interactivity, simple contests that solicit e-mail with answers to questions they can extract from your Web pages incites them to read, and the incremental game administration costs are minimal.

If your company wants to gain information about visitors to your Web site, offering them some sort of incentive or reward for doing so is helpful. Many sites offer premiums, ranging from modems to free software, if Web site visitors will fill out a registration form. Ongoing games or contests help keep the Web site content fresh.

Registration of users and tracking of their activities while on your site also gives you statistical information about how your message is being perceived and whether the demographics your company has targeted are being reached.

Also, don't be afraid to use the full multimedia breadth of the Internet. You may never have produced an audio or video clip because broadcast was too expensive. The Web can make that available at much lower cost. The Web is a great trial ground for experimentation.

Observing Netiquette

No discussion of Web-based marketing would be complete without mention of Netiquette, or rules of etiquette regarding conduct on the Internet and the Web. On the good side, they are not nearly as stringent as they used to be, when all forms of advertising and self-promotion were criticized. This dates primarily to the Internet's beginnings as a research tool. Now that it is a commercial entity, users are learning to deal with the corporate infiltration. On the downside, they have left legacy areas and users that are still sacrosanct, and certain violations will result in *flame wars,* with irritated Internet users flooding your company with negative responses.

Among the practices that should still be avoided are:

▶ Blatant advertising that is intrusive
▶ Uninvited intrusion by a company representative in discussions on newsgroups
▶ Posting of *junk* e-mail to uninterested users, or to numerous related newsgroups (*spamming*)
▶ Posting of press releases about your company and/or products on a listserv or a newsgroup
▶ Outright solicitation of business within particular lists or newsgroups
▶ Use of profanity (or any unprofessional approach)
▶ Making insulting or disparaging remarks (*flaming*)
▶ Not replying to e-mail sent to your company
▶ Allowing out-of-date links to remain on your site
▶ Not being clear, concise, and discreet in your postings

You should always encourage people who represent your company on these lists or newsgroups to only monitor them passively for many weeks before saying anything. That way they can learn how the groups and lists function from the tone and possible flaming of other posters. For more information about Internet Netiquette, visit the newsgroup news.announce. newusers and news.answers.

References

Marketing on the Internet is a popular subject for periodicals; many online articles and professional magazines provide thorough, current suggestions. There are also numerous books available on the topic, including *Marketing on the Internet* by Ellsworth and Ellsworth, published by John Wiley & Sons. Check with your Internet service provider for additional Netiquette guidelines.

CHAPTER 15

Review Performance

So much of this plan has been about communication: sharing vision, goals, plans, and ideas. The final opportunity for doing that before planning your next step onto the Internet is in evaluating your success. We want you to discuss your expectations up front as a team, then again with benefit of hindsight at this stage. Many people discover that the Internet regularly exceeds all expectations, and we believe following this plan will help you do the same.

Motivation

If you had a hesitation when you embarked on your strategy, it centered around the questions of:

▶ What's the company's return on investment?
▶ For all the effort and money that have been invested, what does it mean to the company's bottom line?

Now that your Web site is operational and the Internet connection is working, you can begin to determine the answers to those questions and thus justify whether this project was worthwhile.

Some companies discover answers quickly. They may find that their goals were unrealistic, or that their Web server was inadequate to handle demand, or that expected cost savings were not as much as expected. Each company will have a different set of parameters by which to measure success or failure.

It is important that your company develop a checklist and that the Project Team compiles statistics that can be tracked so that any review is based on fact, not on hunches.

For example, Southern Shores Realty in the tourist Mecca of North Carolina's Outer Banks (see Figure 15.1) had numerous objectives for its plan when it chose to publish its extensive catalog of rental properties on the Web. The firm's team, led by David Watson, established specific and measurable goals. Among them were:

FIGURE **15.1**   Southern Shores Realty is bringing new customers to the Outer Banks of North Carolina through its online catalog Web site.

- Reach new customers without having to print and mail costly, traditional catalogs full of color images
- Stay in touch with existing customers electronically rather than through catalogs and 800 phone services
- Publish new listings immediately rather than waiting for the next catalog printing
- Permit interested renters to get more information about specific properties
- Take reservations electronically
- Respond to competitive pressure created by other Realtors going online

Southern Shores is still on the Web and contemplating expanding its project due to the measurable success of its first phase.

Other case studies cited in this book (First Union, Forté, PC Travel, Indelible Blue) also have precise ways of measuring their success—or failure—in meeting goals. Each had a clear set of objectives, and each is selling some sort of service through its respective Web and Internet connection. The way your company measures success will be determined by the strategic plan's objectives you and your Project Team agreed upon.

Another example of a company that was readily able to measure success was Amazon Books (see Figure 15.2) of Seattle, WA. The objective was simple: Sell books globally through the Internet and its extensive Web catalog of one million titles. Sales are made through encrypted charge-card software.

Shortly after the site debuted (and helped further by extensive publicity from such media as *The Wall Street Journal*), Amazon realized it had succeeded in accomplishing several goals:

- An electronic distribution channel was opened
- New customers could be reached globally, virtually instantaneously
- Customers could get service faster than through many traditional stores
- Books could be sold and orders fulfilled around the clock
- Catalogs didn't have to be mailed to all its customers, thus eliminating any substantial printing, handling, and postage costs
- Charge-card orders were verified almost instantly, meaning the company got its money faster
- Fewer collection problems would occur, since there were no personal checks that might bounce

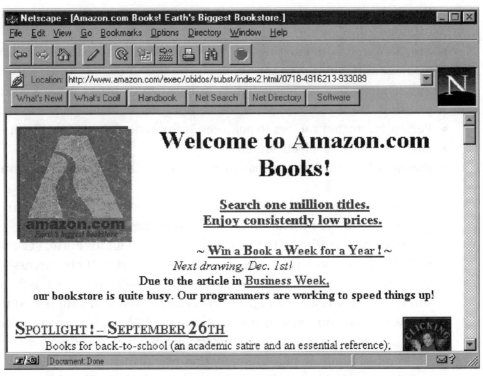

FIGURE 15.2   Amazon Books gives customers access to its catalog 24 hours a day, every day—and doesn't have to print then distribute a conventional catalog.

▶ Special offerings and sales could be handled via the Web site rather than publishing special brochures or notices

▶ By capturing information about visitors to the site, who filled out questionnaires, the company was able to build a database of new prospects

Another sign of success on your business might be the impact of losing access to your site or to the Internet. When hurricane Fran devastated parts of North Carolina in the summer of 1996, one corporate executive was denied access to the Internet for three days. "Without the Internet, I'm out of business," he said.

We also want to stress that for the duration of this project, many of your employees probably put in long hours and made extra efforts to get you online. This is an opportunity to recognize their efforts in pay incentives, perks, or corporate recognition programs.

Dependencies

Several factors will determine how you review the performance of your connection and Web site. Not only does your company have to reach the operational phase in the system's life cycle, but it also needs to allow some time to pass before any meaningful assessments could be made. In fact, since change happens on such a short time scale on the Internet (years are compared to dog years), we caution that you average your results over at least a year in order to get meaningful numbers. However, even with a month or two under your belt, you can begin to notice meaningful trends.

Changes in various applications may force you to alter your site in order to meet customers' expectations. Improvements in technology may require that your Internet connection or Web server be upgraded. An increase in demand may necessitate more bandwidth. And competitive pressures might increase, or force your company on a different tack.

Just as with any other part of your business, your connection to the Internet, your objectives, and your applications are going to go through continual change as long as the company doors are open. And measuring performance will steer your future direction. You will need to know what aspects to scale up and what aspects to scale back. Just because the PERT chart cited at the book's beginning doesn't extend off the right side of the page to cover performance measurement, don't forget to do this important step.

How your company measures performance will be dictated largely by the requirements for the project. Ask yourself the following questions:

▶ What were the goals?
▶ What were the expectations?
▶ What products and services did your company want to offer?
▶ Did unanticipated problems occur?
▶ If so, how were those handled?
▶ What costs did you hope to reduce?
▶ Did other costs increase unexpectedly?
▶ What were the sales objectives?

- ▶ Were those goals realistic?
- ▶ Did you intend to reduce distribution costs?
- ▶ Were those expectations reasonable?
- ▶ Did you intend to reduce travel expenses for corporate staff?
- ▶ Did that in fact occur?
- ▶ Are Web and Internet communications reducing traditional communications costs, such as long distance and fax?
- ▶ Did you intend to improve customer relations?
- ▶ If you did not, what went wrong?
- ▶ How can those errors be corrected?
- ▶ Did your project finish on time and on budget?
- ▶ If not, what went wrong?
- ▶ Are recurring costs within budget?
- ▶ If not, can contracts be renegotiated?
- ▶ Was the budget realistic to begin with?
- ▶ Should the budget be revised for the next stage or budget cycle?
- ▶ Were additional people hired as expected?
- ▶ Conversely, did headcount have to be increased contrary to expectations?
- ▶ Did I learn some things in the process that were valuable?

Goal

The goal of this step in the project is to produce another document or perhaps presenation. It could have components that parallel or are structured like every deliverable created to this point. You are going to take your objective, your requirements, your design, your training plan, your test plans, your system utilization matrix, your cost estimates, and your marketing strategies that were done in the planning phases and you are going to hold them up against empirical data and team feedback.

Company management and the Project Team also may want to review the performance of the team. How well did the members interact and cooperate? Did they stay on task? Each member should be interviewed and asked what worked, what didn't, what could or should have been done differently.

If there are problems with your Internet or Web project, they might be traced to your team and may not have anything to do with the goals, objectives, or technology that were selected.

Given that your project has produced several deliverables to date, the actual performance measurement report could be quite detailed and lengthy. It will be extremely important to create a high-level summary of your project's performance from this report.

For those with existing project tracking tools, the report could include spreadsheets and statistical summaries that track your requirements and goals. This same data can be used to help detect and correct problems, or lead to revisions of sales goals and other items.

People

Think back to Project Team. Either the team conducts the review, or you assemble another cross-functional group composed of representatives from every part of your business. These individuals set out to achieve something by connecting to the Internet, and they are exactly the same individuals who can measure if those goals were realized.

Not only do you want to reestablish the old group, but you also want to include people who have joined since the project began. Look for participation by the external resources you enlisted as well as the additional support individuals (i.e., desktop support, network support, Web development) that were hired to operate your system.

Also, don't forget to include the most important contributing element, which will be your organization's customers or employees. You definitely need to find out how the public received your efforts, and we'll talk about ways to do that shortly.

Location

As with the "Location" phase in the *Requirements* chapter, this step takes place where it is most convenient for the team tasked to measure the results and generate the report. If customers are involved, however, be sure the gathering of data does not cause them any inconvenience.

Specific data can be generated from the Web and Internet hardware itself, assuming your project called for databases to measure sales, monitor e-mail, and record and track information about Web visitors (from simple hits to filling out surveys).

Other measurements, such as satisfaction with the Web server's speed to the Web site's content, will have to be gathered from your customers and end users throughout the organization.

Your team will want to solicit feedback from customers either electronically or by phone, if not in person. The first two are more convenient, and Web or e-mail responses would help your company further measure the effectiveness of the project.

Now that you have an electronic infrastructure, you can look to more efficient ways of gathering information internally as well rather than through pure travel. The team can conduct its survey either through e-mail or through a form on the Web site.

Resources

A great deal of the required resources are already in place. Your operations staff is continually collecting feedback in an informal manner, and they can be invaluable contributors. But to do a more thorough analysis, you could probably benefit from technical auditing utilizing a consultant who can quickly identify the key indicators of your project's performance, and can track down the numbers.

You'll also benefit greatly from simple Web scripts or e-mail-reading applications. (Some of these can be found through shareware that is readily available on the Internet.) These automate the collection and analysis of user feedback.

You will need some word processing and display formatting tools, as well as some part-time documentation assistance.

Duration

Once you've waited long enough to gather meaningful information, you should allow about 15 days for a thorough review. Most of this time will be spent coordinating input from various people across your organization; the actual report preparation should take just a few days.

When your team sets off to assess the impact of the corporate Internet project, they should find a surprising wealth of information. The network applications themselves typically collect more data than people can read. The amount of information from trouble tickets and other experiences of your technical support staff also can grow to fill databases very quickly.

The key time factor is collecting all the information and putting it together in a presentable way. Your team may be able to get all the printouts and files you need in a week's time, but the team should allow members sufficient time to make sense of the data collected, and to consider the data against extenuating circumstances that might have occurred (such as acts of God or failures up the technology chain from your connection that adversely affected you and your customers). Then you must create a report that people will want to read.

Security

If the news is bad, you'll probably want to guard these results from the outside world (and maybe even your boss). On the other hand, if the news is as good as we expect, you'll want to share the results widely within your organization. You may even want to share your Web's popularity with your customers, and possibly with a news release. The media is open for blazing success stories on the Web.

Issues

Having just walked the reader through the process of getting your organization on the Internet, it's only fitting we discuss the special aspects of evaluating its outcome.

Review the Internet Usage Policy

This document was designed to regulate Internet and Web usage by your employees. Are the procedures that were put in place being observed and effective? Your Information Services department or the people directing the Internet project should be keeping logs that show the amount of usage and the destinations being visited by the company users.

If usage exceeds limits, or employees have found ways of evading the controls, then corrective measures should be taken and the usage document should be revised.

Employees who have violated company procedures need to be held accountable if you expect these controls to be observed.

Revisit the Requirements Phase for Your Project

The information that was generated for the matrix we suggested should be checked. Each specific requirement you wanted should be available. But rather than just checking off the box indicating that each function does work, take the matrix a step or two further:

▶ Is each needed service performing as expected?
▶ Is each needed service still relevant?

By this point in the project, your evaluation should ask several questions about the evolution of your service offerings or demands. Among them:

▶ What, if any, additional services are needed?
▶ What do customers want that you aren't providing?
▶ What impact will they have on the infrastructure, from bandwidth to software?
▶ What will the additional services cost?
▶ What specific changes have taken place amongst your competitors that might affect what you are trying to accomplish?
▶ Have your vendors provided adequate service?
▶ Has training of employees been adequate, or is more required?
▶ What new internal needs have arisen that need to be addressed?

Revisit the Design Document

The design phase of the project produced your shopping list and the blueprints to follow for implementation. If you are having difficulties with your project at this point, there may have been a flaw in its design. Even rigorous beta tests don't necessarily find all problems. Just ask Microsoft and Netscape, which keep issuing new versions of their popular Web browsers.

Each step of the design phase may need to be revisited. And the design document itself will become out of date as soon as any modifications are made to your Internet connection and Web site. Did you already deviate in substantial ways? If so, why?

Review the design issues in Chapter 6, and see how or whether they still apply. Does the document still meet the original goals and objectives?

Review Network Design, Client Design, Server Design

The review of the requirements and design documents should help answer many of the questions raised by a review of your bandwidth connection, your software acquisitions, the capacity of your server, and the functionality designed into the Web site. Specific needs or capabilities not being met should be addressed at this point, assuming your company has not already taken corrective measures.

Review Content Services

Are the specifications your Project Team set for Web content being met? Your customers are probably telling you if promised goods, services, and information aren't being posted as promised. What fraction of links are still "under construction"? How many months old is the average document?

This would be a good time to compare your content to that of your competitors. If yours is suffering, take corrective steps. Remember, the Web can't be used to line a birdcage like a day-old newspaper. Unless the information is current, it is no good.

The myriad ways content is provided on the Web also is constantly changing. Your Web master and Project Team should be checking periodically for software updates or new kinds of services that might be appropriate.

Review the Testing and Acceptance Phases

If problems went undetected during these phases, obviously they had an impact on the success or failure of your project. Be sure to ask that the various people involved with the project document unexpected problems or challenges, and then bring these to the attention of the various vendors that were involved in implementing your Internet connection and Web services.

If contract obligations aren't being met, documentation is essential in seeking legal recourse.

If your vendors agreed to provide monthly reports on bandwidth utilization, server hits, and other information, be sure they do so and that the information is filed. This information can be very helpful in determining future changes, expansion needs, technological updates, and/or corrective measures.

Review Your Marketing Program

How effective the marketing plan was for your project could be very subjective. The raw number of stories in the press might look impressive, but if your customers or prospective customers didn't see the publicity then what good was this?

What are more measurable are specific data regarding sales, inquiries, action on your Web site, and feedback from customers, peers, or competitors.

If some of your expectations regarding sales were not met, a review of your marketing efforts is in order. Were the right prospects targeted? Were they likely Internet or Web users? Was the Web site registered with the appropriate lists and search engines to ensure that prospects were likely to find your company?

If you retained an advertising agency or a Web site creation firm, be sure to review their activities.

Corrective steps might be required, from product offerings to price, from Web promotion to a review of customer demographics.

Reviewing Your Training Plans

The answers to a series of questions will tell you whether your training programs were adequate:

▶ How well are employees using the Internet?
▶ Are they comfortable or still struggling?
▶ Are new employees receiving adequate training?
▶ Have your technical people become self-sufficient in network and server administration?

▶ Are the people responsible for Web content maintenance and updates able to do so?

Just as the Internet and Web evolve, so will your training needs. The far-sighted company will be sure its employees stay abreast of the latest technological developments, and this will be especially crucial in the Internet and Web arenas, given the competitive environment and the rapid changes in applications as well as capabilities.

References

The material you need for this step is in your internal usage logs, and in the experiences of your employees. Additionally, consultants and outsource shops should also be invited to participate in this process. They will likely welcome continued involvement as a possible prelude to follow-up work.

CHAPTER 16

Plan Phase II

T he Internet is a moving target. This book didn't describe the entire trip, just the first steps of a very, very long journey. In this final section, we want to help you look ahead to where your system is going, and how your journey may proceed.

Motivation

Congratulations! Your project is online. You now are part of the global Internet. You have earned the right to gather and to share information on the global information infrastructure, with all the privileges and responsibilities that apply. However, your task is far from finished.

As we have stressed throughout the book, the Internet and the Web are as much evolution as they are revolution. Web sites went from static content to dynamic content to animated, multimedia content in the span of less than two years. The Internet backbone bandwidth grows by a factor of 10 every couple of years. The Internet standards groups work continuously and meet three times a year to evolve its capabilities.

Similarly, the number of Internet users continues to grow, demographics change, and usage habits change. An occasional visit to such sites as

CyberAtlas.com and Commerce.Net is called for by the people you want tracking Internet developments (see Figure 16.1).

A wide variety of publications also can help you and your company stay abreast of Internet, Web, and other developments related to internetworking. Among the best are:

WebWeek	*Business Week*	*Information Week*
NetGuide	*Online Access*	*PC Computing*
Internet World	*MacWorld*	*Boardwatch*
Inside the Internet	*Wired*	*Interactive Marketing News*
Inter@active Week	*Network World*	*Internet Business Report*
LAN Times	*Telecommunications*	*Data Communications*
Interactive Age	*Advertising Week*	*Communications Week*

All of these are readily available, and many can be found on the Internet.

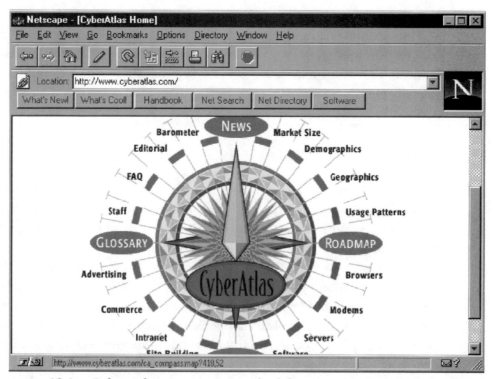

FIGURE **16.1**   CyberAtlas.com is a wonderful site to visit to find the latest news about Internet trends, from usage habits to global growth.

Considered yourself warned: Sitting still on the Internet is like parking your car in the middle of the Washington, DC, Beltway. You can almost guarantee your car will spend some time in the shop.

This chapter isn't laid out like a task, with a finite beginning and end. It also is designed to augment, not mirror, the objects outlined in Chapter 15 for a review of your project's performance. Rather, we do cover some of the issues you need to be aware of as your system grows and the Internet develops. You and your company already have done the most important steps by getting *on* the Internet and getting your feet wet. Now is the time to increase your proficiency and your Internet Quotient (IQ).

Dependencies

Answers to a series of questions will determine whether your project needs to be remodeled or stand pat for a brief period of time. We doubt that the latter will be the case for very long, but if your objectives from the beginning were simple and straightforward, there might not be any need to expand beyond a few desktop connections to the Internet for e-mail and Web access.

We encourage you to revisit the questions raised in Chapter 15. The review suggested there is not a one-time event. It should be done periodically. Used in conjunction with those questions, the information provided in this chapter might be helpful in performing an annual assessment.

Here are some key questions. Perhaps they will trigger more in your mind. If so, add them to the list.

What technological changes have taken place on the Internet that could be of use to your company?

Possible improvements could range from more bandwidth to the desktop, to faster chips for PCs, to faster modems. Your Information Systems people or the systems administrators running the Internet project should be tracking the availability of additional services, such as ADSL, ISDN, ATM, and cable modems. If your company's bandwidth needs are growing, you should get the message from your technical staff.

Similarly, what technological changes have taken place on the Web in terms of applications that could be beneficial?

Possible answers range from improvements in existing applications to entirely new ones. Audio, video, virtual reality, and other multimedia tools are constantly being enhanced. Good Web masters will be tracking those and very likely will be eager to incorporate them into your Web site.

How has the competitive market for your company changed, from both tactical and strategic points of view?

If your competitors weren't online when your project began and have since done so, the market has changed. If you were behind them in terms of online deployment, have they done something to leapfrog back in front of you? What new services or products do they have that you don't? No doubt people at your company are constantly monitoring the marketplace. Keeping an eye on the Internet and the Web should become part of their standard operating procedure.

Given those changes, are alterations in your Internet and Web strategies required? If so, what changes need to be made?

Your competitive analysis could trigger wholesale changes in your strategy. Your catalog may need to be redesigned. You may need to offer encrypted charge-card services that weren't needed earlier. Your original requirements list (see Chapter 5) may have to be rewritten. So be it. After all, Ford did drop the Edsel.

What competitive changes have taken place in the Internet and Web services markets that could impact on your business?

The Internet and Web industries are going through quite a bit of turmoil, with acquisitions and mergers taking place regularly. Some companies simply disappear, having gone out of business with no notice. New companies also are entering the marketplace, such as the Regional Bell Operating Companies, which now offer a full range of Internet access services. All these changes can have a tremendous impact on everything from service levels to prices. Your company may want to shop around for a better contract, or if your service is unsatisfactory there may be another company available that is better suited for your needs.

At this point we suggest you review the terms and conditions of your contract with the Internet and Web providers. Have those services met your requirements?

Did your latest review (as cited in Chapter 15) show similar shortcomings as earlier reviews?

If so, then you have serious problems that may require equally serious remedies. If your service providers aren't delivering as promised, it is time to find new ones. If your technical staff isn't capable of doing the job, personnel changes or additional training are required. If sales aren't meeting goals, you may need to revisit the entire marketing strategy and product offerings.

Were the forecast reductions in costs and improvements in productivity realized? Were the specified objectives met?

The answers to these questions could be as simple as:

Department X is still sending all its packages via overnight courier because its staff says sending information electronically via attachments or through e-mail simply is too difficult to learn.

Department Y is still making all its calls long distance rather than through our computer voice Internet gateway because the staff can't break old habits.

Department Z is still handling hundreds of inbound 800 calls per month from customers, because the customers aren't familiar with how to use the e-mail or Web gateways, or they have never been told.

As a business executive, you know how to respond to each of those answers.

What changes have taken place within the company that might have an impact on the Internet and Web project?

Managers are here today, gone tomorrow. Priorities change. Stock prices fluctuate. Products fail. New ones are needed. All these affect your company's operations across the board. Don't forget that Internet connection and Web site.

Now that the Internet and Web are essential to your business, what is the disaster recovery plan? Has it been altered to reflect the project's growing importance? Are backups in place?

When Hurricane Fran devastated much of Raleigh, NC, in August 1996, a major media outlet's Web server was knocked offline for three days because its one T1 link provided by a local phone company went down. Plans soon were being pursued to set up a server at another location, with multiple links to the outside world to prevent another online disaster. Has your company taken the same precautions, or does disaster loom?

Your technical team has to always assume the worst-case scenario can happen—because it very likely it will.

Given that your company now has a better understanding of the Internet and the Web, are there any pressing corporate needs that could be addressed by these new tools? Are you missing any revenue opportunities or cost savings that weren't identified before your project began?

The more your company works with the Net, the more opportunities may be identified. Later in this chapter we list just a few of the other applications that could help your company in many different areas, from telecommuting to videoconferencing. As more individuals and companies go online globally, your company will face new demands and have new chances to exploit the Internet revolution. But your company must be ready to seize the moments as they occur.

Goal

That's simple: to refine, to improve, to remodel, or to discard the project. Your company saw some advantages in going online, be they competitive or not. Your goals may have been to improve productivity, or to open new markets, or to sell new kinds of products and services. The Internet project needs to evolve for all the reasons you cited in justifying it. If the project has failed, which your in-depth reviews as described in Chapter 15 documented, then the time may have come to pull the plug.

People

If you were satisfied with the work of your Project Team, then many if not all of those team members should be part of the evolutionary process. One of the goals of getting key people involved in this project was to give each a sense of ownership of the process. Why should that be taken away now?

On the other hand, it also would be wise to have your project reviewed and monitored by *outside* sources. This group of people could include peers, customers, and employees who were not directly involved in the project's creation and development. These people can provide a fresh eye and won't be biased about the project's end results. They will spot weaknesses that team members may not. Selecting outside reviewers would be similar to the creation of focus groups to review new brands or products.

This also may be a good time to bring in outside consultants, either the ones retained to help launch your plans or others who might offer a fresh perspective. It is consultants' business to stay abreast of Internet and Web trends. They can offer assessments, critiques, and suggestions about any changes that might be necessary for your company to improve its Internet presence.

Location

Obviously, review and remodeling will take place at your company and at your Web site, whether it is produced internally or not. A full-service

Internet project might allow your employees and customers at other sites to participate in discussion groups, even videoconferences. We encourage you to use the Internet medium so that all involved in the review process become more aware of the Net's possibilities and limitations, as well as the scope of the services your company offers online.

Resources

The primary resources are the people selected to review and to monitor your project as well as Internet and Web developments. But the designation of funds for research and development would be helpful.

The development people will need new Internet and Web tools as they are unveiled. Many are often free during beta testing. However, we caution you not to allow experimentation to take place on your Web server that is used by your customers and/or employees for essential services and information. Rather, a development server should be designated to serve as the prototype center. This will likely need to be linked to the Internet for testing purposes, but access could be restricted only to the developers.

This development server also could serve as a backup, or *mirror*, for your main server. If the primary one goes down, the other could be brought up immediately.

Duration

No time amount can be set, because your Internet and Web projects should be under constant review and undergo constant remodeling. Just as the automobile manufacturers make changes—small or drastic—every year in every model, so should your company when it comes to its online presence. However, the review should be constant and not geared to an arbitrary calendar date.

Security

Apply the same security measures toward your future plans as you learned to apply during Phase I. Decide to what extent the external information is valuable, and protect it accordingly.

Issues

Following are some guidelines for your Phase II work. We hope that by the time this book is in print, these technologies are not too old-fashioned.

Adapting This Book's Project Plan

Managing the life cycle of your Internet connection is in some ways more challenging than the initial build-out. Coordination can be far more complex for a number of reasons:

▶ There are several people representing numerous departments and (perhaps) plant locations already involved.
▶ Your company is now dependent on the Internet project, so you can't afford to have it go down at arbitrary times.
▶ People (staff and customers) want to know more and more when features and capabilities will be available.

A truism of the Web is that once people taste the Web they invariably wonder about new features that they want to try. The phenomenon becomes self-feeding.

Managing your Internet project is therefore more important now than when you started. Communicating requirements, methods, and timetables is a vital organizational behavior. In many ways the Web and Internet enable communication to be improved. Short of circuit-jamming abuse, to limit utilization of the project internally now in any fashion would be taking steps backward for your organization.

We recommend that you lay out your ongoing review strategy in similar fashion to what this book presents. Think about the interdependence of the tasks, structure them to be independent, and flesh out each one in terms of goals, product, people, location, and the other factors we presented as a way of sharing with your company how you will be growing your presence. And share it with them via the medium, either by e-mail or the Web or some means that you already have enabled.

Additional Capabilities

Once your Internet and Web project is online, you and your company are likely to see many other possibilities. It's like buying a car. The first time, you may buy a basic model with few options for many reasons, from financial to skepticism about a new model. Within a few months, you wish you had gotten the sun roof, the CD player with random play, and the leather seats.

Fortunately, unlike with the car, your company can add many, many options to your Internet and Web connection. Bandwidth can be increased for minimal increases in equipment cost (or none at all if you bought routers and CSU/DSUs that can service low as well as high bandwidth). The stringing of cables can add more PCs to your network. And upgrades in memory can increase the power of your servers.

As indicated earlier, new or augmented applications appear for the Web and Internet daily. As your company becomes comfortable with the underlying technology and solves concerns about security, the temptation will be to use the Internet more and to open up your network to more users.

Among the fastest growing improvements to basic Internet strategies are the following:

Intranets

The concept of an *intranet*, where private proprietary networks are converted to (or created with) the TCP/IP protocol, is among the fastest growing segments of the networking industry. It is beyond the scope of this book to talk about intranets, but there are a growing number of books and periodicals that address the issue.

Intranets could help move your company toward the promise of a *paperless office,* as more and more corporate and customer communications take place electronically. However, a headache will be: If your company also has a gateway to the full Internet, which employees get access and which ones won't?

Also, if your company sets up an extensive intranet that is closed to outside use, you may need to acquire a search engine so that employees can find information faster and more efficiently.

Electronic Data Interchange

Many companies use proprietary networks for *electronic data interchange* (EDI), and this information is sensitive, ranging from product orders to financial transactions. The Internet, or an intranet, can be tailored to fit EDI needs with the appropriate authentication, encryption, and security measures.

Virtual Private Networks

Another fast-growing application is a Virtual Private Network, where Internet services provided by other companies are segmented for use by you and your clients. (For example, more and more companies are contracting with Internet service providers for network access, customized Web browsers, order fulfillment, and help desk support that can be used only by their customers.)

Videoconferencing

Videophones are not new, the Picturephone having been introduced by AT&T at the 1964 World's Fair. Three decades later, the time is rapidly approaching for video at the desktop. Videoconferencing over the Internet also is likely to grow as the equipment and the Internet itself become more reliable.

Voice Over the Internet

The appeal of Internet telephony is growing, too. More businesses and individuals are choosing to acquire software that allows them to place voice calls over the Internet through their PCs (or in some cases, regular phones). By doing so, long-distance costs are lowered—or even eliminated.

Real-Time Inventory Control

An increasing number of companies are using the Internet and the Web to link their databases in real time. FedEx and United Parcel Service (see Figures 16.2 and 16.3) are among the leaders. Fierce competitors, both allow their customers to log in electronically and track their packages.

This kind of service allows customers, vendors, dealers, and corporate employees to log in to the company's Web site for a number of reasons as well:

- ► Track inventory
- ► Place or cancel orders
- ► Check on billing
- ► Check on delivery dates
- ► Pay bills electronically
- ► Monitor progress of various projects

These services obviously require substantial programming, secure links to proprietary data, and high-speed connections. But they certainly are doable.

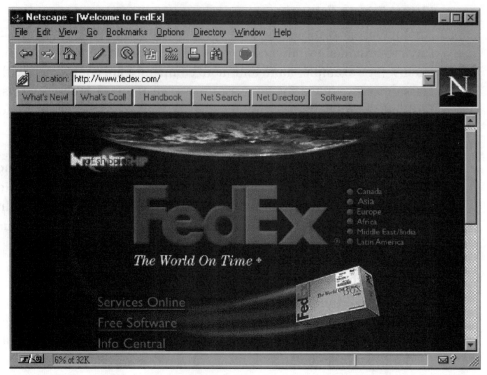

FIGURE 16.2   FedEx uses its Internet and Web project to provide real-time package tracking.

Groupware

Other applications include *groupware* software packages, such as Lotus Notes, which keep all members of a working group informed of developments or changes as they are made by individuals. Microsoft also has a whiteboard application that allows users to simultaneously manipulate documents.

These tools can be shared over the Internet, potentially improving productivity and communications, and reducing travel costs, long-distance costs, even fax and overnight courier expenses.

Remote Access

Your firm also may want to consider remote access by executives or corporate staff (such as sales representatives) who can dial in to your corporate network or Web site from remote locations. This helps create virtual offices and reduces the need for phone tag, voice mail, and paging.

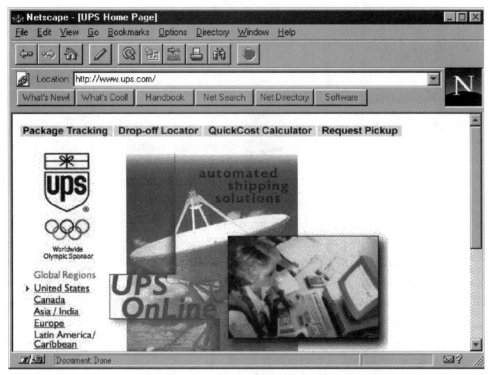

FIGURE 16.3 Not to be outdone by FedEx, United Parcel Service also allows customers to track packages via the Internet and Web.

Telecommuting

As the costs of office space increase and employees seek to spend more time at home with their families, more and more companies are permitting their employees to work from home with their PCs, or *telecommute.* Your Internet and Web project could be ideal for opening the door for this application by your company.

According to the U.S. Department of Labor, there will be 15 million *telecommuters* by the year 2002. That's roughly double the number of 1996. Link Research forecasts that there will be nearly 12 million by 1998.

CD-ROM/Web Links

A number of different companies have unveiled plans to integrate CD-ROMs with Web sites, the idea being that users don't necessarily have to have high bandwidth connections to enjoy multimedia applications. These might be used for games and educational projects as well as high-end catalogs.

Managing the Additions

It would be a mistake to simply assume new tools and capabilities can be added to your Internet and Web project without first seriously studying them. Your technical and manpower requirements have to be revisited, with the latter being especially true if you are suffering from high turnover in your Information Services department.

Videoconferencing and high-end servers to support multimedia Web applications simply can't be added to the demand on a 56 Kbps connection. Frame relay may be an option, allowing incremental increases in bandwidth. But if your company has an ISDN connection and wants to move to a dedicated circuit, chances are equipment such as Terminal Adapters will have to be replaced by routers and CSU/DSUs.

Asking for more multimedia applications also will require more maintenance from your technical team. Do they have the experience? Do they need to be trained? Do they have the time?

The needs of your customers also have to be considered. If your Web presence is constantly changing, with features added or removed, your visitors and buyers may feel uncomfortable or get confused and be unable to use the new tools being offered. Your company should be sure to keep the customers informed of changes, solicit their feedback, and react to their needs.

References

Where will the references be that take you into the next evolution? We're not sure. Keep looking for new books, supplemented with articles for updates on current information. And, of course, you'll rely increasingly on the information at your fingertips on the Internet.

Glossary
of Internet and
Telecommunications
Terms

Applets Small programs incorporated into Web page for various special visual and aural effects.

ARPANET The Department of Defense's Advanced Research projects Agency Network developed the packet-switching network in the early 1970s through the efforts of BBN (Bolt, Beranek and Newman, now a major Internet service provider) with funding from ARPA (and later DARPA). A primary need was to connect different types of mainframe computers using a common set of communications protocols (TCP/IP) in the event of a nuclear war. The ARPANET evolved into the Internet, and the term ARPANET was retired in 1990. The National Science Foundation supplanted ARPA when the need arose to connect the various Supercomputing Centers across the United States with high-speed connectivity.

ATM Asynchronous Transfer Mode, which is a high-bandwidth, low-delay switching and multiplexing technique used to transfer voice, video, images, and character-based data in small, fixed-size cells.

AUP Acceptable Use Policy. This formally was required by the National Science Foundation as a commitment from its users not to transmit what it considered unacceptable traffic across the NSF net (now the Internet). Many Internet service providers still require customers to adhere to AUPs. Some ISPs still have AUPs; these should be reviewed by your legal department.

BBS   Electronic Bulletin Board Systems, typically electronic services designed to meet the needs of people with shared interests or who want easy access to shareware and general news and information.

Cable Modems   Devices currently under development that will deliver data at very high speeds over cable networks to PCs in the home.

CIDR   Classless interdomain routing (pronounced like cider). Although an obscure term, it is important. As Internet usage grows, the number of available unique addresses is threatened. Customers should ask their ISPs who *owns* their addresses. CIDR refers to how ISPs assign and maintain their blocks of Internet Protocol (IP) addresses. This technique is supported by BGP-4 (Border Gateway Protocol) and is based on route aggregation. Allows routers to group routes together in order to cut down on the quantity of routing information carried by core routers. With CIDR, several IP networks are combined, from the point of view of networks outside the group, into a single, larger entity.

CPE   Customer Premise Equipment refers to telecommunications devices and wiring that is located at the user's location.

CSU   Channel Service Unit, which is a digital interface device that connects a customer's equipment to the local digital telephone unit. A CSU/DSU is required at either end of a leased-line connection from a customer's site to the ISP's POP to pass TCP/IP traffic.

DNS   Domain Name System. In the Internet this refers to a portion of a name hierarchy tree. DNS allows the location of IP addresses corresponding to named computers and domains. A DNS name consists of information separated by dots, such as widgets.com (Widgets and Com represent separate domains). In order for a company to have a corporate *address* on the Internet it must provide its own primary DNS or seek it from another company.

DSU   Data Service Unit. A device used in digital transmission from connecting DTE (data terminal equipment), such as a router, to DCE (data communications equipment), such as a modem. Leased-line connections to the Internet require a CSU/DSU at each end of the link from the customer to the ISP's local POP.

E-Mail   Short for electronic mail. Internet users send e-mail over the network to specific addresses, such as: rrsmith@interpath.com. rrsmith stands for the person's name; the @ indicates rrsmith's address is *at* or accessed through the following network, in this case an Internet service provider. E-mail addressing schemes vary but follow the same basic format.

FAQs   Frequently Asked Questions lists. This data, which can be made available on Web pages, gopher sites, or FTP sites, can help information providers deal with questions and problems without having to offer live help desk support at all times.

Forms   An HTML technique of displaying fill-in-the-blank boxes to gather information, as well as check boxes, buttons, and other input types that are used to gather information from the user.

Frame Relay   A protocol used across the interface between user devices (for example, hosts and routers) and network equipment (such as switching nodes). This form of packet switching employs a shared network. Companies may find this a more cost-effective means of using the Internet rather than point-to-point leased lines and dedicated router ports. Frame relay is more efficient than X.25, an older form of packet transfers and the protocol for which frame relay is generally considered a replacement.

Frames   An HTML technique of displaying independent multiple areas within a Web page. Each area, or frame, can be scrollable or remain static on the page, independent of the other frames.

FTP   File Transfer Protocol. An IP application that permits the transferring of files between machines on a network. An FTP machine stores documents and permits users of the Internet to access those documents and download them. Many ISPs have FTP capabilities that you can use. Once files have been moved to your ISP's FTP machine it then can be downloaded directly onto your machine. Not all FTP sites allow public access, using passwords to screen out users.

Gopher   This is both an application and a protocol that enables it. This Internet tool was developed at the University of Minnesota (The Golden Gophers). It is menu based and permits access to online information by using an on-screen pointer. Gophers not only can contain menus of information, but also point to other Telnet sites, WAIS databases, and other sources of information.

GUI   Graphical User Interface (pronounced gooey). This software has helped turn the Internet from a text-based DOS environment into a point-and-click domain with graphics and applications made available with a click of the mouse. Windows and Macintosh operating systems are GUI.

Hits   Visits by Internet surfers to a Web site. However, since a *hit* often includes every graphical element of a Web page, there might be ten hits for one visitor. (Please consult with your Web master or Web service company about a definition of *true hits*.) Similarly, browsers that store information locally may hide page requests by avoiding a rerequest.

Home Page   An HTML page that represents a company's starting point on the World Wide Web. Many companies have several home pages, each for a separate business unit or department—but they are all linked together. Beneath each home page may lie many additional pages that give the site *depth*.

Hot Links   A term that refers to the use of hypertext and HTML to connect sites on the World Wide Web.

Hypertext   This system allows programmers to write *links* to data in other locations, or in other databases or other documents.

HTML   Hypertext Markup Language. Using HTML, World Wide Web site creators establish *links* from one database to another. Simply by clicking on the link, a user can get access to information on the other side of the world without having to enter any complex commands. It also facilitates the formatting of text and images and the insertion of other media types (like video and sound).

IAB   Internet Architecture Board. A group of internetwork researchers who meet regularly to discuss issues pertinent to the Internet. This board sets much of the policy for the Internet through decisions and assignment of task forces to various issues.

InterNIC   Internet Network Information Center. This organization is responsible for the assignment of corporate domains. When a company wants a corporate address, such as widgets.com, its ISP must forward the request to the InterNIC for approval. There now is a $50/year fee for this service. Many ISPs will forward your company's request to the InterNIC at no charge beyond the InterNIC fee.

Internet   This is the term coined to describe what has become the world's largest public packet data network. Developed as the ARPANET, the Internet uses a common protocol (TCP/IP) to connect all types of computers. The definition of the Internet has grown now to include other services (such as the World Wide Web), which all utilize that common TCP/IP protocol. It is estimated that there will be more than 100 million users of the Internet in more than 80 countries before the end of the decade.

internet   Short for internetwork. Generally this is a series of routers linking a number of networks to function as one network.

Internet Address   This is also called an *IP address*. Routers on the Internet send mail and information to you or your company based on this information.

An individual user or a specific machine (*host*) using TCP/IP is assigned a 32-bit address. The address is written as 4 octets separated with periods (dotted decimal format) that are made up of a network section, an optional subnet section, and a host section.

IETF Internet Engineering Task Force. This group of experienced Internet engineers and systems administrators meets regularly to set standards for Internet operations and engineering issues, such as addressing schemes and routing tables.

IP Internet Protocol. This network layer protocol contains the addressing information and some control information that allows packets to be routed.

IP Address See Internet Address.

IP Multicast This routing technique allows IP traffic to be propagated from one source to a number of destinations, or from many sources to many destinations. Rather than sending one packet to each destination, one packet is sent to a multicast group identified by a single IP destination group address, to support applications such as broadcasting.

ISP Internet Service Provider. This is a company that sells Internet access services.

Intranet A growing term in the private sector. This means a company, or a group of companies, constructs a private network linking numerous sites over a TCP/IP network, but it is *closed* and therefore not open to the general Internet. Many companies see *intranets* as ways to improve internal communication.

ISDN Integrated Services Digital Network. This telephone service allows customers to exchange data at faster rates (64K and 128K per second) than over standard analog phone lines. The lines also can be used for two simultaneous voice calls.

Java A programming language, similar to C++, that can be used to develop miniapplications to operate within a Web page.

Listserv This program manages mailing lists, responding automatically to e-mail requests and distributing new messages to addresses listed on a specific directory.

LAN Local Area Network. This is a technology used to connect computers within a relatively small geopgrahic area (usually not larger than a floor or a small building). Compared to WANs (wide area networks), LANs usually are characterized by relatively high data rates, relatively low error rates and smaller sizes. See also WAN.

Mail Server   Often the forgotten piece in a corporate Internet connection, the mail server is a machine that responds to requests for information or to send information. Companies seeking a corporate address with multiple e-mail addresses either must set up a mail server using the SMTP protocol (see definition later in this glossary) or contract for the e-mail service from another company or provider.

MIME   Multipurpose Internet Mail Extensions specifies how nontextual messages can be sent using e-mail. UUencoding offers a related but less versatile mechanism.

Mosaic   This is the graphical tool created at the National Center for Supercomputing Applications at Champaign-Urbana, IL. Mosaic permits access to the World Wide Web and turns the Internet into a point-and-click environment with images, text, and video. Other Mosaic-like tools now include Netscape (currently the most popular), Spyglass Mosaic, and others. These tools are referred to as *web browsers*.

NAP   Network Access Point. The NAPs are where major ISPs converge to exchange Internet traffic. Major NAPs in the United States are located in or near Washington, DC, New York, Chicago, and the San Francisco Bay Area.

Node   Any computer attached to a network is often referred to as a node.

NSF   National Science Foundation. This federally funded group supported the development of the Internet outside the confines of the ARPANET. The NSF has withdrawn financial support of the Internet backbone, turning it over completely to commercial entities.

NFSnet   The NSF network. Its primary focus was to support education and research.

NSP   Network Service Provider. These are ISPs that offer dial-up and leased-line access at multiple locations around the United States.

Newsgroups   Discussion groups on the Internet, where people of similar interests share their opinions.

Packet   Information users send to the Internet is broken into chunks, called *packets*, before being transmitted across the network. Each packet is independent. Routers send the packets on a best-effort basis, relying on the end nodes to verify delivery if necessary.

POP Point of Presence. This refers to a physical location where Internet customers can dial in to the network or secure network access through leased-line access by utilizing phone lines and/or router ports provided by their ISP.

PPP Point-to-Point Protocol. This is a successor to SLIP (see SLIP definition), which provides router-to-router and host-to-network connections over synchronous or asynchronous circuits. PPP and SLIP access is most used to access the World Wide Web from home PCs.

RFC Request for Comments. This document series is used as a primary means for communicating information about Internet operations. Some RFCs are designated by the IAB as Internet standards. Most RFCs document protocol specifications, such as Telnet and FTP, but some are humorous or historical. RFCs are available online from the InterNIC.

RFI Request for Information. An invitation for a company to recommend solutions for its general needs.

RFP Request for Proposal. After soliciting information from various vendors with RFCs, companies often issue RFPs with specific requests for services, requirements, and prices.

Router A specialized computer device (or a regular computer running special programs) that can decide which of several paths network traffic will follow. Routers forward packets from one network to another based on network layer information. A router is often used on the customer's site when a LAN is present.

Server This is a computer that acts as a resource for information on a network. A Web server, for example, is a computer that functions as a site for World Wide Web information.

Shockwave A technique of displaying within a Web page multimedia displays using animation, audio, and interactive development.

SLIP Serial Line Internet Protocol. A standard for point-to-point serial connections using TCP/IP. This was the predecessor of PPP.

SMTP Simple Mail Transfer Protocol. This is an Internet protocol for providing electronic mail services. An SMTP mail server is necessary for corporate Internet connections that involve multiple mail addresses.

TELNET A tool that allows Internet users to log in to and access information from another machine connected to the network.

T1; T3   A Bell system terminology referring to a digital carrier facility used for transmission of data through the telephone hierarchy. The rate of transmission for T1 is 1.54 megabits per second. The rate for T3 is 45 megabits per second.

TCP   Transmission Control Protocol. TCP regulates how information is transported across the Internet and is the Internet's crucial language. Since it is often used with IP, the expression *TCP/IP* often refers to the collection of protocols developed for use on the Internet.

URL   Uniform Resource Locator. This is the address assigned to a company or individual's World Wide Web site. An example would be: http://www. widgets.com (*http* refers to hypertext protocol; *www* refers to World Wide Web; *widgets.com* is the corporate address).

WAIS   Wide Area Information Servers. The WAIS system allows users to do searches across databases using keywords.

WAN   Wide Area Network. A network spanning a wide geographic area.

World Wide Web   The Web is rapidly becoming the most popular feature on the Internet other than e-mail. Using hypertext links, Web sites allow users to connect from the Internet to a wide variety of databases. Written in HTML, a Web site allows users to access data, images, audio, and video.

Web Browser   See Mosaic definition.

APPENDIX **A**

Training Outlines

Abstract. This document lists topics for coverage by internal or external training programs. Plans are given for general, engineering, webmaster, operations, and sales/marketing employees.

Keywords. Education. Training. Engineering. Webmaster, Operations. Sales. Marketing. Curriculum.

Document ID:	EDU-0001	Created:	01-Jan-1997
Version:	1	Modified:	01-Jan-1997
Revision:	1	Effective:	ASAP
Status:	Draft	Expires:	Never

Revision History		
Version	**Date**	**Changes**
1	01-Jan-1997	Document created.

Table of Contents

1 Introduction 2
2 General Employee Training Outline 2
3 Technical Employee Training 3
4 Webmaster Training 5
5 Operations Training 6
6 Sales and Marketing Training 7

1. Introduction

Most formal education is very strategic: school districts, in conjunction with state guidelines, lay out a curriculum for K–12 students. Colleges and universities have degree requirements and course advisors who plan which classes a student will take in advance. Many people thus follow 15 to 20 years of planned learning.

When a person leaves academia for the world of business, training becomes tactical. Organizations send employees to courses immediately before skills are required, when budgets allow, or perhaps in response to an advertisement. In this book, we recommend a more strategic approach—identification of all the subject areas your company may need to be successful, and a plan to reach a level of employee proficiency.

The following training outlines are organized according to general employee responsibilities. Outlines do not generally overlap, so a given employee may reasonably apply for multiple training plans.

2. General Employee Training Outline

2.1 Historic Aspects
    2.1.1 The ARPAnet
    2.1.2 NSFnet
    2.1.3 Internet Commercialization
    2.1.4 Network Access Points/The Routing Arbiter

2.1.5 Growth Statistics

2.2 Technology Basis

    2.2.1 Basic Circuit Switching

    2.2.2 Packet Switching

    2.2.3 TCP/IP

    2.2.4 Presentation Formats

    2.2.5 Intranet

2.3 Using Internet Applications

    2.3.1 Domain Name Service

    2.3.2 Telnet

    2.3.3 FTP and Anonymous FTP

    2.3.4 Gopher

    2.3.5 E-mail

    2.3.6 WWW

    2.3.7 News

    2.3.8 Chat

    2.3.9 Advanced Applications

2.4 Information Resources

    2.4.1 Finding People on the Internet

    2.4.2 WWW Directories

    2.4.3 Archie

    2.4.4 The InterNIC

2.5 Social and Cultural Aspects

    2.5.1 The Internet Culture

    2.5.2 Security on the Internet

    2.5.3 Netiquette

    2.5.4 Legal Issues

    2.5.5 How to Stay Abreast

    2.5.6 Getting Help

3. Technical Employee Training

3.1 Data Communications Basics: Digital Data Transmission

    3.1.1 Baseband Channels: Baseband Encoding

    3.1.2 Passband Channels: Modulation/Demodulation

    3.1.3 Frequency, Time, and Statistical Time Division Multiplexing

    3.1.4 Error Correction and Error Detection Codes

3.1.5 Flow Control and Retransmission Techniques

3.2   Wide Area Network Technologies

3.2.1 Plain Old Telephone Service (POTS)

3.2.2 56k DDS and Switched 56

3.2.3 T1 and the Digital System Hierarchy

3.2.4 X.25

3.2.5 Frame Relay

3.2.6 Switched Megabit Data Services (SMD)

3.2.7 Integrated Services Digital Networks (ISDN)

3.2.8 Asynchronous Transfer Mode (ATM)

3.2.9 Synchronous Optical Network (SONET)

3.3   Local Area Network Technologies

3.3.1 Topology Comparisons

3.3.2 Ethernet

3.3.3 Fast Ethernet

3.3.4 FDDI

3.3.5 Token Ring

3.3.6 Others

3.4   Repeaters and Bridging

3.4.1 Repeaters

3.4.2 Half Bridges/Full Brides

3.4.3 Spanning Trees

3.4.4 Transparent vs. Source-Route Bridging

3.4.5 Scaling Issues

3.5   Internetworking

3.5.1 Routing vs. Bridging

3.5.2 Fragmentation

3.5.3 Addressing Issues

3.5.4 IP over WAN Transport

3.5.5 Internetworking over Dial-Up Networks

3.5.6 Routing Protocols

3.5.7 Filtering

3.5.8 Multicast Forwarding

3.5.9 Priority Queuing

3.6   Transport Layers

3.6.1 User Datagram Protocol (UDP)

3.6.2 Transmission Control Protocol (TCP)

3.6.3 Realtime Transport Protocol and Others

3.7 Applications Layer Protocols

3.7.1 Domain Name System

3.7.2 File Transfer Protocol, Gopher, Hypertext Transfer Protocol

3.7.3 Simple Mail Transfer Protocol, Post Office Protocol, and Others

3.7.4 telnet, rlogin

3.7.5 Network News Transfer Protocol

3.8 Hardware Features

3.8.1 Wiring Guides

3.8.2 LAN Hubs

3.8.3 Bridges and Routers

3.8.4 Modems

3.8.5 CSU/DSUs

3.9 Security

3.9.1 Understanding Threats: Hackers, Viruses, and Mistakes

3.9.2 Preventing Break-ins: Encryption, Firewalls

3.9.3 Testing Effectiveness: Security Audit Tools

3.9.4 Cleaning Up: Logging and Monitoring

4. Webmaster Training

4.1 Design Basics

4.1.1 Visual Design/Style Guides

4.1.2 Page Layout

4.1.3 Navigation Paradigms

4.1.4 Using Audio, Video, Applets

4.1.5 File Structure

4.2 Presentation Formats

4.2.1 Hypertext Markup Language

4.2.2 URL Format

4.2.3 Graphics Image Formats

4.2.4 Audio Formats

4.2.5 Video Formats

4.2.6 Applets and Applications

4.2.7 Virtual Reality Modeling Language

4.2.8 Other Presentation Layers

4.3 Servers

4.3.1 HTTP Version Support

4.3.2 cgi-bin support

4.3.3 Security Considerations: Authentication and SSL

4.3.4 Server-Side Includes

4.3.5 Commercial vs. Shareware Daemons

4.4 Tools

4.4.1 Graphics Production Tools

4.4.2 Sound Production Tools

4.4.3 HTML WYSIWYG Editors

4.4.4 HTML Checking Tools

4.4.5 Revision Control

4.5 Development Languages

4.5.1 Unix Shell Script

4.5.2 PERL

4.5.3 C/C++

4.5.4 JAVA and Active-X

5. Operations Training

5.1 Wiring

5.1.1 Coaxial Cabling

5.1.2 Unshielded Twisted Pairs

5.1.3 Fiber Optic Cables

5.2 Basic Test Tools

5.2.1 Digital Multimeter (DMM)

5.2.2 Bit Error Rate Tester (BERT)

5.2.3 Multifunction Testing Devices

5.2.4 Protocol Analyzers

5.3 Software Testing Applications

5.3.1 Ping and Traceroute

5.3.2 Router Statistics and Troubleshooting

5.3.3 SNMP Packages

5.3.4 Commercial Network Management Software

5.4 Computer Operating Systems

5.4.1 Basic File Structure

5.4.2 CPU Utilization
5.4.3 Basic Test Commands
5.5 Disaster Recovery
5.5.1 Performing Backups
5.5.2 Restoring Backups
5.5.3 Incrementals vs. Full
5.6 Reporting and Accounting
5.6.1 Generating Usage Reports
5.6.2 Monitoring Network Utilization
5.6.3 Counting Web Hits

6. Sales/Marketing

6.1 Internet Organizational Structure
6.1.1 Standards Organizations
6.1.2 Top Tier Internet Service Providers
6.1.3 Second and Third Tier Providers
6.1.4 WWW Directories
6.1.5 Help Organizations
6.1.6 Business Models
6.2 Getting the Word Out
6.2.1 Getting Links from Other Sites
6.2.2 Using Your URL
6.2.3 Effective Newsgroups
6.2.4 Mailing Lists
6.3 Promotional Strategies
6.3.1 Interactive Sites
6.3.2 Online Contests
6.3.3 Driving Further Development

Internet Usage Policy for Employees

Abstract. This document defines the means by which this organization's Internet connection may be used. It provides overall principles for use, and specific constraints as applicable.

Keywords. Internet. Policy. Employee. Business Use. Personal.

Document ID:	POL-0001	Created:	01-Jan-1997
Version:	1	Modified:	01-Jan-1997
Revision:	1	Effective:	ASAP
Status:	Draft	Expires:	Never

Revision History

Version	Date	Changes
1	01-Jan-1997	Document created.

Table of Contents

1. Introduction 2
2. General Types of Use 3
   2.1   Human–Human Communication 3
   2.2   Information Gathering 3
   2.3   Information Dissemination 4
   2.4   Machine–Machine Communication 4
3. Restrictions by Internal User 4
   3.1   By Department 4
   3.2   By Individual 4
   3.3   By Computer 5
   3.4   By Corporate Location 5
   3.5   By Time of Day, Day of Week, Or Other Time-based 5
   3.6   By Type of Application 5
4. By Remote Site 6
   4.1   By Nature of Organization 6
   4.2   By Discussion List 6
5. By Content 6
   5.1   Business Related 6
   5.2   Personal 7
   5.3   Software 7
6. Archiving 8
   6.1   Information to Keep Available Short Term 8
   6.2   Information to Remove Immediately 8
7. Related Documents and References 8

1. Introduction

The Internet offers a wide range of benefits to any organization, and poses a set of risks. This document attempts to minimize the risks by clearly defining the scope of activities permitted, as consistent with our mission, objectives, and common practices. The following terminology is used throughout this document.

- **MUST**—Required; failure to comply may entail consequences as explained in section *xx*.
- **MUST NOT**—Disallowed; violations may entail consequences as explained in section *xx*.
- **SHOULD**—Strongly recommended.
- **MAY**—Optional; up to individual discretion.

Lack of explicit permission does not mean it is permitted; please check with your supervisor if your action seems to be questionable. As you gain experience you will modify this document.

2. General Types of Use

This sections defines the general means by which the Internet connection is intended to be used. It should be possible to determine whether most new applications are permissible based on these general categories.

2.1 Human–Human Communication

This connection will support communications between employees of this organization and others outside the organization. This application is intended to accomplish the following objectives.

- **Improve Availability**—By providing convenient access to our support personnel.
- **Improve Responsiveness**—By being able to leave detailed directions to individuals not at their telephones and without relying on postal delivery.
- **Reduce Costs**—By decreasing the amount of time spent on long distance calls.

2.2 Information Gathering

This connection will support the retrieval of information from and about other organizations and subjects on the Internet, with the following intentions.

▶ **Increase Efficiency**—By providing instant information access to peoples desktops.
▶ **Reduce Costs**—By eliminating time spent doing outside research.
▶ **Improve Accuracy**—By making updated information available easily.

2.3 Information Dissemination

This connection will support the dissemination of information to others on the Internet from and about this company, for the following purposes:

▶ **Reduce Costs**—By making our information available without 800-number costs.
▶ **Improve Availability**—By making information available 24 × 7.
▶ **Competitive Advantage**—By providing an engaging, online information kiosk.

2.4 Machine–Machine Communication

This Internet connection MUST NOT be used to support automated communication between computer systems in this organization and others. While the business advantages do not currently outweigh costs, this may be changed in the future.

3. Restrictions by Internal User

This section defines who within the organization may and may not use the Internet access. While the policy is fairly liberal, all employees should familiarize themselves with the exceptions.

3.1 By Department

All departments MAY have access to the Internet.

3.2 By Individual

Access is available to all full-time employees. Employees MUST complete a beginner's training course on using the Internet that includes information on applications usage and Netiquette. This course may be written, but employees MUST sign a letter acknowledging familiarity with this policy. Part-time employees, contractors, visitors, and all other categories of employee shall require a written request to the Computer Services department, identifying the following:

- ▶ Who is responsible for ensuring the employee is familiar with guidelines
- ▶ The explicit purpose for access
- ▶ How long the access shall be granted

Requests shall be considered by the Computer Services manager, and will be acted upon (approve, deny, or request clarification) within 72 hours.

3.3 By Computer

The Internet may be accessed from any computer system in the company, with the following exception. Computers that hold marketing or accounting information MUST NOT be capable of accessing the Internet, there is no business need, and the consequences of data interception are too high.

3.4 By Corporate Location

All corporate offices SHOULD acquire an Internet connection, either through existing data communications facilities, or through others. The Computer Services group shall determine the exact method and timetables.

3.5 By Time of Day, Day of Week, or Other Time-based

The only time-based restrictions on Internet access are for personal uses:

- ▶ Employees MUST NOT access the Internet for personal reasons during core business hours, 9 A.M. until 5 P.M.
- ▶ Employees MUST NOT access the Internet for personal reasons at any time the office has visitors.

Otherwise, access MAY be conducted at any time. See Section 5 for more details on personal use.

3.6 By Type of Application

Applications like e-mail, character-based chat, and basic Web browsing SHOULD be used. High-bandwidth and extremely delay-sensitive applications MUST NOT be used. This includes, but is not limited to, the following:

- ▶ Network Time Synchronization
- ▶ Real-Time Audio or Video
- ▶ Full News Feed
- ▶ Large Internal Mailing Lists

4. By Remote Site

This sections defines limits to Internet access based on the sites contacted.

4.1 By Nature of Organization

There are no restrictions on the nature of organizations with which employees may communicate—including competitors. Employees MUST comply with the restrictions on information exchanged, as explained in Section 5.

4.2 By Discussion List

There are no restrictions on the types of discussion mailing lists to which employees may subscribe. Employees MUST comply with the restrictions on information exchanged, as explained in Section 5.

5. By Content

There are restrictions on the types of information that employees are permitted to exchange using the organization's Internet connection.

5.1 Business Related

Employees MUST restrict their usage of the Internet—including Web browsing and the composition or reading of lengthy e-mail messages—to activity relevant to the corporate mission during normal business hours of 9 A.M. to 5 P.M. local time. Such relevant activities shall be related to tasks explicitly assigned by a supervisor or to those that are inherently related to one's employment.

Whether browsing or exchanging e-mail for business or personal reasons, an employee SHOULD always apply the following test: If the material retrieved from a remote site would be in violation of existing corporate policies, including but not limited to those on harassment and discrimination, then an employee MUST NOT continue to view the material, and MUST NOT print, save, or retransmit it in any way. All employees MUST be sufficiently familiar with existing guidelines to apply this test. If an employee believes there is a legitimate business need to retrieve additional information from such a site, it should be discussed with a supervisor.

When sending e-mail to an individual or mailing list regarding work, the employee is acting as a representative of this company, and statements may be construed as being contractually binding. Therefore, employees MUST NOT make any promise, explicit or implied, that he or she cannot personally satisfy. Furthermore, employees MUST NOT divulge any information not expressly intended for general use via e-mail, Web, or any Internet application. Everything sent out, whether to a friend or a mailing list, should be considered as being sent to the entire world.

5.2 Personal

The Internet has become for many a basic communications medium, like the telephone. Just as employees are permitted non-toll telephone calls as a basic office necessity, so, too, are the following allowed:

- ▶ Employees MUST NOT use the Internet for personal reasons during core business hours of 9 A.M. to 5 P.M. local time, unless for a brief (~3 minute) e-mail.
- ▶ Employees MAY use the Internet during non-core hours, and such use MUST be consistent with the content and applications restrictions discussed elsewhere in this document.
- ▶ Employess MUST NOT place extreme loads on the Internet connection for personal reasons. Extremely large file transfers (over 2 Mb) for personal use may interfere with the business applications.
- ▶ Employees MUST NOT represent personal opinions to mailing lists with disclaimers as to their association with this organization. Messages sent from here inherently represent this organization.

5.3 Software

Employees MUST NOT download any software from the Internet, for business or personal use. Contact Computer Services if you have specific software requests.

6. Archiving

Information retrieved from the Internet may be stored for varying amounts of time, depending on its nature.

6.1 Information to Keep Available Short Term

All employees SHOULD maintain recent logs of their e-mail activity, from at least six months to one year of receipt. Users MAY elect to keep information longer if desired; suitable support from Computer Services should be requested. The exception to this rule is noted in Section 6.2.

Computer Services MAY keep records of Internet access activity for planning purposes. Such records SHOULD be kept for a period of at least one year, and MAY be maintained longer. These records may indicate which computers have accessed which WWW sites.

6.2. Information to Remove Immediately

Any content of a personal nature MUST be removed from employee personal computers within three business days of being read. Any content failing the test for suitability defined in Section 5.1 MUST also be removed immediately.

7. Related Documents and References

Internet Access High-Level Design

Abstract. This document explains the architecture for this organization's connection to the Internet. It discusses the type of network equipment and services that are required, and their basic operation. It does not include specific configurations, nor explanations of basic networking theory.

Keywords. Internet. Design. Architecture. Router. Leased Line. WWW Server. Browser. Firewall.

Document ID:	DES-0001	Created:	01-Jan-1997
Version:	1	Modified:	01-Jan-1997
Revision:	1	Effective:	ASAP
Status:	Draft	Expires:	Never

Revision History		
Version	Date	Changes
1	01-Jan-1997	Document created.

Table of Contents

1. Introduction 2
2. Physical Architecture 3
   2.1 Network Infrastructure 3
   2.2 Server and Clients 4
   2.3 Power 4
3. Network Design 4
   3.1 WAN Transport 4
   3.2 IP Addressing 4
   3.3 IP Routing 4
4. Logical Architecture 5
   4.1 Address Assignment and DNS 5
   4.2 E-mail 5
   4.3 Chat 5
   4.4 WWW 6
5. Operations Issues 6
   5.1 Configuration Management 6
   5.2 Performance Monitoring 6
   5.3 Fault Detection and Correction 6
   5.4 Accounting 7
   5.5 Security 7
6. Future Expansion 8
   6.1 Increasing Capacity and Availability 8
   6.2 Adding Functionality 8
   6.3 Switching ISPs 8
7. Related Documents and References 8

1. Introduction

This is a same design document explains how a small company with an existing LAN might connect to the Internet. The document provides a significant amount of technical detail that may lose some of the non-technical readers. Therefore, it may be useful to do a companion explanation document or to present it with some assistance. An actual design document would have mentioned specific vendors and perhaps devices by name.

2. Physical Architecture

This section provides a high-level view of how devices are connected. In terms of the OSI model, this deals primarily with the physical layer, although aspects of the data link layer operation are implied. The overall design is presented in Figure 2.1, and specific aspects of the router and server are covered in Sections 2.1 and 2.2, respectively.

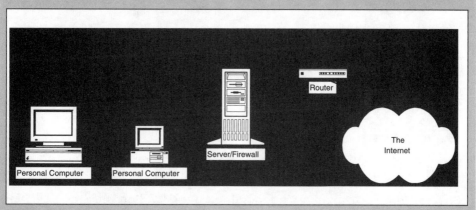

FIGURE C.1   High-level design.

2.1 Network Infrastructure

The approach used is a classical "Demilitarized Zone" or DMZ design, with a dual-purpose server and firewall. The initial connection to the Internet will be through a fractional T1 line running at 128 Kbps. The router used to connect has two high-speed synchronous EIA-422 interfaces, one of which will connect to the fractional T1 multiplexer. The router also has two 10Base-T Ethernet connections, one of which will be attached to a logical LAN segment in the Ethernet hub along with the server/firewall's first Ethernet interface.

The server's second Ethernet interface attaches to a separate logical 10Base-T LAN segment in the hub, which also supports all the personal computers in the Pittsburgh office. When other offices require Internet access, they will receive a similar configuration.

2.2 Server and Clients

The Server/Firewall is a high-end personal computer platform dedicated to use for Internet access. It will not be used by a regular PC user. It will require a total of 32 MB RAM, and 2 GB disk, along with a tape backup. Client PCs may be of any type currently supported by the Computer Services department.

2.3 Power

The router, Ethernet hub, and server will all be co-located in the primary telecommunications closet, and will share a 1000 VA uninterruptible power supply.

3. Network Design

This section describes how the system will function at the Network layer of the OSI model. Some aspects of the data link layer are also discussed here.

3.1 WAN Transport

The fractional T1 link is a frame relay circuit with CIR of 0, which trades guarantee of bandwidth for a lower price. Thus, users may not see consistent performance, independent of the load on this line or server. There is a single PVC established to a router of the ISP.

3.2. IP Addressing

The Internet Service Provider will specify the IP addresses to be used on the WAN link. We will obtain at least 4 bits of subnetted address space from the ISP to use on the LAN connecting the router to the server. (While only 2 bits are needed, the extra will provide room for growth.) Internal addresses will be dynamically assigned by the server using RFC1597 address space.

3.3 IP Routing

The router will have a static default route to the Internet, and the ISP will point a static default to the subnet they allocated to our router; no dynamic routing information will be accepted or transmitted. All client PCs will learn their subnet masks and default router using DHCP. Most importantly, the server/firewall has routing disabled. All access is via application level proxies.

4. Logical Architecture

This section describes how applications work in this design. It relates most strongly to the applications layer, although some aspects of the presentation, session, and transport layers are implied.

4.1 Address Assignment and DNS

As mentioned in Section 3, addresses are dynamically assigned by a DHCP server running on the server/firewall system. This daemon will provide IP addresses, subnet mask, and default router information for any device on the client LAN.

Since the client PCs will not run servers, no DNS will be provided for them. The only DNS service required is for the Internet, and the only address to be mapped is that of the server's first Ethernet. The firewall/server will be configured as secondary, while the ISP will act as primary. The server will be known primarily as "pluto," but also respond to "www" and will be the primary mail exchanger for the domain. The ISP will provide primary and secondary reverse domain name resolution.

4.2 E-mail

As noted, the server/firewall will be the primary e-mail exchanger for the domain; the ISP will provide secondary mail exchanger service, and will forward all stored messages to the primary. All clients will use the Post Office Protocol version 3 to download e-mail from the server. They will send e-mail using SMTP to the server, where it will be queued for delivery.

4.3 Chat

Users wishing to chat interactively with others on the Internet will have to use the Chat daemon running on the firewall/gateway. This prevents them from joining arbitrary chat discussions elsewhere on the Internet, but will allow them to invite customers to connect to their system for interactive online communication.

4.4 WWW

The server/gateway will run a WWW server accessible from the Internet and also from within the company. All content will be produced by the Marketing Department and transferred electronically to the server. The same WWW process will also serve as a caching proxy server for external accesses. Most pages will be stored locally, speeding subsequent accesses and reducing total load on the leased line.

5. Operations Issues

While the preceding sections describe how the system will function, this sections focuses on how it will be maintained. It is organized by the OSI 5 part model for network management.

5.1 Configuration Management

The configuration of the server will be maintained by nightly incremental backups and a full backup performed once each weekend. The full backup tape will be taken offsite each Monday morning and stored in a secure location. The router configuration will be backed up manually onto the server before each full backup, so its configuration will also be maintained.

No special configuration management for the clients (beyond normal backups) need to be performed. It is easy to reproduce any given client configuration given that of the server or another client, and the likelihood of losing the configuration of all clients simultaneously is minimal.

5.2 Performance Monitoring

For the initial phase of this project, no automated performance monitoring will be performed. If users notice a degradation in responsiveness, they will be encouraged to notify the Computer Services group, which can take corrective action.

5.3 Fault Detection and Correction

Automated performance monitoring will be accomplished by a simple computer application that will check the following items:

► Whether the other side of the Internet link is unreachable
► Whether 2 of 5 well-known sites on the Internet are unreachable

► Whether the computer disk, CPU, or I/O are running close to 90% capacity
► Whether the power supply is running off battery

If any of these conditions are true, the computer speaker will beep. An extension speaker will ensure that people sitting in the Computer Services area will be able to hear and respond.

5.4 Accounting

The system will maintain the following logs automatically:

► Undeliverable e-mail messages
► Pages delivered by Proxy
► Pages retrieved via WWW
► Content loading

Accounting information will be used by Computer Services to plan for expansion upgrades.

5.5 Security

It is crucial that the security of this organization's Web site be maintained to the highest degree. Denial of service will reduce productivity and negate all the customer advantages cited in the Policy Document. Additionally, unintentional modification of server data may have an adverse relationship on customer perspective. Therefore, the following steps will be taken to monitor security:

► The server shall not contain any information deemed sensitive to the company.
► The server shall not execute any applications not explicitly mentioned in this design.
► Only full-time employees of the Computer Services staff shall be able to modify server configuration.
► Only Marketing employees shall be provided with the password which allows content loading.
► Once a year the company will hire an outside firm to conduct a Security Audit, which will include analysis of the Internet connection.

6. Future Expansion

This section explains some of the ways this connection may evolve. Many of these were facilitated by conscious decisions in the initial design, based on possible future requirements.

6.1 Increasing Capacity and Availability

This configuration easily scales to handle more users and high speeds. If a large bandwidth frame relay connection is desired, the CIR may be increased, and the external fractional T1 multiplexer can use more the line bandwidth with no additional hardware acquisitions. The second Ethernet port can support an additional LAN, which can be used to accommodate a large number of clients. The server may also be upgraded with more memory and a faster CPU.

If the system availability is not adequate, the second synchronous port on the router can accommodate a connection to an alternate ISP for redundancy. It is also possible to use a second router, and even a second server for higher availability.

6.2 Adding Functionality

The system can be easily reconfigured to support additional capabilities. New applications gateways may be run on the server to support future services, including real-time applications. Alternately, the firewall may be moved to the second router Ethernet, and users may access other applications directly.

6.3 Switching ISPs

The current configuration simplifies the task of switching ISPs. Since RFC1597 addresses are used internally, only the links to the router need to be renumbered. If the organization does obtain a large address space of its own, it can allocate those new addresses dynamically using DHCP.

7. Related Documents and References

Internet Usage Policy, v1, r1, POL-0001, January 1, 1997.

Network Test Plan

Abstract. This document describes tests necessary to ensure proper operation of this company's network. It will be used to verify vendor initial compliance, and on an as-needed basis to confirm continued proper operation or complete fault recovery.

Keywords. Internet. Network. Test Plan. Integration.

Document ID:	TST-0001	Created:	01-Jan-1997
Version:	1	Modified:	01-Jan-1997
Revision:	1	Effective:	ASAP
Status:	Draft	Expires:	Never

Revision History

Version	Date	Changes
1	01-Jan-1997	Document created.

Table of Contents

1. Introduction 2
2. Local Loop Unit Test 3
   2.1 Alarm Verification 3
   2.2 CSU/DSU Loopback Tests 4
   2.3 Multiplexer Loopback Tests 4
   2.4 Power Recovery 5
3. Router Unit Test 5
4. WAN Test 6
   4.1 Routing 6
   4.2 Reachability 6
   4.3 Variable Ping Load 7
   4.4 Variable Packet Size 7
   4.5 Link Failure Recovery 7
5. LAN Test 8
   5.1 Router Reachability 8
   5.2 Variable Ping Load 8
   5.3 Variable Packet Size 9
   5.4 Link Failure Recovery 9
6. System Test 9
   6.1 Reachability 9
   6.2 Variable Load 10
   6.3 Variable Packet Size 10
   6.4 Uninterruptible Power Supply 10
7. Related Documents and References 10

1. Introduction

This document defines the tests performed to the Internet connection upon initial installation, and after significant configuration changes or problems with the network connectivity. These tests are considered necessary but not sufficient to detect many problems; additional tests should be included as experience dictates.

These tests relate only to the network layer components; a companion test document will be used to verify operation of the server, including IP address assignment and system configuration backup.

2. Local Loop Unit Test

This section verifies proper operation of the local loop connection from the premises to the Central Office and Internet Service Provider. These are all unit tests, which also include boundary conditions like all zeroes and ones which can cause some links to fail.

Device	Manufacturer	Model	Serial Number
CSU/DSU			
Fractional Multiplexer			

2.1 Alarm Verification

Test	Procedures	Result
Disconnect Alarm	Disconnect the CSU/DSU telecommunications cable from the demarc, and verify that the CSU/DSU indicates a loss of signal.	
Circuit Operational	Reconnect the CSU/DSU telecommunications cable to the demarc, and verify that the CSU/DSU indicates a signal.	
Additional Alarms	Test additional alarm indicators as documented by CSU/DSU and/or fractional multiplexer equipment vendors.	

2.2 CSU/DSU Loopback Tests

Test	Procedures	Result
All Ones Test	Send loopback command to remote CSU/DSU. When looped, send ALL ONEs test pattern for 5 minutes. Verify Bit Error Rate is less than 10-9.	
All Zeroes Test	Send loopback command to remote CSU/DSU. When looped, send ALL ZEROEs test pattern for 5 minutes. Verify Bit Error Rate is less than 10-9.	
Pseudo-Random Test Pattern Test	Send loopback command to remote CSU/DSU. When looped, send pseudo-random test pattern for 5 minutes. Verify Bit Error Rate is less than 10-9.	

2.3 Multiplexer Loopback Tests

Test	Procedures	Result
Pseudo-Random Test Pattern	Send loopback command to remote multiplexer. When looped, pseudo-random test pattern for 5 minutes. Verify Bit Error Rate is less than 10-9.	
Additional Tests	Perform additional remote loopback tests as supported by particular multiplexer vendor.	

2.4 Power Recovery

Test	Procedures	Result
CSU/DSU	Disconnect the power cord from the CSU/DSU. Wait 30 seconds, then reconnect. Verify equipment returns to normal status.	
Multiplexer	Disconnect the power cord from the multiplexer. Wait 30 seconds, then reconnect. Verify equipment returns to normal status.	

3. Router Unit Test

These tests verify proper operation of the router alone.

Device	Manufacturer	Model	Serial Number
Router			

Test	Procedures	Result
Boot Router	Power down the router using On/Off switch and wait 30 seconds. Restore power and monitor the boot-up sequence for any errors or warnings.	
Indicator Verification	Verify that all router lights read as they should according to the manufacturer's specifications.	
Power Recovery	Disconnect router power cord and wait 30 seconds. Restore power and monitor boot-up sequence for any errors or warnings.	

4. WAN Test

These test verify proper operation of the router and connections to the Internet.

4.1 Routing

Test	Procedures	Result
Routing Tables	Boot the router while connected to the wide area network. Allow 5 minutes for operation to stabilize. View the internal routing table, and verify that there is a single static default to the remote router, and that no routes have been learned dynamically.	
Dynamic WAN Routing	Verify that all routing information on the WAN interface has been disabled— no routes are sent or received.	
Dynamic LAN Routing	Verify that all routing information on the LAN interface has been disable—no routes are sent or received.	

4.2 Reachability

Test	Procedures	Result
Link	From the router console, send an ICMP echo request packet to the remote router using the PING command. Verify that the remote end responds.	
Internet Reachability	From the router console, send an ICMP echo request packet to various well-known locations on the Internet. (*Note:* Unless name resolution is functioning, you may have to specify addresses manually. You may use a dial-up connection to determine some valid IP addresses, or you may guess.) Verify that pings are returned promptly and consistently.	

4.3 Variable Ping Load

Test	Procedures	Result
High Load to Router	Increase the rate of ping transmissions to the remote router. Allow the test to run for 5 minutes. Verify that only a minor fraction of packets are lost.	
High Load to Internet	Select an IP address reachable on the Internet, and ping it at a high packet rate. Verify that a substantial fraction of packets are returned. If not, repeat with additional IP address.	

4.4 Variable Packet Size

Test	Procedures	Result
Increasing Ping Size to Link	Increase the size of transmitted ping packets to the other side of the WAN link. Verify that sizes up to the link's Maximum Transmission Unit work. Larger packets should also take increasingly long to travel the link.	
Increasing Ping Size to Internet	Repeat the above test using other locations on the Internet. Verify that the majority of pings respond.	

4.5 Link Failure Recovery

Test	Procedures	Result
Link Down	Disconnect the cable from the router to the multiplexer. Wait 1 minute and query the router. Verify that the link is reported down.	
Link Up	Reconnect the above cable and wait 1 minute. Query the router and verify that the link is reported operational.	

5. LAN Test

This section verifies proper operation of the LAN interface between the router and the rest of the company network. To perform these, a PC will have to be configured to work on the LAN interface, assigned an IP address and default router.

Device	Manufacturer	Model	Serial Number
10Base-T Ethernet Hub			
Test PC			

5.1 Router Reachability

Test	Procedures	Result
Link	From the PC console, send an ICMP echo request packet to the router using the PING command. Verify that the router responds.	

5.2 Variable Ping Load

Test	Procedures	Result
High Load to Router	Increase the rate of ping transmissions from the PC to the router. Allow the test to run for 5 minutes. Verify that only a minor fraction of packets are lost.	

5.3 Variable Packet Size

Test	Procedures	Result
Increasing Ping Size to Link	Increase the size of transmitted ping packets to the router. Verify that sizes up to the link's Maximum Transmission Unit work. Larger packets should not take noticeably longer to return.	

5.4 Link Failure Recovery

Test	Procedures	Result
Link Down	Disconnect the cable from the PC to the router. Wait 1 minute and query the router. Verify that the link is reported down.	
Link Up	Reconnect the above cable and wait 1 minute. Query the router and verify that the link is reported operational.	

6. System Test

This section tests all of the above components working together.

6.1 Reachability

Test	Procedures	Result
ISP Ping	From the PC console, send an ICMP echo request packet to the remote ISP router using the PING command. Verify that the router responds.	
Remote Ping	From the PC console, send an ICMP echo request packet to any router on the Internet using the PING command. Verify that the router responds.	

6.2 Variable Load

Test	Procedures	Result
High Load	Increase the rate of ping transmissions from the PC to the remote router. Allow the test to run for 5 minutes. Verify that only a minor fraction of packets are lost.	

5.3 Variable Packet Size

Test	Procedures	Result
Increasing Ping Size to Link	Increase the size of transmitted ping packets to the remote router. Verify that size is up to the link's Maximum Transmission Unit work. Larger packets will again take noticeably longer to return.	

5.4 Uninterruptible Power Supply

Test	Procedures	Result
Unplug the Power Supply	Disconnect the uninterruptible power supply from the wall. Wait several minutes, or less if the supply is sized small. Verify that the system remains operational by pinging from the PC to a router on the Internet.	
Restore Power	Reconnect the UPS to the mains. Verify that all components remain operational by pinging from the PC to a router on the Internet.	

7. Related Documents and References

Internet Access High Level Design, v1, r1, DES-0001, January 1, 1997.

Index

Terms followed by lowercase roman t indicate material in tables. Terms followed by italic *illus.* indicate illustrations of home pages.

Accent Soft home page, 243*illus.*
Acceptable Use Policy (AUP), 35, 301
access logs, 96, 281
accounting, 113
acquisition, *see* client acquisition; network acquisition; server acquisition
Adobe Acrobat Reader, 213*illus.*
advertising, *see also* marketing
  policy and, 77
  Web-sponsored, 268–269
Agent, 46
Allen, Cliff, 237–240
Allen Marketing Group, 237–240
  home page, 237*illus.*
Amazon Books home page, 275–276, 276*illus.*
anonymous FTP, 206
Ansardi, Katy, 217–220
applets, 301
Applications Programming Interfaces (APIs), 200
architecture, *see* design
archives, 96, 324
ARPANET, 301, 304
attacks, 112–113
audio, 89, 107, 271

audio conferencing, 109–110
  voice over the Internet, 297

backbone, 35
back-end interfaces, 200–202
bandwidth, 296
banner ads, 269
Bartolomeo, Tom, 30–34
BBSs, 302
Bell South, Internet access from, 151
benefits, of connecting, 27–29
billing, 96, 113
black-box testing, 187
Bohac, Buck, 217–220
boundary testing, 187–188
break-in, 112
browsers, 242, 306
budget, 71–72
bundling, 140

C, 201
catalogs, 265
Catalogue.com, 141
  home page, 142*illus.*
CD-ROM/Web links, 299–300
CGI, 200

Channel Banks, 148
chat, 271
   requirements for access, 108–109
Classless Interdomain Routing (CIDR), 302
client acquisition, 191–198
   issues, 198–206
   people issues, 193–194
   resources for, 194–196
   software selection, 198–199
Cnet Central, 207
collective interaction, 129, 132
Commerce.Net, 288
compatibility, 192
Computer Emergency Response Team
      (CERT), 226
computer modeling/simulation, 138, 186
configuration document, 169
connection, 9
   benefits of, 27–29
   "broken," 210*illus.*
   deciding to connect, *see* decision process
   fragmentation across divisions, 25
   process overview, 9–10
consultants, 58–59. *See also* outsourcing
   for client/server acquisition, 195
   for network testing, 188–189
   for performance review, 285
   for requirements phase help, 102
   for security testing, 224
   for server installation, 224
   for training, 51
content generation, 227–236
   information about (references), 244
   issues, 240–244
   people issues, 232–233
   resources for, 233–234
   reviewing, 283
   style guide, 242–243
   by Web-hosting companies, 140
content (usage) restriction, 93–94, 322–323
contests, as marketing tool, 271
contingency engineering, 174
continuous improvement, 40
costs
   client/server equipment, 205–206
   estimating in requirements phase, 114
   hardware shopping list, 147–150
   information about (references), 153–154

misconceptions about, 35–36
   people issues, 143
   price overview, 143–145, 144t
   and requirements, 145
   savings, as driving force for connecting,
      28–29
   service price factors, 145–146
   telephone charges, 150–151
   Web services, 151–152
Crews, Chuck, 141
cross-training, 51
CSU (Channel Service Unit), 148, 300, 302
customer base, expanding, 28
customer premise equipment (CPE), 302
CyberAtlas.com home page, 288*illus.*
cyberbanking, 30
cybercasts, 227

Daniels, Walter E., 62–69
databases, 201
data formats, 111
decision process, 23–27
   authority, 26
   benefits of connection, 27–29
   information about (references), 37–38
   Internet myths, 34–37
   issues, 27–29
   reevaluation, 37
   resources for, 26
Demming Philosophy of Continuous
      Improvement, 40
denial of service attacks, 113
departments, 57
   usage limitations by, 92
design, 121–128
   high-level design, 121, 124, 325–332
   information about (references), 140
   issues, 133–140
   methodology, 137–138
   outsourcing WEB hosting, 138–140
   people issues, 124
   resources for, 125–127
design document, 123–124
   goals of, 133–134
   organizing, 135–137
   OSI models for, 135–137
   production tools, 126
   reviewing, 282–283

directed cross-marketing, 267–268
documentation, 255–256
document production tools, 126
domain names, 113
    list of, at InterNIC, 119
    registration, 27, 171
Domain Name System (DNS), 302
downloading software, 93–94, 323
downtime, 255
drop-and-insert, 148
DSU (Data Service Unit), 148, 300, 302

EDI (electronic data interchange), 296
education, *see* training
electronic white board, 110, 271
e-mail, 28, 87–88, 302
    as marketing tool, 268
    requirements, 107
    server testing for, 221
    usage policy, 94–95, 323
    user feedback and, 280
    World Wide Web, 89
e-mail signature files, 269
employee usage policy, *see* policy
employee user manuals, 256–257
engineering plan, 185
    writing, 220–221
ESPN home page, 228*illus.*
Eudora, 269
executives, *see* upper management
external resources, 58–59. *See also*
        consultants; outsourcing
    locating, 60
    security issues, 61–62
    Web design houses, 244

FAQs, 303
FedEx home page, 298*illus.*
file transfer protocol, *see* FTP
firewall systems, 148–149
    costs, 206
    testing, 18t
First Union Corporation, 30–34
    home page, 29*illus.*
flame wars, 272
forms, 303
Forté, 45–48
    home page, 45*illus.*

Fox Network home page, 229*illus.*
frame relay, 91, 303
    vs. ISDN, 158–159, 300
frames, 303
Free Agent, 46
FTP (File Transfer Protocol), 205, 212, 303
    anonymous, 206

games, as marketing tool, 271
generating content, *see* content generation
gophers, 212, 303
Graham, Doug, 161–168
graphic design, 233–234
groupware, 110, 298
GUIs (graphical user interfaces), 107, 303

hackers, 36, 108
hardware
    buy/lease/rent decision, 150
    cost estimation, 147–150
    selection, 169
    servers, *see* server acquisition
high-level design, 121, 124, 325–332
hits, 75, 269, 303–304
home pages, 304. *See also* specific home
        pages
host, 305
hosting services, *see* Web hosting
hot links, 261, 304
hot spare switch, 189
HTML (Hypertext Markup Language), 304,
        308
    authoring tools, 234
human-human communication policy,
        87–88, 319
human resources department, 57
hyperlinks, 89
hypertext, 304

Indelible Blue, 217–220
    home page, 215*illus.*
Indianapolis Star/News home page, 228,
        230*illus.*
information collection, 90, 319–320
    for requirements phase, 104–106
information dissemination, 88–89, 320
information redistribution, 95
Infoseek home page, 268*illus.*

insurance malls, 85
Integrated Services Digital Network (ISDN),
    see ISDN
intellectual property, 61, 94
  and content generation, 236
internal resources, see project leader;
    project team
internal survey, 58, 70–71
internet (internetwork), 304
Internet, 304. See also e-mail; World Wide
    Web
  etiquette, see Netiquette
  improvements to capabilities, 295–300
  maximizing benefit from, 24–25
  myths about, 34–37
  new business models enabled, 29
  price overview, 143–145, 144t
  publications on, 288
Internet addresses, 304–305
Internet Architecture Board (IAB), 304
Internet connection, see connection
Internet Czar, 83
Internet Engineering Task Force (IETF), 35,
    305
Internet Information Center, 304
Internet marketing, see marketing
Internet Network Information Center
    (InterNIC), see InterNIC
Internet newsgroups (USENET), see
    newsgroups
Internet policy, see policy
Internet project leader, see project leader
Internet project team, see project team
Internet Relay Chat (IRC), 108–109, 271
Internet requirements, see requirements
Internet Service Providers (ISPs), 305
  The List site, 153, 171
  network testing assistance, 178–179
  price overview, 143–145, 144t
  questions for prospective, 169–170
  ratings information, 171
  service price factors, 145–146
Internet Society home page, 190
Internet strategy, need for coherent, 36
Internet usage policy, see policy
Internet WWW directories, 28, 266–267
InterNIC, 35, 304
  address, 119

as design phase resource, 127
Interpath, 41, 250
intranet, 296, 305
inventory control, real-time, 297, 298illus.
IP (Internet Protocol), 305
IP addresses, 304–305
IP multicast, 305
ISDN (Integrated Services Digital Network),
    139, 151, 305
  hardware support for, 149
  vs. frame relay networks, 158–159, 300
ISDN terminal adapters, 149, 300

Java, 41, 201, 212, 305
Java World magazine home page, 235illus.
junk e-mail, 107, 272

Knuff, Charles, 46–48

landline access, 151
LANs (Local Area Networks), 305–306
  test plan for, 340–341
Lea, David, 181–184
listservs, 305
local loop, 151
  unit test plan, 335–337
local machine usage limitations, 92–93
logs, 96, 281
Lotus Notes, 298

machine-machine communication policy,
    90–92, 320
Macro*World Research Corporation,
    161–168
  home page, 161illus.
magazines, marketing in, 264
mailing lists, as marketing tool, 270–271
mail servers, 306
maintenance procedures, 254–255
Maloff, Joel, 83–86
Maloff Company, 83–86
  home page, 82illus.
marketing, 257–263
  information about (references), 272
  Internet-specific techniques, 266–272
  issues, 263–272
  people issues, 261–262
  resources for, 262

reviewing, 284
spamming, 272
success factors, 258–260
traditional techniques, 263–266
Marketing on the Internet, 272
MBONE broadcasts, 109–110
media announcements, 264–265
memory upgrades, 296
MIME (Multipurpose Internet Mail
    Extensions), 111, 306
mirror, for server, 294
mission creep, 162
modems, 149
    cable modems, 150, 302
Mosaic, 306
multicasting, 109–110
myths, about the Internet, 34–37

National Science Foundation (NSF), 35, 306
Netiquette, 94, 97
    marketing and, 271–272
    sales and, 108
Netscape, 270
Network Access Point (NAP), 306
network acquisition, 155–160
    information about (references), 171
    issues, 160, 168–171
    people issues, 157
    resources for, 158–159
networks, 91. *See also* LANs; WANs
Network Service Providers (NSPs), 35, 306
network testing, 173–180
    basic elements of, 185–188
    information about (references), 189–190
    issues, 184–189
    people issues, 177–178
    resources for, 178–179
network test plan, 177, 333–342
newsgroups, 306
    as client/server acquisition resource, 199
    as marketing tool, 270–271
    requirements for access, 108
    as resource, 190
newspapers, marketing in, 264
nodes, 306
noncompete agreements, 62
nondisclosure agreements, 27, 61, 104
    network acquisition phase, 160

NSFnet, 306
NT-1 devices, 149

online banking, 30
online commerce, 110
online reservation systems, 182
open database compliant interfaces, 201
operations, 140
operations turnover, 245–251
    issues, 254–256
    people issues, 247–248
    resources for, 248–249
organization, 8–9
    key departments, 57
OSI model for systems management,
    136–137
OSI reference model, 135–136, 140
outside partners, 59
outside vendors, *see* vendors
outsourcing, *see also* consultants
    of network testing, 188–189
    for performance review, 285
    server installation, 224
    of Web hosting, 138–140, 193, 202–205

PacBell home page, 138, 139*illus.*
packets, 306
paperless office, 296
PC Travel, 181–184
    home page, 181*illus.*
peak load requirements, 110–111
peering agreements, 110
people issues
    in client/server acquisition, 193–194
    in content generation, 232–233
    cost estimation, 143
    in decision process, 25
    in marketing, 261–262
    in network acquisition, 157
    in network testing, 177–178
    in operations turnover, 247–248
    in performance review, 279
    in phase II, 293
    policy definition, 79–80
    in requirements phase, 101
    in resource identification, 55–59
    in server installation, 214
    in training, 42

performance review, 273–281
  issues, 281–285
  people issues, 279
  resources for, 280
periodicals, 51–52
  as client/server acquisition resource, 199
  marketing in, 264
  Web server applications, 225–226
PERL, 41, 201
personal use, 323
personnel, *see* people issues
PERT task representation, 12–13, 14*illus.*
phase II, 287–294
  issues, 295–300
  key questions during, 289–292
  people issues, 293
  resources for, 294
physical architecture, 327–328
PointCast, 75
  home page, 258, 259*illus.*
Point of Presence (POP), 307
policy, 75–82
  information about (references), 97
  issues, 86–96
  penalties for misuse, 95–96
  people issues, 79–80
  record keeping, 95–96
  resources for, 80
  reviewing, 281–282
  sample employee usage policy, 317–324
  usage limitations, 87–97, 320–324
pornography, 75, 76
Portable Document Format (PDF), 212
PPP (Point-to-Point Protocol), 307
prices, *see* costs
problem procedures, 255
procedures list, 254–255
product life-cycle model, 9
project leader, 10
  choosing the team, 57–58
  role in architecture/design phase, 123
  role of, 56
  team assignments, 72–73
project plan, 12, 295
  phase II, *see* phase II
project team, 10, 57–58
  assignments, 72–73
  availability, 103–104
  "dream team," 59

role in architecture/design phase, 124
role in content generation, 229, 231
role in marketing, 260, 262, 266
role in network acquisition, 156, 158
role in network testing, 175
role in performance review, 275, 278,
    279, 283
role in phase II, 293, 294
role in policy development, 79–80
role in requirements phase, 101, 107, 152
role in server installation, 210, 213, 214,
    221
role in Web requirements determination,
    152

real-time inventory control, 297, 298*illus.*
record keeping, for usage control, 95–96
reflectors, 109
remote access, 298
requirements, 99–104
  and costs, 145
  "creep," 105
  format, 106–111
  information about (references), 119
  issues, 104–114
  people issues, 101
  resources for, 102
  reviewing, 282
resource identification, 53–62
  information about (references), 73
  issues, 70–73
  people issues, 55–59
  resources for, 60
resources, 11. *See also* external resources
  for client/server acquisition, 194–196
  for content generation, 233–234
  for decision process, 25
  for design, 125–127
  for marketing, 262
  for network acquisition, 158–159
  for network testing, 178–179
  newsgroups as, 190
  for operations turnover, 248–249
  for performance review, 280
  for phase II, 294
  for policy definition, 80
  for requirements phase, 102
  for resource identification, 60
  for server installation, 215

for training, 43
reviewing performance, *see* performance
    review
RFC (Request for Comments), 307
RFI (Request for Information), 58, 126, 307
    in design phase, 126
    submitting to consultants, 58
RFP (Request for Proposal), 126, 307
    in design phase, 126
risk estimation, 112
routers, 148, 300, 307
    network testing, 174
    test plan for, 337
rule-of-thumb design, 138

SAS Institute, 251–254
    home page, 250*illus.*
scheduled downtime, 255
search engines, 38, 266–267
security, *see also* firewall systems
    in architecture/design phase, 127–128
    in client/server acquisition phase, 197,
        206
    consultant testing, 224
    in content generation phase, 236
    in decision process, 26–27
    external resources, 61–62
    in marketing, 263
    in network acquisition phase, 160
    in network testing phase, 180
    in operations turnover, 251
    in performance review phase, 281
    in phase II, 294
    in requirements phase, 104, 111–113
    risk estimation, 112
    in server installation phase, 216, 223,
        224, 226
    in training, 44
    usage policy, 81–82
security audit, 137
server acquisition, 191–198
    issues, 198–206
    people issues, 193–194
    resources for, 194–196
    software selection, 198–199
server installation, 209–216
    information about (references), 224–226
    issues, 220–224
    outsourcing, 224

    people issues, 214
    resources for, 215
    test plan, 209, 221–224
servers, 41, 90, 307
    cost estimation, 149
    demand estimation, 152
    information about (references), 226
    mirror for, 294
    programming language, 201
sexually-explicit material, 75, 76
Shockwave, 212, 307
signature files, 269
Site Security Handbook, 97
SLIP (Serial Line Internet Protocol), 307
SMDS (Switched Megabit Data Service), 91
SMTP (Simple Mail Transfer Protocol), 307
software downloading, 93–94, 323
Southern Shores Realty home page,
        274*illus.*, 274–275
spamming, 272
spiders, 266
sports pages, 228
Star/News home page, 228, 230*illus.*
strategy, need for coherent, 36
structured query language (SQL) interfaces,
        201
stub network connection, 176
style guide, 242–243
switched access, 139–140
system testing, 186

T1 lines, 308
    cost, 142, 145
    delivery time, 159
    hardware support for, 148
Taylor, Frank, 115–119
TCP/IP protocol, 304
TCP (Transmission Control Protocol), 308
teams, *see* project team
technical training curricula, 49
technical writers, 125–126
TechSolv, 128–133
    home page, 128*illus.*
telecommunications bill, 76
telecommuting, 298
telephone charges, 150–151
telephone usage policy, 77
Telnet, 307
terminal adapters, 149, 300

test plan
   networks, *see* network testing
   reviewing, 283–284
   server installation, 209, 221–224
time usage limitations, 93
top-level domains, 113
training, 39–44. *See also* operations
      turnover
   consequences of inadequate, 40
   information about (references), 51–52
   issues, 49–51
   outlines for various employees, 309–315
   people issues, 42
   resources for, 43
   reviewing, 284–285
   user manuals, 256–257
Transport Finder, 138
TriNet Services, Inc., 115–119
   home page, 114*illus.*
turnkey installations, 160, 168–169
turnover
   in Internet businesses, 41, 247
   to operations, *see* operations turnover

under construction graphics, 231
United Parcel Service home page, 299*illus.*
unit testing, 186–187
UNIX Guru Universe home page, 49,
      50*illus.*
upper management, 10
   role in decision process, 25
URL (Uniform Resource Locator), 308
usage policy, *see* policy
USENET, *see* newsgroups
user feedback, 280
user manuals, 256–257
UUencoding, 306

vendors
   as client/server acquisition resource, 196
   security aspects, 61–62
   training provided by, 49
verification, 186
video, 89
video conferencing, 109–110, 271, 297, 300
   cost estimation, 150
videophones, 297

virtual private networks, 297
voice over the Internet, 297

W3 consortium, 207
WAIS (Wide Area Information Servers),
      308
WANs (Wide Area Networks), 308
   test plan for, 338–339
Watson, David, 274
Web, *see* World Wide Web
Web authoring, 234. *See also* content
      generation
Web browsers, 306
   support for multiple, 242
Web directories, 28, 266–267
Web hosting
   content generation, *see* content
      generation
   evaluating services, 199–200
   outsourcing of, 138–140, 193, 202–205
Weblint, 225*illus.*
Web master, 214, 283
Web scripts, for user feedback, 280
Webweek home page, 195*illus.*
white board, 110, 271
white-box testing, 187
Wide Area Networks (WANs), *see* WANs
World Wide Web, 308. *See also*
      Internet; servers; Web browsers;
      Web hosting
   CD-ROM/Web links, 299–300
   content as key to success, 227
   cutting-edge sites, 241–242
   external design houses, 244
   growth of, 258
   hits, 75, 269, 303–304
   information dissemination on, 88–89
   publications on, 288
   requirements for access, 107
   service costs, 151–152
   sponsored advertising, 268–269
   statistics on, 37
   success factors, 258–260

Yahoo home page, 176*illus.*, 267*illus.*
Yeo, Curt, 251–254
Yost, Kevin, 128–133